# Postcolonial Imaginings

For Josh and Miranda, my two children
of a different geography;
and in memory of Amos Tutuola,
blacksmith and ghost

# Postcolonial Imaginings

## Fictions of a New World Order

David Punter

Edinburgh University Press

ATLANTIC®

PUBLISHERS & DISTRIBUTORS

**ATLANTIC®**
PUBLISHERS & DISTRIBUTORS
7/22, Ansari Road, Darya Ganj
New Delhi – 110 002
Tel: 2327 3880, 2327 5880, 2328 0451
Fax: 91-11-2328 5873
E-mail: info@atlanticbooks.com
Website: www.atlanticbooks.com

Published in India by
Atlantic Publishers and Distributors, New Delhi
in association with
Edinburgh University Press Ltd
22 George Square, Edinburgh, U.K.



First published 2000 by Edinburgh University Press Ltd
**First Indian Reprint 2005**



ISBN 81-269-0554-9

Typeset in Monotype Apollo by
Koinonia, Bury, and
printed in India by
Pushp Print Services, Delhi

# Contents

# Preface

The process of mutual postcolonial abjection is, I suppose, one that confronts us every day in the ambiguous form of a series of uncanny returns. I have three moments in mind.

When I was small, a neighbour in our London suburb used to like to come and talk to my mother on occasions, perhaps once a month. He was a huge man with a grey military moustache, who had spent his working life as an engineer in the Sudan; he had been invalided 'home', and in fact died, of a massive haemorrhage, in our kitchen. He had, I noticed from my low vantage-point at the time, a strange voice, one I had not heard before; it was not until some years later that I realised that this bloated imperial lackey, who was also a destroyed victim of empire, was in fact not 'at home' at all; he was an Irishman from Limerick.

Years later in Hong Kong I worked in a Cantonese-speaking university that had very close contact with mainland China. There, at a drinks party, I met a sad bureaucrat called Eddie who spent some time laboriously explaining his job to me. All day, every day, he worked through the mountain of mail between the university and the higher education officials in Beijing, which had already been translated into *putonghua*, for the sole purpose of introducing into each missive the necessary honorifics that were required in order that mail from Hong Kong, then still of course a British colony, was not immediately dumped in the waste bin. I should perhaps add that one of my roles as expatriate Professor of English was to check through the English versions of the Vice-Chancellor's public pronouncements and speeches and, as it was delicately called, 'improve the text'.

In Scotland only two years ago I met a moderately famous Scottish writer, and provided her with a formal introduction before she gave a reading to an audience of students. While talking briefly afterwards over a coffee, she was for some reason explaining the intricacies of Glaswegian junk food; then, after falling momentarily silent, she asked me: 'Where are *you* from?' The strange anger I felt at that question, I have since realised, was a politically inappropriate response; it nevertheless brought home to me that the question is in many contexts a terroristic one, and it was thus part of the stimulus that drove me to write this book.

The book is the second in a series of three on modern and contemporary writing. The first, *The Hidden Script: Writing and the Unconscious,* was published in 1985; the third, on the postmodern, will appear in about two years' time. It is, as I explain later, a ghost of what it might have been; but it is not an elegy, although it is predicated on a certain 'politics of despair'. These are the words of Dipesh Chakrabarty in an article called 'Postcoloniality and the Artifice of History'; the project there described is to 'return the gaze' by 'provincialising Europe', a project that 'must realise within itself its own impossibility'. 'This is a history', Chakrabarty continues, 'that will attempt the impossible: to look towards its own death by tracing that which resists and escapes the best human effort at translation across cultural and other semiotic systems, so that the world may once again be imagined as radically heterogeneous'.

My book is predicated also as a response to a certain problematic elevation of an ill-thought-out notion of 'theory', which I read as based in a stony-eyed, guilt-induced insistence on an abstract focus as a deflection from issues of both joy and loss. And it is further predicated on the assumption that the collapse of a certain part of the Marxist project finishes an area of hope for the future. There are those who say that all we are left with is the future of capitalism, but we should all know that the words 'future' and 'capitalism' do not consort easily together, that the future of profit is, for most people, an imagining of destitution and death.

I say 'a certain part' of the Marxist project because there are, again, those who seem concerned to forget China; but it seems to me that the arguments about the perils of convergence and 'development' to which I shall frequently allude in the following pages can ultimately now tend only towards a conflict – not necessarily military – with China, and also that China, grim as it is, is now the only 'alternative' to obliterative modernisation; I am not presuming for that reason that it will prove able to provide a better one. Were I a materialist, much of this might appear to have a more self-evident political force; because I am not, and also because I seem to think of literature in a fashion radically different from most 'postcolonial critics', such force may appear more diffuse, dispersed, elliptical. That, I believe, intellectually and politically, is as it should be.

# Acknowledgements

Intellectual concerns have, in the conception of this book, been inseparable from urgent practical and political ones. Thus my acknowledgements begin with Isobel, conceived in Shanghai, and must include Ravi, Samjhana and Rusli, my 'other children', whom I have not yet met. But intellect there has certainly been, on the part of others if not myself: in particular, Sudesh Mishra, valued colleague and model bohemian; Ackbar Abbas for his triumphant conclusion to Hong Kong; Maggie Nolan, my unwitting Australian informant; and Bob Hodge and Vijay Mishra, neither of whom I have seen for many years but whose work continues to revitalise. Thanks also to Jackie Jones at Edinburgh University Press for not tearing up my contract, and to many others, including Alan Bissett, Louise Ho, Alan Nicholson, Chris Powici, Angela Smith and Dennis Walder.

# I Introductory

At the beginning of the twenty-first century, according to the dating imposed on the world by its dominant socio-theological order, it is worth remembering that the beginning of the twentieth marked the peak of the colonial empire. In fact, by far the larger part of the land surface of the world was then formed into empires, if we take the word 'empire' in its broadest sense. The ancient Chinese and Ottoman empires were still in existence, although in precarious condition. The Habsburgs and Romanovs ruled over vast empires within and adjacent to Europe. But when thinking of a *colonial* empire specifically, we usually mean an empire that has overseas 'possessions', rather than simply a large collection of adjacent states or territories under a single regime (see Fieldhouse, 1973; Pagden, 1995).

The colonial empires – which were almost exclusively European in provenance – can be divided into two broad categories: the older ones (Dutch, Spanish and Portuguese), which dated back to the sixteenth century, and the more recent ones (principally the British, German, Italian and French) whose zenith was during the nineteenth. The whole of Africa, with the single exception of Abyssinia, was under European rule. Most of South America, it is true, had recently gained independence from the European imperial powers, principally Spain and Portugal, but Canada, Australia, New Zealand, the Indian subcontinent, most of Indo-China, parts of the Middle East, and the islands of the Indian and Pacific oceans as well as those of the Caribbean all remained imperial possessions.

This is no place in which to attempt a detailed history of empire, which would in any case be an impossibility considering the vast range of social formations, the varieties of ruling apparatus, that typified the European empires. Nor is it possible to attempt a history of the 'colony' in particular, since again colonies took a wide range of forms. Some of them we might refer to as 'settler colonies', territories like Canada and Australia where large numbers of

Europeans emigrated and inhabited the land, usually treating it as empty despite the plentiful evidence of previous indigenous inhabitants. Some were 'invader colonies', where the Europeans acquired power by more overt force of arms, subjugating local structures of authority by means more or less violent. In some cases, in many African countries for example, local communities never acquiesced in imperial rule; in others the invaders were successful in forming at least temporary alliances with sections of the native population or in manipulating local alliances and disputes so that, for a time at least, rule could be presented as largely administrative rather than military. India was the prime example of such a situation. Still other colonies, notably in the Caribbean and on islands like Fiji, were based on slave labour transported by Europeans from other countries – from Africa principally, but also, in the case of the Pacific, from India and elsewhere.[1]

Behind these manifold situations lay, obviously, an enormously complex machinery: a machinery dedicated to the continuance of European rule, the exploitation of natural resources, and the spread of European culture as an accompaniment to the continued subordination of native peoples. Yet during the course of the first two-thirds of the twentieth century, almost the whole of this apparatus fell apart. Historians cite many reasons why this should have been the case: they point to inherent instabilities in the system; to the difficulty of continuing to control territories many thousands of miles away; to the rise of independence movements across a wide range of colonised lands (see, e.g., Morris-Jones and Fischer, 1980; Darwin, 1988). One factor universally recognised as of major significance was the Second World War. Some of its effects were straightforward: the German, Italian and fledgling Japanese empires were destroyed and re-appropriated by the victor powers. But the wider effect was to threaten the whole notion of European rule, both because the European powers were in practice more concerned with handling the terrors of the war in Europe than with its effects in more 'far-flung parts' of the world, and because, in India for example, the war clearly revealed the underlying weakness of the European powers, allowing nascent drives towards independence and self-determination to come closer to the surface. Although there are still small colonies dotted around the world, mostly territories that are too small, or which occupy land too inhospitable, for independence to appear a realistic option, the last European overseas colony of any size was Hong Kong, which Britain handed back to China in 1997 (see Abbas, 1997). The era of the formal colony is dead.

This, at least, is a normative sketch of empire and colonialisation, but it begs many questions, and they are ones that will recur throughout this book. The first is: in what sense has colonialism really ended? To take but one example: it has become conventional to accept that the United States, the world's only remaining superpower, regards most of South America as within its 'sphere of influence' – as its 'backyard', as the usual phrase has it. Regimes with which it disagrees for one reason or another – in Chile, Grenada, Panama, for example – find themselves violently removed from power; regimes with 'Yanqui' support have their time prolonged, even when the consequences may include mass murder. Is this colonialism? Was it, for instance, an act or consequence of colonialism when, during the war between the USA and the Philippines at the very end of the nineteenth century, a million Filipinos were killed?

I use the example of the United States in this context for two reasons. First, because if there continues to be neo-colonial influence around the world then it does not emanate merely from the ex-colonial powers themselves, although there is certainly plenty of that, as we can see, for instance, in the attitude of France to its former colonies in Africa, and as we have also seen recently in Portugal's sudden memory of its earlier role in the catastrophe that is now East Timor. It comes also, and overwhelmingly, from the force that now controls the bulk of the world's resources, which is the United States, frequently as mediated through the apparently independent but in practice US-dominated international organisations, the World Trade Organisation and the World Bank, about whose influence I shall be saying more later.

Second, it is the United States that has of recent years been saying most about the notion of a 'new world order', and this is a notion I want to place under continual question in this book.[2] Such a notion, it should immediately be added, is not of itself 'new': for example, such a 'new order' was much spoken of between the wars, principally by Germany, Italy and Japan, who took it as a code for the replacement of the post-First World War settlement, driven by Britain, France and the United States, which had, according to at least some accounts, been directly responsible for the catastrophic economic slump of the 1930s.

What is meant, however, by the 'new world order' as it is spoken of today? The answer, I think, has to be given at two levels. The rhetoric of the United States and, by a curious coincidence of which one ought obviously to be wary, that of the United Nations has to do with the end of the Cold War, with the fragmentation of the

Soviet Union, with the pragmatic recognition of US power, and with the supposed emergence of a will to use that power both to solve military and territorial disputes in the world and also to do something to bridge the increasing wealth gap between areas of the planet – I say 'areas of the planet' because it is also part of this new order that the old opposition between 'west' and 'east' is now much more seen as between 'north' ('developed') and 'south' ('developing'), although I shall return to all these terms in various contexts later. The second level, however, suggests that the 'new world order' consists principally in an absolutist subjugation of the world to a particular economic theory, which goes by the name of 'free trade' and which, despite its name, appears designed to tie the entire planet into a US-dominated arrangement of production and markets. Again, I shall have more to say of this below.

Clearly one matter that would be important in any 'new world order' would be the putative independence of states and territories, and this takes us directly to the question of the 'postcolonial'; of what we might mean by saying, or more frequently assuming, that we live in a 'postcolonial' age.[3] One crucial dispute is whether we thereby mean to refer to the world as it is *after the end of the colonies* (if they have ended) or to the world as it has been *since the beginning of colonisation*. I shall adopt the first meaning, fraught with uncertainties as it is, but that is just the beginning of the difficulty. A critic speaks of the complexities of using the term at all in a cultural context:

> Such has been the elasticity of the concept 'postcolonial' that in recent years some commentators have begun to express anxiety that there may be a danger of imploding as an analytic construct with any real cutting edge. ... the problem derives from the fact that the term has been so variously applied to such different kinds of historical moment, geographical region, cultural identities, political predicaments and affiliations, and reading practices. As a consequence, there has been increasingly heated, even bitter, contestation of the legitimacy of seeing certain regions, periods, socio-political formations and cultural practices as 'genuinely' postcolonial. (Moore-Gilbert, 1997, 11)

Bart Moore-Gilbert, in this passage, is being quite restrained. The usage of the term 'postcolonial' with which I am concerned in this book has to do with its applicability to writing, to literature, but clearly, and rightly, it is impossible to divorce this usage from others. The fact is that the postcolonial is, in cultural and political terms, a bitterly contested field. The question of whether you should even spell the word with or without a hyphen, and what the implications of that might be; the issue of what areas of the world can be properly regarded as postcolonial; the issue of the relation between texts, creative and critical, produced in ex-colonies and those produced in Europe and North America; the question, to which I shall return in a moment, of the relation between primary text and 'theory'; the connection between different summary terms like 'postcolonial', 'neo-colonial', 'Third World', 'developing world' – all of these are sites on which the conflictual and often violent politics of the postcolonial world necessarily spills over onto cultural terrain, and thus becomes the very substance of our dealings with textuality.

> 'Post-colonialism', as it is now used in various fields, de-scribes a remarkably heterogeneous set of subject positions, professional fields, and critical enterprises. It has been used as a way of ordering a critique of totalising forms of Western historicism; as a portmanteau term for a retooled notion of 'class'; as a subset of both postmodernism and post-structuralism (and conversely, as the condition from which those two structures of cultural logic and cultural critique themselves are seen to emerge); as the name for a condition of nativist longing in post-independence national groupings; as a cultural marker of non-residency for a Third World intellectual cadre; as the inevitable underside of a fractured and ambivalent discourse of colonialist power; as an oppositional form of 'reading practice'; and ... as the name for a category of 'literary' activity which sprang from a new and welcome political energy going on within what used to be called 'Commonwealth' literary studies. (Tiffin and Lawson, 1994, 16–17)

Stephen Slemon in this paragraph puts the 'literary' aspect last even though, as he also says, it was his first encounter with the term; I shall in this book put it first, and state that my concern is with the relation between the postcolonial and the literary. What do I mean by the 'literary'? Perhaps I can best start by putting it in negative terms. I mean by it all that is omitted in this statement by a 'post-colonial critic': 'Literature is defined as an instance of concrete political practice which reflects the dynamic process of the national democratic revolution in the developing countries' (San Juan, 1998, 254).

By the 'literary', what I shall mean has very little to do with such an account. I shall instead think of the literary as the uncanny, as the haunting and the haunted; as that which resists pinning down, that which will always squirm away and produce 'other', 'unauthorised' meanings; as that which conjures phantoms, which banishes phantoms, and which always leaves us uncertain whether or not we are alone; as intimately connected with hallucination and dream; as constantly reflecting upon its own state of loss, that loss of the object which is capable of plunging writer and reader into a state of the most profound melancholy; as constantly in a state of becoming, of never reaching a 'fixed point', as infected at the heart with an ineradicable absence; as constantly in exile and in flight, dealing in false signatures, forged passports, unthinkable alibis; as always imbricated with the passions, with rage and hatred, with elation and triumph, with jealousy and love; as a phenomenon of lies and truth, of narratives that wind and twist and go nowhere, of history and trauma endlessly and impossibly rewriting each other; as trace and supplement, without origin, without closure, and thus as the distorted mirroring, the per-version, of the worlds in which it functions. All these things I take to be true of the literary in general; what I shall be testing in the pages that follow is the ways in which they are specifically visible in the postcolonial, and what relations between the two might thereby be suggested.[4]

There has been a long recent argument about whether or not postcolonial writers are necessarily writing a 'national allegory' (see Jameson, 1986; Ahmad, 1992); I shall not be concerned with that, since I do not believe that such reductivisms are possible. Neither shall I be much concerned with formal categories like modernism and postmodernism, although on the whole I agree with Vinay Dharwadker when he writes of a 'literary paradigm-shift in post-colonial countries [that] is *not* the same as the transition from modernism to post-modernism in First World societies', but is part of, to use precisely my own key term, a 'wider international movement' towards a 'new world order' (Dharwadker, 1996, 71). I need also to make a far more important disclaimer about the geographical coordinates for the postcolonial I have adopted.

Any book is, I assume, only a shadow or a ghost of a book that might have been written. The book that this shadows, the one that is needed, is 'needful', is the one that would be able lucidly and accurately to compare different postcolonial writings across a variety of societal formations and, more importantly, across the many languages – the languages of the colonisers, the 'native' languages – concerned. Such a study would also be able adequately to compare the different imperial formations themselves; it would be able to situate the British and, as it were, 'post-British' experience – if that were the primary focus – among other comparable materials; it would be able to effect a wider sweep and judgement than this book will be able to do.

I can only say that such a book is beyond my powers, and the evidence seems to suggest that so far it has also proved beyond anybody else's powers.[5] This should not prevent me, however, from flagging up that although almost all the texts discussed in this book were first written in English I am well aware that there are other huge literatures of the postcolonial. Sometimes, as in the Francophone situation, they are known by that name; in other cases, particularly in Latin America, lapse of time seems to have banished the label and enabled its replacement by other ones of which, of course, 'magic realism' has been the most recent instance. 'A study', Ketu Katrak says, 'that focuses only on English-language post-colonial writers involves some loss, even distortion in terms of the complex reality of linguistic situations in post-colonial areas' (Katrak, 1996, 230); I think this is a remarkable understatement, but all I can say in response to it is that at various points in this book I have tried to address the *issues this raises*, even though I am not myself able to offer sufficient inwardness with any relevant language other than English to be helpful.

Within that limitation, however, I hope to offer some comment on a wide range of texts, and they are listed in the first part of the Bibliography. They were all published after the Second World War. With the single exception of the anthology of new writing in India, they were all originally published in English. Some of them are recognised postcolonial classics by established authors (Achebe, Brathwaite, Harris, Naipaul, Narayan); others are texts of non-canonical status (Chandra, D'Aguiar, Kiran Desai, Kureishi, Roy). Some have entered the canon, or at least *a* canon, as serious works of literary originality, whatever that might mean; others are deliberately more slight. Some have an obvious connection to acceptably postcolonial issues, others less so. I have chosen texts from India (Behl and Nicholls, Chandra, Desai), black Africa (Achebe, Armah, Dangarembga, Soyinka, Tutuola) and the Caribbean (Brathwaite, Harris, Naipaul, Narayan, Walcott), from white South Africa (Coetzee) and from Sri Lanka (Ondaatje), from Canada (Atwood, Gibson), Australia (Keneally) and New Zealand (Hulme); but I have also selected texts from Scotland (Banks, Kelman, Welsh) and Ireland (Deane), on the now commonly recognised assumption that these too are cultures that have, at least in the British context, a post-colonial dimension.[6] I have included 'diasporic' texts, written (perhaps) in Britain but having a bearing on colonial and postcolonial history and on the fate of diasporic and immigrant communities (D'Aguiar,

Gupta, Gurnah, Kureishi, Riley, Rushdie, Syal). I have also included texts by two US writers: the black writer and Nobel Prize winner Toni Morrison, whose work is inseparable from the history of slavery, and Susan Power, who raises native American issues. Some of the texts, as one might already see from this list, run across the boundaries, challenge the whole sense of the 'location' from which they come. Where was Michael Ondaatje's *Running in the Family* 'written', where did its textuality originate? Where does a writer like Arundhati Roy 'belong' when her writing – like that of so many others – and indeed her activism, is about the whole vexed question of 'belonging'? What do we do about a Scots writer, Giles Foden, writing with pungent comicality about Uganda? Or about William Gibson's *Neuromancer*, whose take on 'location' threatens, or perhaps merely suspends, any sense of national boundary?

By juxtaposing, and indeed on occasion intertwining, these texts I hope to do two things. I hope to achieve a pedagogic end; I believe the selection of writings listed in the first part of the Bibliography could form the basis for a recognisable academic course in the postcolonial – not one that answers questions, but one that provides a sense of boundaries which is at the same time a sense of the inevitable crossing and contamination of those boundaries.[7] I hope at the same time to achieve a critical purpose, which is to challenge some of the stereotyped ways in which postcolonial criticism is developing, and to reconnect its concerns with those concerns which are properly literary.

Behind this lies a polemic; that polemic has to do with what I take to be the continuing and damaging misuse of the term 'theory' in postcolonial criticism. Katrak, for example, tells us that 'social responsibility must be the basis of any theorising on postcolonial literature', and asks, 'What theoretical models will be appropriate for this task?'; 'How can we make our theory and interpretation of postcolonial texts challenge the hegemony of the Western canon?' (Katrak, 1989, 157–8), and so on and on; Teshome H. Gabriel, in similar vein, talks of a theoretical 'matrix' (Gabriel, 1989, 31). The dictionary, in my view, gives the game away when it defines theory as 'speculation as opposed to practice'. Theorists in the realm of the postcolonial have become accustomed to sharing a common supposition, whatever their internal rivalries, which is that theory is the next 'stage' on a path to truth. But this is an Enlightenment model writ large; theory is not a 'stage of progress', it is a stepping aside – of interest in itself, to be sure, but only insofar as it might, at some deferred point, resume its part in a dialectic with 'practice', which I take to include the literary as well as the political.

What lies behind all this, of course, is the recent history of postcolonial criticism, which has been dominated by a series of figures, a series of authorities, and a series of debates. Very crudely (because I shall be recurring to this throughout the book), we can say that one group of dominant figures in recent postcolonial criticism has included Edward Said, Gayatri Spivak and Homi Bhabha; their authorities have been taken to be, respectively, Foucault, Derrida and Lacan. This is a caricature, but a significant one. My claim will be that in their deployment of 'Western' theory they have become involved in prolonging and repeating imperialist subjugation, to the point at which Spivak can solemnly claim, in the teeth of the evidence, that the subaltern 'cannot speak'.[8] This disavowal, this wishing away of the complexities of the voice, of the defiles of the literary, is a move designed to silence, and it has only been very recently that alternative voices have spoken up, at least within the hearing of the all-listening ears, the patrolling listeners of the Western arena. They have spoken up in two ways. First, they have spoken up, in the emblematic cases of Aijaz Ahmad and E. San Juan, for example, to confront the claims of 'high theory' with the exigencies of political reality (see Ahmad, 1992; San Juan, 1998). Second, they have spoken up, from a variety of perspectives, to remind – with a surprising tentativeness – that the significant critical work in the postcolonial theatre of action has been going on all the time; it has been going on where it should have been going on, in the closest of embraces with the literary and with the political, in the work of postcolonial writers themselves. The endless 'theorising' exemplified in the seemingly authoritative collections of anthologising critics like Bill Ashcroft, Gareth Griffiths and Helen Tiffin, or like Patrick Williams and Laura Chrisman (see Ashcroft, Griffiths and Tiffin, 1989, 1995; Williams and Chrisman, 1993), even though these collections include African, Indian and Caribbean voices, is continuingly revealed as in the end a further extension of globalism; I own to having more political sympathy with the positions of Ahmad and San Juan, but here again the question of the literary raises itself to put uncomfortable questions, as do the limitations of any philosophic 'materialism'.

It is my conviction – and the conviction on which this book rests – that what is specifically not needed, in the West in general and in the encounter with the postcolonial in particular, is more theoretical 'frameworks' or 'matrices', which inevitably repeat a prior subjugation and exploitation, a kind of mining and transportation of natural resources reinscribed at the cultural level. What *is* needed is perceptions and ideas: perceptions of what might be *in the text* (however broadly the 'text' might be conceived) and ideas about how and why it might be there. I could recast that in a different language by saying that what is not needed is a debate that relies on shaky and usually misunderstood terms like 'essentialism' and its presumed alternatives, but rather a discourse carried out in the spirit of what Stuart Hall refers to in an admirable essay as 'positionality', a discourse that recognises the temporary, that eschews the teleological, that does not try to classify or define but seeks instead to work reflexively, in however humble a way, with the complexities of the literary as it emerges in an unending flow of ideas and images (Hall, 1990, 222–37).

Thus what I am saying is, in a sense, very simple: if we are to engage with postcolonial writing, then we have to do it through an encounter between the postcolonial and the literary, in all its peculiarities, its exemplary unyieldingness, its intransigence, its resistance not only to political appropriation but also to theoretical oversight. We have to find a kind of criticism which is less panoptical, which ebbs and flows with the complex rhythms of the text. This is not for a moment to say that we have to envisage some kind of 'naturalism', that we should abandon thought in order to plunge into some prior world, for what is crucial here is precisely that *there is no prior world*. The literary tells us, among many other things, that there is no return, no 'recourse' beyond text; just as for the postcolonial there can be no return, no recuperation, only a painful and already damaged work with the materials that history has left us, distorted though those materials must inevitably be.

Although keeping a distance from 'theory' as presently – and in my view wrongly – conceived, I trust that this book is not devoid of ideas. Some of the main ones, I should say, derive from the history, practice and cultural encounters of psychoanalysis and from the revisionary work of Gilles Deleuze and Félix Guattari.[9] But I have at all points tried to avoid recasting these ideas as a *framework*; they will be seen to be of value only insofar as their encounter with postcolonial texts succeeds in producing a conjuncture for further thought. The postcolonial is a field in which everything is contested, everything is contestable, from one's reading of a text to one's personal, cultural, racial, national standpoint, perspective and history. This is as it should be, but that contestation will nevertheless remain sterile unless it begins and continues on the basis of a certain openness, a beckoning but unassuageably thirsty openness which is precisely the province of the literary; it is such an openness that I have tried to keep available in writing this book.

# II Impossibility and Loss

> In the ruins, a population of ragpickers,
> bent over stones, deciphering their graves.
> Hoses plied the shambles
> making the ashes mud.
> Here were the broken arches and the vines
> ascending leisurely, with the languor of fire.
> Your ruined Ilion, your grandfather's pyre.
>
> (Derek Walcott, *Another Life*, in *Collected Poems 1948–1984*)

> We hear this uncanny whispering behind: Never question the legitimacy of this new dispensation, for it's the same old thing – unequal exchange on a world scale – lest you unleash the barbarism of Prospero and Ariel against Caliban's hordes. (E. San Juan, Jr., *Beyond Postcolonial Theory*)

> When I wake in the morning I know they have gone finally, back into the earth, the air, the water, wherever they were when I summoned them. The rules are over. I can go anywhere now, into the cabin, into the garden, I can walk on the paths. I am the only one left alive on the island. (Margaret Atwood, *Surfacing*)

It is, then, only with the greatest of trepidation that the field of the postcolonial can or should be approached. This is at least partly because the issue of what is and what is not postcolonial is a complex and open one, and nowhere more so than in the European nations whose history has already indelibly stamped, and been stamped by, those other parts of the world that might consider themselves to be more obviously in a postcolonial situation. In an attempt at a beginning, I want to offer some facts, but facts are, of course, very much disputed territory in the realm of the literary, in literary criticism and theory, and equally if not more so on the terrain of the postcolonial. One might think, for example, of the influence of Foucault on Edward Said, and the consequent complexities over the course of his work in terms of the construction of reality through discourse (see Said, 1978, 3, 22ff.; 1993, 1–72); or of the influence of Derrida on Gayatri Spivak, and the constant tension in her work, perhaps best summarised in her phrasings around 'strategic essentialism', between rhetorical analysis and political activism (see Spivak, 1987, 46–76, 197–221; 1990, 35–49); or one might think of the influence of Lacan on Homi Bhabha, and the consequent arguments about the intercultural validity of psychoanalysis and the effect of its devices if they are seen as 'frames' for the raw psychic materials, if such exist, of different colonial and postcolonial formations (see Bhabha, 1990, 291–332; 1994, 40–65).

All of these developments – and they are among those considered major in postcolonial studies – serve to put the notion of 'fact' into question; but I want to bracket these epistemological concerns for a moment – although I shall return to them later – and lay out several facts, accompanied by the question: 'What has this to do with the postcolonial?'

Fact 1: The richest fifth of the world's population consumes 86 per cent of all goods and services while the poorest fifth consumes just 1.3 per cent. Indeed, the richest fifth consumes 45 per cent of all meat and fish, 58 per cent of all energy used and 84 per cent of all paper.

Fact 2: The Ganges River symbolises purification in the Hindu religion, and Hindus believe that drinking or bathing in its waters will lead to salvation. But 29 cities, 70 towns and countless villages deposit about 345 million gallons of raw sewage directly into the river. Factories add another 70 million gallons of industrial waste and farmers are responsible for another 6 million tons of chemical fertiliser and 9,000 tons of pesticides.

Fact 3: The three richest people in the world have assets that exceed the combined gross domestic product of the 48 least 'developed' countries, and the world's 225 richest individuals, of whom 60 are from the USA with total assets of $311 billion, have a combined wealth of over $1 trillion – equal to the annual income of the poorest 47 per cent of the entire world's population.

Fact 4: Americans and Europeans spend $17 billion a year on pet food – $4 billion more than the estimated annual additional total needed to provide basic health and nutrition for everyone in the world.

Fact 5: It is currently estimated that the additional cost of achieving and maintaining universal access to basic education for all, reproductive health care for all women, adequate food for all and clean water and safe sewers for all is roughly $40 billion a year

– or less than 4 per cent of the combined wealth of those same 225 richest people in the world.

Fact 6: Transactions in foreign exchange markets have now reached the sum of around $1.2 trillion a day – over fifty times the level of world trade. Around 95 per cent of these transactions are speculative in nature, many using complex new derivative financial instruments based on futures and options. The *daily* volume of transactions in the world is now equal to the *annual* gross domestic product of France, and is at least $200 million more than the total foreign currency reserves of the world's central banks.

Fact 7: At the end of 1994, just over 5 million people in the USA were under some form of legal restraint. According to Department of Justice figures, around a million and a half of them were in jail – state, federal or local. That means that one in 193 adult US citizens is a prisoner.

Fact 8: In 1992, one of the most recent years for which there are clear records, over 40 per cent of all black males between eighteen and thirty-five years of age living in the District of Columbia were in prison, on probation, on parole awaiting trial, or on the run.

Most of these facts are drawn from a recent United Nations Human Development Report, although a few are from John Gray's 1998 book, *False Dawn: The Delusions of Global Capitalism*.

There are, of course, several obvious things that literary and textual critics might dwell on in the 'presentation' of these facts. For example, the consumption of paper might commend itself especially to the attention of academics, and might provide a further perspective on the ever-receding possibility of the 'paper-free office'. Perhaps more importantly, we see the frequently used phrase about the world's 'least developed countries', and this of course marks the crucial ideological precipice over which, for example, the United Nations is in constant danger of falling: namely of acceding to the notion, sponsored by the global monetary organisations and their US controllers, that there is a single, unidirectional route towards 'development', and that nations shall be judged by their ability to walk this narrow path, no matter what disastrous uncertainties may await them along the way or at the end.[1] Or one might note the curious contortions of meaning through which the term 'speculative' has historically gone in order to reach the point where it is now descriptive of a system which possesses, as figures as diverse as Dr Mahathir Mohammed of Malaysia and the Swedish government have complained in recent years, the power to distort or destroy entire national economies and thus the ways of life sanctioned by, or in thrall to, those economies.

To return, however, to the question: What have these facts to do with the postcolonial? An initial, oblique response would be to quote some passages from the admirable introduction, by Ania Loomba and Suvir Kaul, to volume 16 of the *Oxford Literary Review*, published in 1994 and titled *On India: Writing History, Culture, Post-Coloniality*:

> The question that often underlines these exchanges [exchanges, in this context, mostly between scholars living and working on the postcolonial in different national and cultural environments] is whether 'post-colonialism' continues to serve a useful purpose or whether it now deflects attention from the complexity of disparate situations in 'third world' societies? ... Such discussions cannot be conducted without a detailed understanding of the power relations and hierarchies within these [different] countries, or indeed without differentiating between them (so that 'Africa' and India, for example, cannot be conveniently lumped together as 'post-colonial').
>
> New scholarship in the last two decades has done much to indicate the cultural, psychic, and discursive operations and effects of post-colonialism, but overarching theories of colonialism or indeed *the* post-colonial moment/predicament/mind-set also minimise the differences between colonial encounters the world over. It becomes easy to generalise when we work from a particular, dominant, and highly visible analytic paradigm, and forget that the visibility and dominance of particular paradigms may have more to do with the state of either the archive or of conditions of research. (Loomba and Kaul, 1994, 4–5)

In these complex sentences, several areas are broached which tend not merely to render the concept and study of the postcolonial difficult but actually to expose its impossibility. For example, the first sentence directly and, I presume, unwittingly reflects the overall problem of aggregation and disaggregation to which Loomba and Kaul are otherwise drawing attention in its attempted replacement of the term 'post-colonialism' by the phantomatic notion of the 'Third World'.[2] It has, of course, for many years been of some passing interest to ask where the Second World has gone; some political and cultural thinkers have started speaking of a dispossessed 'Fourth World'; but more importantly, we need constantly to enquire as to who is doing the numbering here. We need also to ask by what insidious process the Third World might be supposed to 'develop naturally' into the First World when, as

John Gray puts it, the 'hallucinatory vistas of a New World Order' may be seen to serve merely to provide an acceptable face for what is in fact increasingly 'a chaos of sovereign states and stateless peoples struggling for the necessities of survival' (Gray, 1998, 205, 208).

To these notions of hallucinatory order and stateless people I shall return later in the book. There is here also, however, the problem expressed as the presence of 'particular, dominant, and highly visible analytic paradigm[s]' and how they may inflect to the point of totally determining what the nature of evidentiary status – economic, social, cultural – might be. A further turn, we might say, of the screw: where literary theory used to make much of saying, thirty years ago, that the task was not to impose theory but to bring to light the way in which everybody, even someone in the virtually subhuman position of an F. R. Leavis, in fact had a theory but was unable to bring it out into the light, here truth is being implicitly sought in a realm where theory has not intruded and, therefore, in a realm which remains precisely 'invisible' (see Belsey, 1980, 11–13). The truth, if truth there is, can be found only – rather as we might conclude it ought to be from, for example, a reading of Slavoj Žižek on Lacan – by looking *away*, by losing focus (see Žižek, 1992, 3–47). This losing of focus in the set of encounters with the postcolonial needs also to be set aside as a trope to be returned to.

It certainly appears to be the case that, in approaching the perhaps hallucinatory, at the very least constantly disappearing, condition of the postcolonial, it is both by and towards a certain sense of loss that we are led. We might think, for example, of Edward Kamau Brathwaite's investigation of the ways in which 'creolisation' involves a continuing recognition that loss is an inevitable part of the evolving process (see Brathwaite, 1975); or of Derek Walcott's thoughts in 'What the Twilight Says' on the loss involved in the 'anguish' of the race (see Walcott, 1972, 3–40). We might place these writers, along with Wilson Harris, here in opposition to Homi Bhabha's influential notion of 'hybridity'.[3] One danger in Bhabha's thinking is that, despite protestations to the contrary, he seems so frequently to be thoroughly in hock to a Western Enlightenment project – in other words, to be convinced that the process of hybridity, whatever its local and temporary difficulties, will nonetheless end up by adding to the sum of positive cultural experience (see Bhabha, e.g., 1994, 37–9). We might perhaps be reminded of some relevant lines from Philip Larkin's 'Dockery and Son': 'Why did he think adding meant increase?/To me it was dilution' (Larkin, 1990, 153). Brathwaite, Walcott and Harris, on the other hand, remind us constantly that this rhetoric of local and temporary difficulties – not that Bhabha is overt enough to phrase them that way – is uncannily redolent of the equally 'convergent' rhetoric of the Raj, and that what is lost in the promulgation and sustenance of this rhetoric is, precisely, loss. That Enlightenment rhetoric of convergence, of course, is also – and according to an unassailable political logic – the rhetoric of convergence constantly employed by the World Bank.

We might equally say that what is *lost* is also impossible to register. How can the scale of loss be measured when, as Bhabha quite rightly points out, even concepts as apparently basic as 'the family', 'ageing' and 'mothering' stand revealed as agents – to what degree unwitting is a source of disagreement between the major figures of postcolonial theory – of an ideological world order, whether new or old (see Moore-Gilbert, 1997, 125) And, perhaps more to the point in this context, how might these considerations impact on the literary?

In this chapter I want to look at three texts and to trace in them some of the operations of loss and its bearings on our dealings with and in the postcolonial. The first one, Chinua Achebe's *Things Fall Apart*, is perhaps an unsurprising choice, because loss is very overtly its theme. The book, one of the best-known of all postcolonial texts, concerns the career and downfall of one Okonkwo, a great man in traditional Igbo society in Nigeria. Exactly what his downfall means has been the subject of much critical debate, but at the very least it is clearly associated with the spread of British colonial rule, and the memorable conclusion to the novel effects a brilliant apparent replacement of one narrative by another (see Weinstock and Ramadan, 1978; Innes, 1990, 21–41; Gikandi, 1991, 24–50). The text we have in our hands, as it were, disappears; it becomes clear that its point of view will be lost to history as it is replaced by the other book, the book that the white District Commissioner is writing, under the splendidly imperial – or is it anthropological, and is there, has there ever been, any difference? – title *The Pacification of the Primitive Tribes of the Lower Niger*.

And so already we are confronted with a contradiction, an impossibility. The text assures us of its own vanishing, its passing beneath the written sign of colonialism; but at the same time this very structure is a fiction, it is the text *Things Fall Apart* itself which has 'survived' (having indeed in one sense created) this encounter, or at least has reinscribed itself on top of the decades of history symbolised in the imperial/anthropological textuality of white colonisation, been resurrected from the ashes of the textbooks of the imperial project.

If the process stopped there, there would, after all, be much to be said for Bhabha's Enlightenment notion of hybridity; and indeed, there *is* much to be said for it. *Things Fall Apart*, more than any other work of African fiction, marked the emergence of its own culture into Western consciousness, and it is very largely due to that process, ambiguous as one may think it, that many students in the West now study those literatures which are variously, and sometimes to their own peril, designated as 'postcolonial', 'Commonwealth', 'the new literatures in English'. It could thus be argued that 'new' voices are being heard, that a multicultural liberalism is spreading apace throughout the West. Some of the 'facts' I mentioned earlier might thus appear mere temporary aberrations against this spreading backcloth of improvement.

But what, I think we have to ask, can we find to place against this ameliorative view – for after all, *Things Fall Apart* does not appear to be about amelioration, indeed clearly the reverse. In a resonant phrase in the final paragraph the District Commissioner, musing on his projected book in the aftermath of Okonkwo's suicide, decides that because there is 'so much ... to include ... one must be firm in cutting out details' (Achebe, 1996, 148). This, then, might be seen as part of the price that will have to be paid. It is the price paid, for example, to the World Bank and the International Monetary Fund: the exclusion of all the local detail that belongs to a particular way of life so that national and cultural systems can be subsumed under a single rubric, so that they, and the course of local histories, can be rewritten – under another name. This, it seems to me, is a point on which there is a need to be absolutely clear. There has been much debate in recent years about the importance and role of writing in political and economic development, and much criticism of what is sometimes termed the 'exorbitancy' afforded to writing by the 'high theorists' of the postcolonial – Said, Spivak, Bhabha.[4] But despite the significant objections to this over-promotion of history as simply an effect of textuality, it remains crucial to keep in mind that power *is* a process of writing, of inscription: we do not need Foucault to tell us that, we can see it more clearly in the everyday processes of bureaucratic documentation, self-serving legal obfuscation, media distortion which are around us all the time and with which, as readers of whatever sort, we are obliged to tangle. Or, more simply, we can listen to a resonant phrasing in the experienced voice of Ngugi wa Thiong'o: 'The bullet was the means of the physical subjugation. Language was the means of the spiritual subjugation' (Ngugi, 1986, 9).

'Cutting out details', to return to *Things Fall Apart*; cutting them out, perhaps, because the devil is in them. Again, we might say that Okonkwo at the end of the book has become a detail – an instance, an example in more than one sense of the word – to be cut down from a tree. But in any case, who owns the details? The most recent edition of *Things Fall Apart* was published in 1996 (the original dates from 1958) and it is, it proudly informs us on the front cover, an 'expanded edition with notes'. The back cover goes further: it tells us that the book 'includes essays, maps, illustrations, and reference material'. In some ways it might appear surprising that it does not contain a pop-up model of an African village and a small replica of a gallows. There is much that could be said about this intricate peritextual apparatus. Perhaps the most obvious general point is how 'differently' it locates the text. Of course there are 'student editions' of all sorts of things available, and some of them are very helpful, but not many contain a list of 'Principal Characters in the Novel' or a 'Glossary of Words and Phrases Used in the Text'. The latter, of course, is particularly important, for there are two ways – at least – of seeing the way in which Achebe deploys languages, writing as he does in English with Igbo terms dropped in from time to time. One way would be to say that this is a successful, hybrid accommodation between two sets of cultural assumptions, achieving maximum communicative force while respecting the untranslatability of certain local terms; the other would be to say that what is exposed is that contradiction between the general and local which is, precisely, the conflict of thought-patterns which is responsible for Okonkwo's doom.

In any case, on the political terrain of the postcolonial the processes of interpretation will always be complex. It would be necessary to consider, for example, these sentences from one of the introductory essays in *Things Fall Apart*:

> it is quite striking how rapidly the Igbo people, despite their attachment to their customs, succumbed to European civilisation. The fact that it took barely a hundred years (1857–1960) for the British to tear apart a society that had taken thousands of years to evolve suggests that European colonialism was a potent agent of change. (Achebe, 1996, xlviii)

Reading a comment like this is, I suggest, like listening to a multitude of voices. It is like trying to read a palimpsest, like trying to determine irony in a funeral oration. What it is *not* like – and this seems to me crucial – is the simple binary voice, the forked tongue adumbrated in much contemporary postcolonial criticism;[5] what we do not have here is a simple 'revision' of history. What there is, for example, is the mild phrase 'quite striking', which modulates into the passivity of 'succumbing'. We have the violence of 'tearing apart' succeeded by the extraordinary – or is it ironic? – bathos of 'potent agent of change'. This supposedly heuristic text reads, I suggest, as though it is a replacement for another one, a replacement for a text that has been lost, that was in any case perhaps written in a different language, a text in which real, detailed experiences could somehow have been written down, and of which the existing text is merely a shadow, an inexact and confusing reminder of a haunting. We are here, and not for the last time, in the presence of the 'text instead'.[6]

Thus there is a sense – as indeed we know from other sources – in which the postcolonial, in the very act of naming itself, inevitably succumbs to the temptation of 'rewriting' (although it might also be asked, following Derrida, what else there is anyway but the trace, the nervous system running through the body of literature without beginning or end (see Derrida, 1978, 196–231)). What else, one might however more specifically ask in the postcolonial context, can the body which has already been inscribed again and again in the process of colonisation do? There is no neutral starting point, no *fons et origo*, only the traces of a violent past, as we also see running through the work of Toni Morrison, to whose novel *The Bluest Eye* I now want to turn. It is a book of great formal complexity, interweaving different voices, different streams of thought, different perspectives. One of the most potent counterpoints Morrison uses involves some sentences from what appears to be a white child's reading book (is it a 'real' book or an invented composite?):

> Here is the house. It is green and white. It has a red door. It is very pretty. Here is the family. Mother, Father, Dick, and Jane live in the green-and-white house. They are very happy. See Jane. She has a red dress. She wants to play. (Morrison, 1979, 1)

And so it goes on; but as the book progresses, so the passage is reproduced in ever more bizarre and chaotic forms, with the punctuation slipping and sliding, repeating itself, moving into what we might consider to be a hallucinatory version of itself as we increasingly experience the conflict between this idealised view of family relations and the utterly catastrophic facts of the family life we are being shown in the novel.

What is gradually though violently lost in the progress of the text is this illusory sense of social completeness, which is necessarily also a linguistic completeness. There is at the beginning an apparently perfect mirroring between the psychic containment offered by the symmetrical, safe family and the mental containment on offer in the simple, neat, well-ordered phrases of a language which matches at all points the reality it purports to describe.

Yet to put it in that way, of course, is in one way nonsense, in that it is obviously purely fictive to claim such a propensity for language; but it is nonetheless a fiction, so Morrison claims, by which we might live or die. 'How Late It Was, How Late', James Kelman reminds us in the title of a book which is also about loss of language, about having one's words taken away, distorted, ridiculed and flung back to devastating effect. Too late for Morrison too, as she says at the end of the novel: 'It's too late. At least on the edge of my town, among the garbage and the sunflowers of my town, it's much, much, much too late' (164).

Too late, in this postcolonial context, because too much damage has been done, although along quite what timescale remains an impossible matter to measure. We might be speaking here of individual lives ruined by poverty, disenfranchisement, the collapse of structures of relationship and nurture; or we might be talking about a phantom shaping which repeats itself down the centuries, a history written in blood and slavery. It is necessary to ask whether, at the end of the long day, there is any difference, whether the nature of an inevitably traumatised recapitulation, the relationship between the individual mind and wider, deeper histories, will always subvert any attempt to isolate the subject or to interpret clearly the origin of the present plight.

Whichever way we take it, it may be helpful to suggest that we are here in the presence of what Nicolas Abraham and Maria Torok speak of in *The Wolf-Man's Magic Word* and elsewhere as a crypt (see Abraham and Torok, 1986, 49–54). There are various significant objections one might immediately make to the ideas in *The Wolf-Man's Magic Word*, quite apart from the standard controversies about using arguments derived from Western psychoanalysis in postcolonial contexts.[7] For example, it is not at all clear from a psychoanalytic point of view that a reopening of the wolf-man's case purely on the basis of the endlessly re-authored textual materials left to us over the years is a process that can ever have a very clear focus.[8] One might also suspect that the wish to find a single word which will unlock psychic secrets says more about the ways in which Abraham and Torok instantiate a European rage for order while at the same time succumbing to the admittedly compelling logic of the fairy-tale than it does about the wretched wolf-man and his exasperating fantasies. But having said these things, it does seem that the notion of the crypt as they elaborate it – in other words, to put it very simply, the notion of a psychic space which contains transgenerational phantoms of which the bearer may be entirely unaware – *is* useful, and not least in a postcolonial context where we may be looking at texts which are freighted with their own unacknowledged phantoms, which may be structured by specific forces of fracture which are beyond ready authorial control. In *The Bluest Eye*, then, we might say that the passage from the child's reading book becomes the site of an unnerving paradox: precisely where, and because, it appears transparent it serves also to carry a vast weight of hidden pain and loss. That this pain and loss in some sense 'belongs' (exactly insofar as it *does not belong*) to the central character Pecola is inescapable; but equally, like a crypt, it brooks no completion of ownership or possession among the living or the present, and its effects, those effects by which it can only be known, ripple on through our apprehension of the authorial presence/absence, through our readerly apprehensions, and through the histories of suppression and slavery.

To come at the text of *The Bluest Eye* briefly from another angle: by far the most terrifying scene in it is the one where the remarkably named Cholly Breedlove rapes Pecola, his daughter. The passage is complex and full of emotional contradiction, full of love and hatred, self-disgust and arrogance, protectiveness and violence feeding off each other in the damaged environment of Cholly's consciousness, the place where Cholly cannot but feel the deepest impossibility of being ever 'at home'. What is important is that the point of 'provocation', the curiously inverted primal scene, that moves Cholly to the ambivalent passion which ends up with his violent assault is the potential sight of his daughter's eyes, eyes that are loving and challenge him to return that love, but eyes that are also, so we are told, 'haunted' (Morrison, 1979, 127). Haunted by what? By fear, perhaps; perhaps even by a premonition of doom, by an anguished sense of the impossibility of evading repetition, so that past violences will project themselves endlessly into the future. If this is the case, then we can see that what afflicts Pecola is indeed, as Cholly seems dimly to suppose, not unlike that which afflicts him too: namely, the impossibility of replacing that which has, down the years and down the generations, been lost. A relevant comparison would be with the remarkable passage in Salman Rushdie's *Shame* where a description is given of the inside of Sufiya Zenobia's mind (see Rushdie, 1983, 212–15). Sufiya Zenobia is an innocent monster in a postcolonial setting, driven to madness and murder by the violent shamelessness (shamelessness which is also shamefulness) that is going on all around her; her mind is described as a storehouse, a place full of good experiences and bad experiences, in some sense alienated from her ownership, but with all the attendant anxieties about what would happen if items were lost from the shelves.

Shortly before this scene in *The Bluest Eye* the author tells us, in a phrase that has been the source of much controversy, that Cholly is 'free' (Morrison, 1979, 125). What might this mean in the context of his immediately subsequent actions? What indeed might it mean in the immediate context of the postcolonial? I suggest that one way of interpreting it would be like this. When loss in the past has been painful, then indeed it might be as though, to use those oft-repeated words, 'the dreadful has already happened'. All that can happen now falls under the sign of the repetition compulsion; there is nothing new under the sun, and therefore no possibility of acting badly; all that can happen has already occurred – under the guise of transportation and slavery. Pecola's loss, the loss of everything good that Pecola might want, the loss of Pecola herself, these multiple and intertwined losses are doomed to come anyway given her home circumstances and the 'colonised' history of her race; what does it matter when or how? The haunting that is in her eyes – a haunting that is inseparable from the way in which Cholly also is 'haunted' by the hallucination of his daughter's eyes – would then not be from the past alone. That haunting would then also come, as it does emblematically in D. M. Thomas's *The White Hotel*, from the future whence, as has been said before, the most dangerous and frightening ghosts arrive (see Thomas, 1981).

The third text I want to look at is Elspeth Barker's *O Caledonia*, the first novel of a Scottish exile living in England. The themes which I hope are beginning to emerge, the postcolonial themes of loss, ghosts, rewriting, and the instability of language – and thus, indeed, of memory – are set out in a passage from the beginning of the novel:

> Halfway up the great stone staircase which rises from the dim and vaulting hall of Auchnasaugh, there is a tall stained-glass window. In the height of its Gothic arch is sheltered a circular panel, where a white cockatoo, his breast transfixed by an arrow, is swooning in death. Around the circumference, threaded through sharp green leaves and twisted branches, runs the legend: 'Moriens sed Invictus'; dying but unconquered. By day little light penetrates this window, but in early winter evenings,

when the sun emerges from the backs of the looming hills, only to set immediately in the dying distance far down the glen, it sheds an unearthly glory; shafting drifts of crimson, green and blue, alive with whirling atoms of dust, spill translucent petals of colour down the cold grey steps. At night, when the moon is high it beams through the dying cockatoo and casts his blood drops in a chain of rubies on to the flagstones of the hall. Here it was that Janet was found, oddly attired in her mother's black lace evening dress, twisted and slumped in bloody, murderous death.

She was buried in the village churchyard, next to a tombstone which read:

*Chewing gum, chewing gum sent me to my grave.*
*My mother told me not to, but I disobeyed.*

Janet's parents would have preferred a more rarefied situation, but the graveyard was getting full and, as the minister emphasised, no booking had been made. (Barker, 1991, 1)

If we were to want to begin by analysing the linguistic registers of this passage, we could probably establish five. First, there is the high pictorial discourse of most of the first paragraph, with heraldic and feudal overtones, and anchored firmly in Scotland by the early mention of Auchnasaugh, which Barker will later translate, for those who need it translated and for those beyond the grasp of onomatopoeia, as the 'field of sighing' (32). Second, there is the Latin motto; it might appear culturally irrelevant, belonging, after all, to a dead language, but here as so often the biographical tantalises us, for Barker, as well as being a Scot, is by profession a teacher of Latin. Third, we have the register that begins with 'Here it was that Janet was found ...', which is surely an ironised version of the beginning of any popular detective novel, replete with 'bloody, murderous death', which is only one step away from the mysterious plethora of 'pools of blood' that victims seem to make a habit of dying in according to the newspapers. Fourth, there is the bathos of the tombstone inscription, reminiscent mainly of children's books like *Charlie and the Chocolate Factory*, or of the thinly disguised moral savagery of Hilaire Belloc. And finally, and probably most importantly as the next part of the text develops, there is the everyday, conversational, petit-bourgeois tone of the last sentence about the graveyard being full. How dreadful that no booking had been made; as if one could not have *told* that this death would occur ...

What then, to repeat my earlier question, is the postcolonial? Can we properly distinguish it, in this Scottish novelist, for example, from some more general category, which would have to do with the clash and contradiction between rival languages of power and victimisation? We might ask here, for example: does power reside in the language associated with Auchnasaugh itself, which we might consider either lushly beautiful or absurdly over-ornate, depending perhaps on taste or perhaps on cultural background; or does it lie in the heroic but, of course, to most contemporary readers initially unintelligible terseness of the Latin motto? To go a little further, we might ask whether a language even needs to be understood to carry weight, or whether the cultural example of legal language, relevant surely in both Latin and Scottish contexts as well as most other imperial ones, suggests that power has less to do with knowledge than with secrets.

Certainly those two languages of power, the one represented in the feudal ancestry of Auchnasaugh and the other suggested in the motto, are lost languages. They are, therefore, in some way inextricably associated with the ability to portray, to suggest, loss; even in its own absence, in its own inability to show itself as other than a series of disturbances in the smooth hallucinatory flows of language, in the coherence of a child's reading book, in the humorous and deadly inevitability of an admonitory inscription over a child's crypt. We might even take these registers as characters in their own right and watch them in these sentences being first subdued by the more contemporary but less emotionally rich language of the detective story, then coshed over the head by the ludicrous tomb inscription, before all these ghosts from the colonised past can be conveniently disposed of to make room for an entirely pragmatic language, a 'new world order' that eschews such resonances, attempts to rid itself of the trace. 'No booking had been made'; this new language, however banal (and perhaps its strength and future resides in its banality), has no truck with the ornate historical and geographical localisations of Auchnasaugh; it sets its face resolutely towards practical matters and is thus, in its small way, a model of 'development', setting aside irrelevancies and considering only economic and temporal necessities. Where Auchnasaugh and Rome may have their secrets, and the detective fiction model parades its own association with the very topic of secrecy, this brave new language has no secrets, or rather will profess to none; like estuarine English, like the rhetoric of convergence, it seeks a mid-point which will involve no necessity of translation, no need for a glossary to preserve the tongue from extinction.

And this returns me to the central thrust of my argument. Loss is crucial to *O Caledonia*; indeed, the whole text is about the impossibility of living in Scotland, the necessity of living in Scotland, the status of Scotland as a hallucination, the vanishing point of cultural and linguistic evidence for national survival or resurrection. And if loss is one of the subtexts with which we need to deal in the context of the postcolonial, then one way of figuring that loss is precisely as the loss of the untranslatable. We need to be fully aware that to say this places us firmly on the terrain of the paradox, but it is a paradox which has to be faced and lived. A language that can survive only by being translated into another one is, as we all know, a language in considerable trouble – not necessarily terminal trouble, but that appalling species of trouble that may result in it being confined to the infirmary of the heritage industry. On the other hand, there are difficulties too for languages that seek to modernise themselves. One graphic emblem of the advantages and disadvantages which attend upon this course of action can be found in Wales, where one penetrates the skin of the language to discover that quite a lot of the time you are speaking in English, except that you have not recognised the orthography. This is but a small emblem of the complexity of relations between language and the postcolonial.

But it is possible to become lost in the detail, and I want now to try to offer some generalisations. First, it is necessary to return to one of the matters to which I alluded, if a little elliptically, at the beginning of the chapter. John Gray in *False Dawn* makes it very plain that many Western commentators on globalisation, including the vast majority of environmental activists, are decisively missing the contemporary political and economic point when they quixotically take on the multinational corporations. According to Gray, although it is perfectly true that there are multinationals that are now as big, in terms of gross product, as nation-states, they are not at all more secure; they are, in fact, equally at the mercy of the real 'culprit of difference', which is the international monetary organisations and their US-inspired ethos of convergent development.[9]

It then seems to me that it would be important to look at the literary under that light of convergent development, and that one way in which such a concept figures in specifically literary terms is in the matter of translatability: Achebe's use of Igbo terms, Morrison's use of white children's books, Barker's multiple shifts of genre and register. But precisely here, I suggest, is where the critical problem with the notion of the postcolonial arises with full force, and this is because there are three interlinked levels at which loss can be examined in its inalienable connection with the literary.

First, of course, there is the general psychoanalytic theory of loss, about which a huge literature exists running from Freud and Klein to John Bowlby and beyond.[10] Essentially, what this literature is talking about is the inevitability of loss as a primary field on which personality, individual or social, constructs itself, loss primarily of the mother, but also loss as a site for the scenario of repetition which will structure the psychic life. Without loss or the fear of loss, there would be no movement, there would be, quite literally, lifelessness. Only loss 'prepares the ground'; thus the ground is marked by loss, 'marked out' by loss; all boundaries involve loss, just as all boundaries, and especially those set up to contain the 'colony', are hallucinatory (which is not at all to deny that they are protected by the power of the gun).

Second, and on top of this, we can suggest that the literary in general is based on loss, that it is inherently nostalgic in its desirous attempt to bring into being something which is not there, although clearly it has in some sense once been there before, in the imagination of the writer, in the cultural tradition or repertoire, along the lost nervous system of the trace.[11] This would be a condition general to all literature, perhaps to all writing, and it would also imply that all writing is rewriting, an attempt to conjure manifest content from latent content; although I am perfectly conscious that in using these terms while attempting to remain on the terrain of the postcolonial I am risking challenge on the grounds of attempting to import Western psychoanalytic terminology into situations which are, to use the word in its strongest sense, different.

To say, however, one further word about this controversial matter: we might argue that the question of the imperialism of psychoanalytic terminology and practice, and its association with a rhetoric of the subjugation of savagery, has become confused with a different set of issues to do with reproduction, maturation, childhood and parenting, family relations. What seems important is to suggest that psychoanalysis occupies a particular location in the cultures of the West, and then to ask where one might find – in other cultures – discourses, rhetorics, practices that can be usefully compared to psychoanalysis. This enquiry would not be simple, for several reasons: it is, for a start, exceedingly difficult to define that location, because to do so inevitably brings one up against the intractability of the 'unconscious'; it is also the case that there are global complexities to psychoanalysis itself, perhaps most emblematically in South America, and these are themselves bound up with wider questions about cultural forms – in this case, about the relation between a certain imagining of the unconscious and the hallucinations of magic realism.[12]

Which brings me to my third and final reading of loss: that in a postcolonial situation it will be given an added twist, perhaps one with the gravest and most appalling of consequences, by the sense of the crowding memory of all that has been lost in the colonising process, not only in the overt act of violent domination – the bullet – but also in the external and internal repetition of that act through the coercion of language. We might, both in order to pursue this thought further and also to subject to further inspection my no doubt controversial classification of Scotland as a postcolonial culture, consider the following sentences from *O Caledonia*:

> While Janet agreed that the Dibdins had a ridiculous surname she had nothing against the English *per se*. After all, most of her favourite poets were English. And she thought that she might like people who talked a lot. (Barker, 1991, 64)

Clearly here stereotyping and irony are inextricably intertwined in this looping between the grandeur of the past and the ludicrousness of the present, this complexity of assertions about control of and submission to the processes of cultural and social domination. But then, the overall notion of these three layers of loss returns me again to my original question. One might ask: how might it be possible to discern a specificity of the postcolonial, considering the omnipresence of loss? But one might also more potently ask: if the, as it were, real story of what is going on is not about the replacement of one culture with another, or about the cosmopolitan versus the nativist, then what might the real story of convergence be?

In one sense, and for the moment to submit to the conventional critical elision of the 'postcolonial' with the 'post(British)colonial', we already know the answer clearly enough. The promulgation of the English language began as an imperial enterprise, as has been so often and repeatedly demonstrated; but it is now a thoroughly commercial one, and its aim is not the validation or promulgation of any nation-state but the banalisation and integration of markets in the name of economic convergence.[13] And so we might feel left, before we move on in the next chapters to look at a variety of other postcolonial texts, with a question to think about. If local cultures are what have to be swept aside, rendered ultimately convergent and translatable for the purposes of economic assimilation, then what quite is happening with the application of the label 'postcolonial'? Is it the case that, as Gareth Griffiths suggests, 'post-colonial theory may act as a globalising international force to wipe out local differences and concerns' (Griffiths, 1996, 168), implying that the only feasible site of resistance would then be an attention confined to local detail? Or might it rather be that there is some way in which postcolonial writing and postcolonial theory can be 'read' for their very evasions, for the sense that, in fact, the problems they address are, as it were, allowed to be addressed precisely because, while we are spending our time 'examining the "post"', the world has, probably malignly, certainly secretly, moved on? Neither of these conclusions are particularly attractive; but then, while we spend time celebrating the success of native, indigenous, or simply national literatures, perhaps we ought also to spend time wondering about what these temporary, 'postcolonial' successes really amount to in the wider terms of economic, linguistic, cultural power.

Perhaps what they amount to is hinted at in a brief passage from Amos Tutuola's *Feather Woman of the Jungle*, a book written, like all of Tutuola's extraordinary books, in a unique variety of English:

> I noticed that the main gate had a portico which resembled that of an ancient palace of the olden days king. Several images like that of the lions, tigers, deers, antelopes, monkeys, crocodiles, lizards, men, women, etc. were carved on that portico from bottom to top. But some parts of them had been washed away and all together with the portico were very old. In the veranda, there were several sprouts of the small trees. The frames, roof, ceiling, etc. were nearly eaten off by the white ants. (Tutuola, 1962, 39–40)

Here we have a conjuration of an ancient, singular world, a trace of previous empire, a hint of things hidden and overlaid; but the shape this can assume is not the shape of a resurrection, of a new springing into life, but a shape which is decayed, eaten, washed away; a shape that, in its ambiguous, hallucinatory presence, figures forth the very faces of loss.

# III Violent Geographics

> What was civilisation anyway but itself an edge, a space afforded by the absurd ... (Sunetra Gupta, *The Glassblower's Breath*)

> It was understandable that in Arabanoo's geography ... the Camarai headlands, layered in sandstone and covered with the coarse and distinctive foliage of the new earth, shone like remembered combats and desires ... (Thomas Keneally, *The Playmaker*)

> In a borderless economy, the nation-focused maps we typically use to make sense of economic activity are woefully misleading. We must ... face up at last to the awkward and uncomfortable truth: the old cartography no longer works. It has become no more than an illusion. (Kenichi Ohmae, *The End of the Nation-State*)

Margaret Atwood's novel *Surfacing*, which, like so many other postcolonial texts, is structured around loss, is also a book about maps. Her heroine, returning to the scene of complex past trauma, says that she does not bring a map with her because she assumes she knows her way, although she finds that there is in any case a map tacked to the cabin wall (Atwood, 1973, 6, 29). The book's maps, however, shift and change, not so much depicting fixed territory as gesturing towards a continuing and inescapable series of deterritorialisations and reterritorialisations.[1] Running through them like a disabling fracture is the dividing line between Canada and the United States; yet perhaps this is less a fracture than an infected wound. It certainly has the power to spread its infection into language, as the character David discovers:

> We ought to start a colony, I mean a community up here, get it together with some other people, break away from the urban nuclear family. It wouldn't be a bad country if only we could kick out the fucking pig Americans, eh? (83)

The mistaken mention of 'colony' serves precisely to undermine this neat view of history, development, progress; behind it lurk some less easily answerable questions, to do with borders, or rather the absence of them, and to do also with who, if anybody, might be 'at home' in the foreign space Atwood depicts. 'Now we're on my home ground', the nameless heroine, Atwood's *alter ego*, says: 'foreign territory', she immediately continues. 'My throat constricts, as it learned to do when I discovered people could say words that would go into my ears meaning nothing' (5).

Home ground (in a colonial/colonised space?) is foreign territory. And the effect of this impossible conjunction, this inconceivable distortion of boundaries and of the sense of place, is to constrict the throat – to prevent, therefore, the possibility of language, to erode meaning. Birds, Atwood tells us, 'sing for the same reason trucks honk, to proclaim their territory: a rudimentary language' (35). But in this sphere, which is both postcolonial (in relation to the British) and neocolonial (in relation to the USA), even the proclamation of territory is shrouded in mystery. When the group of principal characters meets a group of intruders onto their space, they initially assume they are from the USA because they 'had a starry flag like all of them, a miniature decal on the canoe bow. To show us we were in occupied territory' (115), but in fact the canoeists turn out to be Canadian, the decal is not a flag but an entirely different sign; in this world, if signals are legible at all they are susceptible only of being read wrongly.

It is for this reason that the heroine's search for origins – for her father, for the cave paintings which had apparently been absorbing him (in more senses than one) before his disappearance – becomes so contorted, that she enters so many dead ends in the labyrinth. She is searching for a painting she has found represented in her father's notes:

> 'It might be hard to see at first', I said, 'Faded. It ought to be right here somewhere'. But it wasn't: no man with antlers, nothing like red paint or even a stain, the rock surface extended under my hand, coarse-grained, lunar, broken only by a pink-white vein of quartz that ran across it, a diagonal marking the slow tilt of the land; nothing human.
>
> Either I hadn't remembered the map properly or what he'd written on the map was wrong. (121)

Would it be possible, one might wonder, ever to remember a postcolonial map properly, ever to put together a coherent account of a world where histories are mysteriously overlaid? In one sense, what we have here is a version of the world depicted so graphically by Deleuze and Guattari in *A Thousand Plateaus* and elsewhere, a world which is radically inhuman, where the 'subject', no longer conceived of as at the centre, is

> 'produced as a mere residuum' of the processes of the desiring machines, the nomadic offshoot of striated mental spaces and of the body defined as longitude and latitude: 'Individual or group, we are traversed by lines, meridians, geodesics, tropics, and zones marching to different beats and differing in nature'. (Young, 1995, 168)[2]

There are, as Robert Young among others has shown, clear parallels between this world of tectonic plates and geological formations and the inhumanity of colonisation, the realisation of the colonial desiring machine within which people, and peoples, are consumed, exhausted, deadened, robbed of meaning (see Young, 1995, 171–4); as Toni Morrison puts it in an emblematic episode in her novel *Beloved*, 'the whitefolks had tired her out at last' (Morrison, 1987, 180). Just so, in *Surfacing*, there are clear connections between the traumatised condition of the heroine, her blankness, the unbreakable (yet in another sense already broken) window between her and the world, and the multiple violences enacted on the troubled soil of Canada. Not, of course, only or even primarily the invasive presence of the USA; but here more the residual trace of an earlier people, a First Nation, whose unreadable marks and signs come to signify the only possibility for the unravelling of a contorted history.[3]

This, at any rate, is what the vanished father appears to have been trying to do although, as his daughter realises, the actual relation between his notes and the signs held on and in the rocks of the lake is more complicated than that:

> The map crosses and the drawings made sense now: at the beginning he must have been only locating the rock paintings, deducing them, tracing and photographing them, a retirement hobby; but then he found out about them. The Indians did not own salvation but they had once known where it lived and their signs marked the sacred places, the places where you could learn the truth. There was no painting at White Birch Lake and none here, because his later drawings weren't copied from things on the rocks. He had discovered new places, new oracles, they were things he was seeing the way I had seen, true vision; at the end, after the failure of logic. (Atwood, 1973, 139)

The attempt to recapture the past, Atwood is therefore saying, can take place only under the sign of a new geography, a 'radical' geography (one, that is, which is committed to uprooting or 're-discovering' its own ancestors), eventually an 'imagined geography' in which the map takes on its own life and becomes a source rather than a representation of incarnation.[4] Yet even in this putatively hopeful scenario there remains room for doubt, a doubt fully present in the closing words of the text where the trees are 'asking and giving nothing' (186), the heroine's request for an interpretation of the map within which she is herself enclosed has fallen on deaf and stony ears.

'The prevalence of the map topos', says Graham Huggan, 'in contemporary post-colonial literary texts, and the frequency of its ironic and/or parodic usage in these texts, suggests a link between a de/reconstructive reading of maps and a revisioning of the history of European colonialism' (Huggan, 1989, 123). Indeed it does; yet the question of irony or parody may seem somewhat beside the point when confronted with the violent clarity of, for example, R. Parthasarathy's 'The Attar of Tamil':

> Your country is not a suitcase:
> you are not a traveller
> shuffling, with tongue in cheek,
>
> the loose change of words.
> For twenty years you have tried
> to pry this book open.
>
> Tall and attentive, the rose-apple tree
> stands in your uncle's backyard
> in Trichinopoly, undefiled
>
> by the passing English dog.
> You arrive there, unscathed and with a whole skin,
> with the attar of Tamil for a map.
>
> (Behl and Nicholls, 1995, 55)

Or, for that matter, with the submerged passion of this fragment from Brathwaite's *The Arrivants*:

> the fisherman's boat is broken on the first white inland hills,
> his tangled nets in a lonely tree,
> the trapped fish still confused.
> After this breach of the sea's balanced

treaty, how will new maps be drafted?
Who will suggest a new tentative frontier?
How will the sky dawn now?

(Brathwaite, 1973, 184)

Parthasarathy's map will, perhaps, still be a guide when the 'English dog' has retreated; but what is crucial here is to recognise that, because empire retreats, that does not mean that the namings that have accompanied it will also fade into the shadows. Rather, they remain to haunt. In Giles Foden's peculiar novel about Idi Amin, *The Last King of Scotland*, an odd mixture of sharp observation and imperial nostalgia, Bonney's father, we are told, used to be 'Chief Headman for the Directorate of Overseas Surveys' – in other words, he used to assist his imperial masters in the making of maps – and because of this he knows a huge amount about European geographical misnamings; but this knowledge does not protect him from a vicious and ugly death (Foden, 1998, 80).

One of the phenomena with which we are presented in postcolonial writing is, then, a whole panoply of maps, a treasure chest of charts, piled in heaps, lapped one over another, imaginary geographies, but ones in which the root of power that has nourished them is in the slow process of being exposed. Geography, we might say, would be the key to resistance, even though geography is itself not immovable, as we remember when we see the Yangtse dammed, the Indonesian forests in flames. Would it be possible to find a human image that would approximate in some way to this resistance, that would in the terms of Deleuze and Guattari appropriate the position of the absolute nomad, would enact a final rejection of the state apparatus, the war machine and all their cartographic works?[5]

Perhaps the best example would be found in J.M. Coetzee's *Life & Times of Michael K.* During times of unrest in South Africa, Michael, who is black, poor and disabled, sets out to take his sick mother back to the only place where she can ever remember being happy, a farm on which she worked when younger. She dies on the way and Michael finds himself, as it were, at a loss. He has no papers and no possessions; he also has no clear idea of where to go. His sense of self is precarious and his grip on language even more so. He gradually descends through a series of locations, geological strata, barren mountainsides, including a labour camp and other manifestations of apartheid rule, until he is living in a hole in the ground; he ceases to need to eat, his thought processes dry up, he becomes a mere withered stump, a dry leaf. Yet at the same time he inescapably enacts a new geography: he becomes a cultivator, planting pumpkin seeds, watching the fruit grow. Later a doctor at a re-education camp where Michael is taken, appalled and fascinated by his condition, tries to find meaning in this mysterious, inexplicable life, a life that owes much to Kafka's bureaucratic Gothic but has also the inescapable inflexions of colonial exploitation (see Kafka, 1930, e.g., pp. 108–9). 'Let me tell you', says the doctor,

> the meaning of the sacred and alluring garden that blooms in the heart of the desert and produces the food of life. The garden for which you are presently heading is nowhere and everywhere except in the camps. It is another name for the only place where you belong, Michaels, where you do not feel homeless. It is off every map, no road leads to it that is merely a road, and only you know the way. (Coetzee, 1983, 228)

This attempt at explanation is confusing and confused. Michael's plight (he is addressed as 'Michaels' in an error of naming typical both of the apartheid state and of the postcolonial condition in general[6]) is to be continually reinterpreted. Insofar as he represents absolute resistance, then a map has to be found – to show the visitor the way round the exhibit. The miserable and dangerous hillside on which he grew his pumpkins has to be renamed: a 'sacred and alluring garden'. A paradise of productivity has to be incarnated in fantasy on a site of devastation.[7]

The guilt at the root of this postcolonial cultural narrative is perhaps obvious – the need to suppose that, despite all the reterritorialisations, the partitions, the redrawing of boundaries for imperial convenience, something rocklike remains, something that has survived the violence and exploitation and thereby demonstrates the salving possibility that all can be made whole again, that new maps can be drawn on fresh paper, that the legacy of domination can be erased. Then again, we might say that such erasure is in another sense not only possible but even unavoidable as part of the attempt to continue to live with an unspoken and unspeakable past. In his story 'Shakti', Vikram Chandra shows us how the composure of a wealthy Bombay socialite is nearly but not quite shaken by the memories of her father:

> Later, she would remember the old story of schisms and horrors, how he had left half his family murdered in Lahore, two brothers, a sister, a father. They had a shop, which was burned. Partition threw him onto the streets of Bombay, but he still spoke

> of his Lahore, his beautiful Lahore. It was something of a family joke. (Chandra, 1997, 66–7)

Here indeed history and geography are ironised, passed through the grid of a memory of a memory (are these the memories 'of' her father, or are they rather her memories 'of' him?), sifting down through time; whether and to what extent this constitutes a 'cure' for cultural and social trauma is a crucial topic, and one to which I shall return.

The maps that provide the background for Abdulrazak Gurnah's alluring and frightening novel *Paradise*, however, clearly permit of almost nothing in the way of cure, and at the same time they serve precisely to undermine the paradisal fantasy generated as a compensation for loss and ruin by the colonial desiring machine. Yusuf, the protagonist, is sold into slavery at the beginning of the novel; at the end, with no other choices available to him in a changing but still devastated world, he joins a German-led militia. The setting is East Africa as European war dawns, but the story is more concerned with the Arab traders' experience of encountering the expansion of the European empires in general in Africa:

> Everywhere they went now they found the Europeans had got there before them, and had installed soldiers and officials telling the people that they had come to save them from their enemies who only sought to make slaves of them. It was as if no other trade had been heard of, to hear them speak. The traders spoke of the Europeans with amazement, awed by their ferocity and ruthlessness. (Gurnah, 1994, 71–2)

Here geography is changing at every moment; the very relations between inner and outer, between centre and margin, alter as European incursion changes the basis of the relations between trader and 'native'. Yusuf's role is to travel with his 'uncle' Aziz into the 'interior', but the final trading mission is a disaster and it is clear that the old maps will no longer suffice, they no longer give clear or accurate directions.

It is again obvious that geography itself is dependent on power, as Aziz tells Yusuf when he has almost finished recounting the complex geographical history of Tayari and its division among Arab lords:

> Now there's talk that the Germans will build their railway all the way to here. It's they who make the law and dictate now,

> although it has been that way since the time of Amir Pasha and Prinzi really. But before the Germans came, no one travelled to the lakes without going through this town. (131)

This is in one sense, of course, simply the 'logic of the bypass', one of the more familiar narratives of development, but here it carries a greater than usual weight. There is the question, which we have come across before in the context of Achebe's District Commissioner, of whose story is going to be told, of what version of the tale will survive the vicissitudes of history. One of the phrases in commonest use in postcolonial criticism is 'The Empire Writes Back' (see Ashcroft, Griffiths and Tiffin, 1989); but amid the manifold – and still unfolding – ambiguities of that phrase, there is the question of what then happens to the 'original letter', whether it is contradicted by a new account, sealed into place as part of a continuing dialogue, or set up as a fetish for a past locked in presence and absence.[8]

Insofar as any dialogue on this terrain concerns maps, there would then be a further question as to how far it might permit the persistence of the inexplicable, what space there might be for the old sign that read 'Here Be Dragons' on a map whose contours have been radically redefined by, for example, the railway. In *Paradise*, that possibility remains, although it will soon be extinguished by the European invasion: 'When you get as far as the lakes in your travels', says one of the characters,

> you'll see that the world is ringed with mountains which give the green tint to the sky. Those mountains on the other side of the lake are the edge of the world we know. Beyond them, the air has the colour of plague and pestilence, and the creatures who live in it are known only to God. The east and the north are known to us, as far as the land of China in the farthest east and to the ramparts of Gog and Magog in the north. But the west is the land of darkness, the land of jinns and monsters. (Gurnah, 1994, 83)

Which 'west', the novel encourages us to ask, is being spoken of here: the 'west' which, for the Arabs of the East African coast, represents the interior, the impenetrable (yet at the same time thoroughly penetrated) 'heartland' of Africa, or that further 'west' from which come the Europeans, with their meaningless armies, their false accusations, their violent redrawings of boundaries? Either way, there is a space on the map which is filled with darkness, a world of 'plague and pestilence', from which monsters emerge. It is that space which generates the monstrous German officer who, Yusuf at first thinks, looks young; but on closer inspection,

> Yusuf realised that the officer was not as young as he had looked from a distance. The skin on his face was stretched tight and smooth, as if he had suffered burning or a disease. His smile was a fixed grimace of deformity. His teeth were exposed, as if the tightly stretched flesh on his face had already begun to rot and slough off round his mouth. It was the face of a cadaver, and Yusuf was shocked by its ugliness and its look of cruelty. (245)

This, then, is one composite face of the 'new world order'; the face of the man who now has the law on his side, who dictates to the rest of the world; the man who, in a bitter twist, leads the ramshackle army that Yusuf comes to see in the end as his only hope of survival. Yet still, and despite the horrifying nature of the description, there are questions to be asked: the 'look of cruelty', for example, seems to operate reflexively, the suffering inflicted by the colonialists and the military is itself, it may be suggested, the product of previous cruelty, the continuing unfolding saga of violence in terms of which the war machine claims its victims.

Geography claims its fixities and certainties; but below this there continues a world in which a radical displacement has paradoxically taken the centre of the stage. We might think, for example, of Beatrice in Achebe's *Anthills of the Savannah,* and of her reactions when confronted by the traditions of what we might call – under a certain erasure – 'her people':

> Beatrice Nwanyibuife did not know these traditions and legends of her people because they played but little part in her upbringing. She was born ... into a world apart; was baptised and sent to schools which made much about the English and the Jews and the Hindu and practically everybody else but hardly put in a word for her forebears and the divinities with whom they had evolved. So she came to barely knowing who she was. (Achebe, 1987, 105)

What is at stake here is the very status of stable identity, the nature of an emblematic 'decentred subjectivity' that is at the same time the product of a 'subjection' rigorously enacted through the imperial attempt to eradicate – place under erasure – previous histories and geographies.[9] The eponymous lead character in V.S. Naipaul's *A House for Mr Biswas* is another of many in postcolonial fiction who have been deracinated by imperial education. Mr Biswas was, we hear in a resonant phrase, never taught anything useful; he was taught 'other things' – things, we might literally suggest, *of the other* – by Mr Lal, his teacher:

> He learned to say the Lord's Prayer in Hindi from the *King George V Hindi Reader*, and he learned many English poems by heart from the *Royal Reader*. At Lal's dictation he made copious notes, which he never seriously believed, about geysers, rift valleys, watersheds, currents, the Gulf Stream, and a number of deserts. He learned about oases, which Lal taught him to pronounce 'osis' ... He learned about igloos. (Naipaul, 1961, 46)

It has often been said that anthropology, in its conceptual isolation of 'primitive peoples' as a specific object of study, acted as the intellectual handmaiden of the imperial project, and there is no doubt that this is true;[10] but at the same time a forcible redrawing of maps was being instituted by an 'imperial geography', under the guise of a scientistic neutrality. It is the after-effect of this substitutive intellectual project that resonates through so much postcolonial writing, along at times with a sophisticated understanding that a simple further redrawing of boundaries will not suffice and may serve only to repeat the destructive errors of colonisation.

Coetzee's Michael K becomes, in some sense, a cultivator, enacting a history of human development that sometimes seems curiously inverted;[11] Iain Banks, the Scottish novelist, provides us with another perceptive reworking of the history of farming that simultaneously remaps the relations between exploiter and exploited when the main character in *The Wasp Factory* reflects on his prior assumptions about the nature of sheep:

> After I'd come to understand evolution and know a little about history and farming, I saw that the thick white animals I laughed at for following each other around and getting caught in bushes were the product of generations of farmers as much as generations of sheep; *we* made them, we moulded them from the wild, smart survivors that were their ancestors so that they would become docile, frightened, stupid, tasty wool-producers. We didn't want them to be smart, and to some extent their aggression and their intelligence went together. (Banks, 1984, 145–6)

Set as *The Wasp Factory* is on a small Scottish island, and bearing in mind the historical relation between the introduction of sheep to

Scotland and the Highland clearances, it would be difficult not to read in this an allegory for the colonial relations between Scotland and England. The questions, in this particular novel, would then become: if sheep have developed as the mirror image of their human masters, to what extent is the psychopathy of the central character (who is, among other things, a triple murderer) separable from the violence practised upon him (imaged in the text in the entirely apposite terms of imagined castration); and to what extent can we read this further as a metaphor for the maddened and maddening relations between the rulers and the ruled?

He who draws the map 'articulates', we may say, the available space: similarly, as so many postcolonial writers remind us, articulacy itself is removed and set apart by the colonial project as a 'gift' – to be returned, if at all, only when a certain price has been paid. Dennis Lee puts it this way:

> To speak unreflectingly in a colony … is to use words that speak only alien space. To reflect is to fall silent, discovering that your authentic space does not have words. And to reflect further is to recognise that you and your people do not in fact have a privileged authentic space just waiting for words; you are, among other things, the people who have made an alien inauthenticity their own. You are left chafing at the inarticulacy of a native space which may not exist. So you shut up. (Lee, 1974, 163)

But at the same time, of course, it is also to search for other modes of articulacy, other ways of drawing the map that will permit the opening of spaces against this threat of permanent closure. Wilson Harris, in his Note on *The Palace of the Peacock*, provides us with an extraordinarily vivid example of a way of re-envisioning geography:

> A great magical web born of the music of the elements is how one may respond perhaps to a detailed map of Guyana seen rotating in space with its numerous etched rivers, numerous lines and tributaries, interior rivers, coastal rivers, the arteries of God's spider. (Harris, 1988, 7)[12]

'Guyana', Harris goes on to remind us, is derived from an Amerindian word meaning 'land of waters', but this kind of 'originary' re-envisioning can only properly occur while one remains aware of the social and cultural dangers that threaten it, dangers into which his next sentence, after a mystical beginning, descends with precipitous force:

> The spirit-bone of water that sings in the dense, interior rainforests is as invaluable a resource in the coastal savannahs which have long been subject to drought as to floodwaters that stretched like a sea from coastal river to coastal river yet remained unharnessed and wasted; subject also to the rapacity of moneylenders, miserable loans, inflated interest.

It is as if this very sentence – which in its very windings, repetitions, curves and loops, vividly represents the river gods – cannot but descend into a reminder of all that threatens the return to a vitalised, 'native' geography: precisely that alternative 'new geography', that 'new world order' of capital that can have no truck with difference, that can see rivers no longer even as conduits of trade, let alone as the 'arteries of God's spider', but merely as abstract emblems for wastage, superfluity, impediments in the way of the smooth free flow of commerce and development.[13]

Michael Ondaatje's fragmentary memoir of his journey to recapture his past in Sri Lanka, *Running in the Family*, can take us a little further in our consideration of geography and maps; indeed, it provides us with an example of the kind of 'geo-graphics' to which I have intended to allude in the title of this chapter, a 'graphics' or writing, inscription that takes as its primary model an attempted reincarnation of geography. Opening with a map of the island which he unflinchingly refers to throughout as 'Ceylon', despite the fact that its named was changed in 1972, the text moves to his planning of the journey that will form its main subject. 'During quiet afternoons', he says, 'I spread maps onto the floor and searched out possible routes to Ceylon', but it is not only maps he spreads on the floor; it is, inevitably, names as well, and in this case one particular name: '*Asia*. ... The word sprawled. It had none of the clipped sound of Europe, America, Canada. The vowels took over, slept on the map with the S' (Ondaatje, 1982, 22).

He finds, perhaps unsurprisingly, that the land to which he wishes to return is no longer there. He walks with other relatives 'around the house, through the depressed garden of guava trees, plantains, old forgotten flowerbeds. Whatever "empire" my grandfather had fought for had to all purposes disappeared' (60). Atwood's heroine's vanished father; Yusuf's lost family; Ondaatje's vivid yet unsustainable memories – all of these are phenomena of the redrawing of maps, the restless search for a moment of geographical stability. But 'Ceylon', according to Ondaatje, has always *been* an unstable geography:

> On my brother's wall in Toronto are the false maps. Old portraits of Ceylon. The result of sightings, glances from trading vessels, the theories of sextant. The shapes differ so much they seem to be translations – by Ptolemy, Mercator, François Valentyn, Mortier, and Heydt – growing from mythic shapes into eventual accuracy. (63)

'Sextant theories'; by a slip of the tongue, by a conventional parapraxis, one might detect an allusion to 'sexual theories', growing as Freud optimistically supposes them to do from the 'mythic' towards 'accuracy'; and indeed it would only be by means of some such teleological fiction that one could accuse these older maps of being 'false'. Nevertheless, the point about 'translation' is important, for all maps are, in some sense, translations; they take data in a particular medium and, in the equivalent of what now happens under the aegis of computer modelling, they throw the resulting construct over the 'real' in an attempt to capture what is there (see Harvey, 1985, 25, 136–9).

But what *is* there? Ondaatje, in the end, really does not seem sure. The passage continues:

> Amoeba, then stout rectangle, and then the island as we know it now, a pendant off the ear of India. Around it, a blue-combed ocean busy with dolphin and sea-horse, cherub and compass. Ceylon floats on the Indian Ocean and holds its naïve mountains, drawings of cassowary and boar who leap without perspective across imagined 'desertum' and plain. (Ondaatje, 1982, 63)

Is this really how we 'know' Sri Lanka now, as a 'pendant off the ear of India'? What is at work here, of course, is a set of old orientalist, or perhaps in this case one should say 'subcontinental', myths: according to these myths this pendant, this jewel, may well 'depend' from an ear, but it is not a human ear, as Ondaatje himself goes on to reveal:

> At the edge of the maps the scrolled mantling depicts ferocious slipper-footed elephants, a white queen offering a necklace to natives who carry tusks and a conch, a Moorish king who stands amidst the power of books and armour. On the south-west corner of some charts are satyrs, hoof deep in foam, listening to the sound of the island, their tails writhing in the waves. (63–4)

An elephant's ear, one supposes, the ear of Ganesh; the discourse is crossed with the other 'Indianist' myth of fabulous wealth and somewhere not far away, despite Ondaatje's frequent reviling in the book of the English ('transients, snobs and racists' (41)), echoes the imperialist rhetoric of the 'jewel in the crown'.[14] But then Ceylon itself, in these meditations of Ondaatje's, is the source of jewels:

> The maps reveal rumours of topography, the routes for invasion and trade, and the dark mad mind of travellers' tales appears throughout Arab and Chinese medieval records. The island seduced all of Europe. The Portuguese. The Dutch. The English. And so its name changed, as well as its shape, – Serendip, Ratnapida ('island of gems'), Taprobane, Zeloan, Zeilan, Seyllan, Ceilon, and Ceylon – the wife of many marriages, courted by invaders who stepped ashore and claimed everything with the power of their sword or bible or language. (64)

Ratnapida, 'island of gems'; any of these names is perhaps preferable to the unutterably contemporary, Sri Lanka, which again figures nowhere in this list; thus, we might say, the 'dark mad mind of travellers' tales' is still being re-enacted through this reincarnation of the exotic. But names, as we see, do change, change under the irresistible impress of naming by the other, naming *as* the other; just as shapes change, maps change; this too is an inevitable part of the postcolonial narrative.

'The dark mad mind of travellers' tales'; those travellers' tales are not the property of the imperial explorers alone, they at all points become merged with, melded with, the discourse of the colonised. Kiran Desai's *Hullabaloo in the Guava Orchard*, a book amusing in its conception but flawed by an apparently irresistible attraction to farce, tells the story of a boy, similar to Melville's Bartleby in his passive resistance to work, who decides to spend his time living in a guava tree and as a consequence becomes treated for a while as a guru (see Melville, 1993, 95–130). His mother Kulfi, unbalanced since her son's birth in various ways and specifically by her yearning to cook increasingly 'exotic' foods, has clearly internalised this 'dark mad mind':

> She was the royal cook of a great kingdom, she imagined. There, in some old port city, ruthless hunters, reckless adventurers, fleets of ships and whole armies lay at her beck and call, were alert to her every command, her every whim. And sitting in a vast kitchen before an enormous globe, imperiously she ordered her supplies, sent out for spices from many seas away, from mountain ranges and deserts that lay beyond the horizon, for

> spices that existed only in the fantastical tales of sailors and soothsayers. She sent out for these and for plants that grew on islands no bigger than specks in the ocean, or on mountain peaks devoid of human habitation. She sent out for kingdoms to be ruined, for storehouses and fields to be plundered and ransacked. She asked for tiger meat and bear, Siberian goose and black buck. For turtles, terrapins, puff adders and seals. For armadillos, antelopes, zebras and whales ... (Desai, 1998, 154–5)

What operates this myth, we might suppose, is precisely the 'enormous globe', the incarnation of a fantasy of imperial domination. Here, swinging before Kulfi, are empires and powers, thrones and dominations, all the riches and treasures of the world. The madness of a parody of travel is called forth by the map; on its surface lines of flight are planned, imaginary narratives and fabulous creatures meet and interlock (cf., e.g., Rushdie, 1995, 36–42).

Behind these maps, of course, lie the colonial 'realities' of migration, the refugee, slavery, the Middle Passage. Brathwaite's *The Arrivants* is suffused with imagery of travel, the after-effects of the journeyings of slaves across the Atlantic:

> And so it was Little
> Rock, Dall-
> as, New Orleans, Santiago
> De Cuba, the miles
> of unfortunate islands: the
>
> Saints and the Virgins. L'Ouverture's Haiti
> ruined by greed and the slow
> growing green of its freedom; golden Guiana:
> Potaro
> leaping in light liquid amber
> in Makonaima's perpetual falls. And as if
> the exhaustion of this wasn't all – Egypt,
> Meroë, the Congo and all –
> in the fall we reached De-
> troit, Chicago and Den-
> ver; and then it was New
> York, selling news-
> papers in Brooklyn and Harlem.
> Then Capetown and Rio; remember how we
> took Paris by storm: Sartre, Camus, Picasso and all?
> (Brathwaite, 1973, 36)

Here we have the very process of reterritorialisation caught in the lines' uncertain rhythms; namings which have become conventionalised are rendered strange again, a foreignness is reincarnated in the shaping of the text. 'Now we're on my home ground, foreign territory', as Atwood puts it; part of the challenge that she and Brathwaite both issue to their readers is to ask whether, for any of us, there is a 'home ground' that is not 'foreign territory', a map that makes perfect sense, or a language fully adequate to the articulation of experience.

Perhaps that perfect map would be held only in fantasy, in dream, where the impossibilities of the home ground that is foreign territory can be held in stasis, names that are merely the product of the 'colonial arbitrary' can still be held and reinvested with meaning. As Harris puts it in *Palace of the Peacock,*

> The map of the savannahs was a dream. The names Brazil and Guyana were colonial conventions I had known from childhood. I clung to them now as to a curious necessary stone and footing, even in my dream, the ground I knew I must not relinquish. ... I pored over the map of the sun my brother had given me. The river of the savannahs wound its way far into the distance until it had forgotten the open land. The dense dreaming jungle and forest emerged. (Harris, 1988, 24)

Whose dream, we wonder, is this; or, perhaps better, what is it that dreams, what is it in the land that dreams its own shapes, that forms its own geography?

# IV Rage and Hatred Chaos and Ruin

... observe the débâcle in which I now exist, the utter ruin that I say is my life ... (Jamaica Kincaid, *A Small Place*)

'Pure' cultures do not exist, and neither do 'mixed' ones, but only cultures which recognise and value their diverse character, and others which deny or repress it. (Tzvetan Todorov, 'The Coexistence of Cultures')

It is not
it is not
it is not enough
to be pause, to be hole
to be void, to be silent
to be semicolon, to be semicolony;
(Edward Brathwaite, *The Arrivants*)

Among the most damaging results of colonisation, as is now well recognised, were the pervasions/perversions of education and of literature; which in the case of the British colonies, because of the peculiarly nationalistic place assigned to the literary within the imperial 'English' curriculum, can scarcely be separated.[1] George Lamming is among many in his reporting, with an admirable light-heartedness that does not conceal – nor is it meant to – a continuing bitterness, on the experience and effects of this series of acts of exploitative imposition:

> The West Indian's education was imported in much the same way that flour and butter are imported from Canada. Since the cultural negotiation was strictly between England and the natives, and England had acquired, somehow, the divine right to organise the native's reading, it is to be expected that England's export of literature would be English. Deliberately and exclusively

> English. And the further back in time England went for these treasures, the safer was the English commodity. So the examinations, which would determine that Trinidadian's future in the Civil Service, imposed Shakespeare, and Wordsworth, and Jane Austen and George Eliot and the whole tabernacle of dead names, now come alive at the world's greatest summit of literary expression. (Lamming, 1960, 27)

Within this compelling rhetoric we might isolate two elements. There are the 'treasures', themselves the construct of the imperial imagination, reminiscent perhaps of those emblematically delivered and in a sense withheld in the (ironically Scottish) text of Robert Louis Stevenson's *Treasure Island*; there is also the issue of 'dead names', which touches both on the crucial question of (mis)naming but also on a whole range of further questions about the way in which the rhetoric of the imperial is always simultaneously a rhetoric of haunting, the installation of the names of the dead (the 'tabernacle') as a propitiation against an understanding of the names of the living.

The notion within colonial rhetoric that treasure and death might be inextricably linked is, of course, one of the controlling myths of empire.[2] 'Fifteen men on the dead man's chest' is only the most enduring of many such formulations, and indeed it is so precisely because of its incorporation within the corpus of a children's literature, a literature that has a long-lost yet still hovering function of training, even in infancy, the next generation of (male) imperial explorers and adventurers.[3] What might now arrest us in the face of postcolonial writing is the way in which the real focus of this thanatic urge might be redirected onto a different object, mirrored back onto the 'originary' focus of discontent. The point is graphically put by Jamaica Kincaid:

> [The English] don't seem to know that this empire business was all wrong and they should, at least, be wearing sackcloth and ashes in token penance of the wrongs committed, the irrevocableness of their bad deeds, for no natural disaster imaginable could equal the harm they did. Actual death might have been better. ... no place could ever really be England, and nobody who did not look exactly like them would ever be English, so you can imagine the destruction of people and land that came from that. The English hate each other and they hate England, and the reason they are so miserable now is that they have no place else to go and nobody else to feel better than. (Kincaid, 1988, 41)

What is particularly important is to register the term 'hatred'. Often subsumed into the more ameliorative discourses of 'envy' and 'mimicry', the issue of hatred has nonetheless continued to cry out from the time of Frantz Fanon,[4] inviting inspection, not merely of the ruin as Kincaid puts it, but also of the 'irrevocableness' (the impossibility of 're-vocalising' the depth of humiliation) of that ruin,[5] the impossibility of restoring anything from the loss created. What is registered in the postcolonial is not so frequently the possibility of a hybrid rapprochement but instead the recognition that the construction of boundaries, borders, 'false maps', has rendered such a rapprochement impossible; there is literally no language in which 'negotiation' would be possible. English, one would of course want to add, is not the only site of demolition: among the major empires at the turn of the nineteenth century, as we have seen, were many that were not English-speaking, they were Chinese, Russian, Austro-Hungarian, and before that, until for example the Spanish-American war, they had also been Iberian; one might say that there is even a certain adventitious element in the way a ghostly perpetuation of the English language as the major means of oppression has been preserved not through the perpetuation of any active British hegemony but through the expansion of the US empire and now the consequences of US domination of cyberspace. Nevertheless, the issue of the removal of the 'native tongue' remains firmly attached to the spread of the English language in particular. Kincaid puts it like this:

> what I see is the millions of people, of whom I am just one, made orphans: no motherland, no fatherland, no god ... and worst and most painful of all, no tongue. ... For isn't it odd that the only language I have in which to speak of this crime is the language of the criminal who committed the crime? (Kincaid, 1988, 43)

There is, one might say, no way of evading the indictment of criminality, precisely because the old colonialisms arrogated to themselves the right of a usurped 'law'.[6] What would be very convenient for that western rhetoric which perpetuates itself in ghostly fashion above all in the presumed 'rule' of 'high theory' would be to claim that such 'criminality' can be explained (and explained away) in a specific reading of passages such as this, whereby the rhetoric of the mother, the father, the orphan come to stand as essentialist expiations of a specific set of local dominations; but this is precisely the point at which the writ of psychoanalysis as 'framework' refuses to run.

For those fatherings, those motherings, those orphanages (as conditions and as institutions) stand here revealed in the terms now ascribed to them emblematically in the 'rediscoveries' of Australia, the rediscoverings of the cost of the presumption of 'racial purity', the thousands of children removed from their parents in order to cover up the criminal consequences of colonial desire, the wish of white men to father children on 'native' women and the further wish to obliterate the trace of this crossing of the boundary by removing those same children from situations in which they might learn something of the truth of their parentage.[7] Here too we come across a further aspect of that ruin of which Kincaid speaks, and we can find a cognate rhetoric at work in Harris's attempts to coin new terminologies, terminologies which may appear at times idiosyncratic, to represent these senses of hidden histories, disguised births, realms of forcing and rape. We might consider his curious description of his usage of the term 'fossil': 'The word *fossil* is used in an idiosyncratic sense to invoke a rhythmic capacity to re-sense contrasting spaces and to suggest that a curious rapport exists between *ruin* and *origin* as latent to arts of genius' (Harris et al., 1975, 16).

There are many ways in which one might try to understand this passage. One would be by suggesting that the experience of colonisation suggests in particularly vivid form that, as Derrida might say, there can be no exploration of the mythical 'point of origin' that does not involve us in the forcible and frequently unwelcome discovery of the ruin that is there concealed (see Leavey, 1986, 61, 76, 80); to take up the Blakean echo in the mention of the 'arts of genius', we might be reminded that it was also Blake who said, 'Drive your cart and your plow over the bones of the dead' (Blake, 1966, 150). The 'fossil' in this sense would then represent that which has been deposited down through past ages, the 'relic' of the past that cannot be disturbed without the gravest risk to the stability of the present and yet which continues to exercise a malign, even fetishistic, influence over the possibilities of the future.[8]

Here is Achebe, in *Anthills of the Savannah*, describing or perhaps reconstructing one such fossil:

> the chief was full of praise for my father for the good training he was giving the children of the village through his whip. My father, with a wistful look I had never seen on his face before, was telling the chief of a certain headmaster in 1940 who was praised by some white inspectors who came from England to look at schools in their colonies and found his school the most quiet in West Africa. (Achebe, 1987, 85–6)

The fossil, we might say, is silent, it has no tongue to call its own; but at the same time it is absolutely constitutive of its successor strata, it dominates the passage down the generations just as, here, the image of the 'white inspectors' continues to reverberate through a whole system of education, a system where silence is the most prized of commodities, wordless acquiescence in the face of the whip is the only possible guarantee of submission before the colonial and postcolonial imperative.[9]

But these ruins, these fossils, these aftermaths are everywhere in postcolonial writing. We might equally well consider the aftermath of the Ascendancy in Ireland, one image of which is provided for us in John Banville's *Mefisto*, replete with barren, ruined landscapes, the fossils of dead enterprises, the dangerously preserved relics of past ages:

> Now the stables were falling, the forge where Jack Kay had worked was silent. One day, on an overgrown path, under a huge tree, we met Miss Kitty, the last of the Ashburns of Ashburn Park, a distracted and not very clean maiden lady with a great beaked nose and tangled hair, who talked to us calmly enough for a bit, then turned abruptly and ordered us off the estate, waving her arms and shouting. (Banville, 1986, 11)

'The stables were falling': that which had appeared stable collapses, a fundamental (mental or societal) instability emerges, what is left of past empire, past certainty, is burnt ash, tangles, rubble, the impossibility of purity, contradictory discourses (the polite and the violent) which threaten to shake apart whatever fragile synthesis appears to have been achieved on the remains of the site of domination.

We can trace the operations of this sense of ruin and chaos further through *The Healers*, a novel by Ayi Kwei Armah. The text recounts an episode in the fall of the Asante empire, but it does so in an oblique manner, through the eyes of Densu, a villager who, after a series of disastrous encounters with his own local authorities, takes up a calling to become a 'healer'. The shape of the text is in some ways very similar to that of Scott's Waverley novels, at least as influentially interpreted by Gyorgy Lukács (see Lukács, 1962); in other words, the central figure is to some extent a bystander on historical events. There is, however, an interesting difference, in that it is not merely Densu as an individual who is the 'bystander', it is also his whole local culture that is shown as thrown about among the power struggles that herald and accomplish the end of the Asante empire.

If Densu is the bystander, then the 'voice' of understanding is a senior healer, Damfo. He offers these remarks in relation to the troubling, indeed disastrous, times in which he lives:

> Things go wrong when we do violence to ourselves. Yes, we have more than one self. The difficulty is to know which self to make the permanent one, and which we should leave ephemeral. You set one of the passing selves above your permanent self: that's doing violence to your self. Things will go wrong then, and you'll never know why as long as you remain in the same situation and don't move out of it. (Armah, 1978, 69)

What is important to bear in mind about these comments as they occur in the context of the novel is that they do not represent a psychologisation of a historical condition; on the contrary, they are to be taken also as an analysis *of* that historical condition. That historical condition is one of many possibilities; the crucial thing is to hold to that choice, among the multiple selves, which will lead through the tangle, but in the historical context Armah is describing this frequently proves impossible because the force of resistance, the sense of cultural integration that might have proved strong enough to hold against the oncoming march of the white aggressor, has already been fatally dissipated by internal feuding and the corrupt weakness of the Asante kings.

A consequence of this is that, against the always delayed possibility of 'healing', the imposition of false selves, false gods, becomes irresistible. 'In my blindness', says another character in the text, 'I had almost killed my true self. I had embraced false selves and set them up to dominate my real self. They were not even of my own making, these false selves. They were pieces of other people, demands put out by others to whom I used to give respect without stopping to think why' (69). What is being talked about here is a bowing before unexamined authority, what in psychoanalytic terms might be referred to as capitulation in the superego, and Armah portrays with great clarity what the dire consequences of this imperial kowtowing can be. What happens is that within the multiple personality (the diverse body of the village, the tribe, the nation) we undergo a process of internal colonisation: foreign bodies within the self, personalities that are perhaps distant from the main source of power, are gradually converted – infected, contaminated – and cease to be part of ourselves altogether. As though we were reading Conrad's *Heart of Darkness* from the 'other side', viewing it from the dark into the light, portions of the map of ourselves become occupied by the foreign, they become precisely 'stations' that will be capable of sustaining the enemy as he makes the long march towards the heartland of the kingdom.[10]

The image of the kingdom supplies the essential bridge between the different levels of the text. What is being talked about here is the habit of blind submission before the charisma of the 'royals', a black culture based on internal slavery (see Armah, 1978, 204ff.). Armah paints a devastatingly angry picture of these kings: drunkards, fools, but mostly children, they are entirely insulated from the world outside. What is lacking, the text says, whether we are now talking about the Asante or about their rival collaborationist kings, is any 'healing' vision of unity: they are too busily engaged in fighting each other to notice how the corners of their map are getting frayed, how the broad highway of invasion is being laid down right through the heartland of their territory, how models of both independence and mutual partnership are disappearing in a sea of colonisation precisely because of its fatal similarity to the bases of their own rule (see 271–7). They are exploiters and cynics: at the end of the day the Asante kings according to Armah preferred to give up all power and flee, in the hope that this enactment of loss would be temporary and they would be put back on their cardboard thrones by the whites who had already refused to negotiate with them, rather than allowing anybody the slightest internal chance of saving the kingdom if that would also entail their own fall from power (300–1).

These kings, Armah says, are already ruins, fossils, or in a different rhetoric they are 'false selves' and are thus things of transience, as they so clearly demonstrate in their own actions; they are thus also 'pieces of other people', they think and behave as though they are themselves locked firmly and forever under a foreign sign, the transubstantiated sign of 'king'. What stands over against this fragmentation is the notion of 'healing' itself, the work of perceiving harmony. The general Asamoa has this to say of his plan for defeating the white army:

> I also knew their greatest weakness. A warrior needs to know his enemy's weaknesses. I saw the weakness of the whites. It wasn't military at all. It was a weakness of the spirit, the soul. The whites are not on friendly terms with the surrounding universe. Between them and the universe there is real hostility. Take the forest here: if they stay long in the forest, they die. Either they cut down the forest and kill it, or it kills them. They can't live with it. (182)

Asamoa's diagnosis is, of course, perfectly correct: the problem is that he does not see the process of actually *killing* the forest as imaginatively possible. Demonstrably utopian in this unthought optimism, he finds he is wrong.

The principle of multiplicity – as opposed to the military and theological monotheism of the whites – is crucial to the novel. Armah describes it in terms of the 'shadow', that many-ness which is too big even to be incorporated into our understanding, which must stand or hover outside ourselves, as the entity in whose dark light our actions are to be performed. Just so is the forest the essence of multiplicity, the pathless, the trackless, the very moving form of loss, the wild wood where every tree turns into every other; but what is more important about this (white) apprehension is that what we lose in the forest is not only 'our own way', in all senses of that phrase, but also our sense of ownership of the self. It is in the teeth of these problematic multiplicities – Deleuze and Guattari would refer to them as 'nomadic assemblages' (see Deleuze and Guattari, 1988, 351–423) – that the rage that fuels the whites, Wolseley and Glover, grows. Against the dark multiple shadow rises the unilateral emblem of the Great White Mother of empire, who serves both to embody and to control the passions, to translate them for the blacks into a supposedly recognisable image which in fact serves only as an unsuccessful cover story for the flood of rage that keeps the lust of conquest afloat (see Armah, 1978, 201).

But Armah's text has also a more complex twist, for this is not just a search for another lost paradise, for something to hold against the irruption of the undead fossil. While Densu is engaged on his Zen-like quest for the status of healer, which involves gazing into a bowl of water,

> A hurtful thought arose. Suppose the need for completion was merely a disease? A second thought took the hurt away: the search would not be any the less natural for that. In the water the gazer saw a world in which some, a large number, had a prevalent disease. The disease was an urge to fragment everything. And the disease gave infinite satisfaction to the diseased because it gave them control. There were those with a contrary disease, an urge to unite everything. If that was a disease, the gazer thought, so let it be. But there would be nothing to keep him from choosing it for his own disease, and following its natural course, reaching for its natural aim. (230)

This rhetoric of disease also needs to be traced through postcolonial writing. It is central, obviously, because it represents a prevalent form of encounter between unequal cultures. Europeans, suffering in Africa or India climates for which they were wholly unsuited, experienced unknown diseases, ranging from malarial scourges to the anomie of the isolated settler, discovered that their repertoire of symptoms was inadequate as a directory to the fate of their bodies in unaccustomed tropics. But to an incomparably greater extent colonised peoples and First Nations – aboriginals and native Americans, most emblematically – were decimated by plagues brought from other climates, other regimes: the history of colonial contact can be written as a medical history, as a history of infections, contaminations, symptoms both real and phantomatic.[11] Against these threats of disease fetishistic solutions had to be found on both sides – the Great White Mother, for example – and perhaps it is this that helps to explain some puzzling lines in Brathwaite's *The Arrivants*, where he is speaking of the emergence of a terrible new god:

> From this womb'd heaven comes the new curled god
> with goblin old man's grinning, flat face smiling,
> crouched like a frog with monkey hands and
> insect fingers. This we will carve and carry
> with our cooking pots, wood mud and wattle;
> symbol sickness fetish for our sickness.
>
> (Brathwaite, 1973, 116)

Amid the multiple contemporary rewritings of the history of the 'science' of anthropology, we might say *apropos* of this passage, nothing is clear (see Okely, 1996; Gupta and Ferguson, 1997). In one of Michael Taussig's accounts of his work in South America, for example, we find that the attribution of magical skills arose from nothing in the culture of the native peoples themselves but was rather a direct result of the white settlers' desire to be 'cured' of their disease, a desire which propelled them to attribute magical powers to the very host body upon which they were parasitic (see Taussig, 1993). Similarly, it should remain an open question whether the notion of the 'fetish' relates to some assumed primordial state of the 'native', or whether it is rather a talismanic after-effect of European desire, the power of the shrunken head, for example, a mere extra-version of a need to propitiate in the face of overwhelming guilt.

The surgeon's knife, at any rate, is customarily applied to multiplicity and, as Achebe reminds us, things consequently 'fall apart'.

'Does the white man understand our custom about land?', a character asks in *Things Fall Apart*:

> How can he when he does not even speak our tongue? But he says that our customs are bad; and our own brothers who have taken up his religion also say that our customs are bad. How do you think we can fight when our own brothers have turned against us? The white man is very clever. He came quietly and peaceably with his religion. We were amused at his foolishness and allowed him to stay. Now he has won our brothers, and our clan can no longer act like one. He has put a knife on the things that held us together and we have fallen apart. (Achebe, 1996, 124–5)

What happens when this knife is placed 'on the things that held us together' is that a forcible singularity is imposed upon a prior multiplicity, assemblages are torn limb from limb; unanswerable questions are asked in a foreign tongue, and the whole site of possible resistance is subjected to the forces of repetition and surveillance (see Foucault, 1977, 195–228). In 'Preparations of War', Kunwar Narayan depicts the colonial panopticon, but for him the apparatus of surveillance (like a fossil, like a relic) has never gone away:

> After thousands of years
> like the same beaten-up question
> the same beaten-up man is still being asked
> 'Who are you?
> Where do you live?
> What's your name?'
>
> The prisoner who patrols
> a motionless octagonal cell
> holds three guards captive at the same time.
>
> Everywhere outside
> a forest of iron bars has spread its stranglehold
> like a magnet's invisible lines of force.
>
> And this is the solid proof of the success
> of a massive build-up of arms
> that as soon as we have a gun in our hands
> enemy heads
> begin to appear all around us.
>
> (Behl and Nicholls, 1995, 148)

Despite the self-evident reductivism of Fredric Jameson's assertion that all postcolonial narrative is 'national allegory', it would nevertheless be difficult to ignore in this poem the drag back into history, the continuing prevalence of learned habits of surveillance, the 'invisible lines of force' that hold old-fashioned concepts like centre and periphery in a fascinated, terrified embrace.

What is being spoken of, I take it, in at least some of these texts is the passional undertow of the postcolonial situation. There is the mutual rage of incomprehension, the rage that stems from the tearing out of the tongue, the tearing out by the tongue, the 'tonguelessness' that lies behind the most sophisticated of narratives, that renders the gesture of writing in the language of the conqueror forever an activity of pollution. There is the mutual hatred of that same incomprehension, the sense of a wilful withholding of secrets, the exasperation of the meeting that is denied common ground and instead takes place only under prescribed conditions. There is the sense of ruin at the origin that attends these aftermaths of empire, the awareness that what was destroyed can never be reconstructed. And there is the sense of the hovering of chaos around these sites of depredation, the uncertainty about what, if anything, will be 'met':

> When the lamplighter, his head swung by its hair,
> Meant the dread footfall lumping up the stair:
> Maman with soup, perhaps; or it could well
> Be Chaos, genderer of Earth, called Night.
>
> (Walcott, 1992, 36–7)

This, though, from Derek Walcott's 'Orient and Immortal Wheat', is perhaps less compelling as an account of the postcolonial condition than the ending of his 'The Swamp', in which that 'limbo of cracker convicts, Negroes', haunts 'the travellers of its one road':

> Deep, deeper than sleep
> Like death,
> Too rich in its decrescence, too close of breath,
>
> In the fast-filling night, note
> How the last bird drinks darkness with its throat,
> How the wild saplings slip
>
> Backward to darkness, go black
> With widening amnesia, take the edge
> Of nothing to them slowly, merge

> Limb, tongue, and sinew into a knot
> Like chaos, like the road
> Ahead.
>
> (59–60)

The swamp here is the frightening reminder of the ruin, the remains; that limbo into which history always tries to retreat unless its sleep is rudely disturbed, the fossils of the past brought struggling to the surface. The amnesia of which Walcott speaks will always be the easy option, for all the struggles and violations of the past to sink down into the undifferentiated soup of a tongueless history, for the mementoes of the distorted and abused body ('limb, tongue, and sinew') to be slowly dissolved into chaos, into that which cannot, will not, submit itself to re-membering, to being put back together as a whole, intelligible history. Lest one be in any doubt that this repeated 'chaos' is the fate of Africa, Walcott draws the knot tighter in 'Goats and Monkeys', a poem that partially rewrites *Othello*:

> The owl's torches gutter. Chaos clouds the globe.
> Shriek, augury! His earthen bulk
> buries her bosom in its slow eclipse.
> His smoky hand has charred
> that marble throat. Bent to her lips,
> he is Africa, a vast sidling shadow
> that halves your world with doubt.
>
> (83)

The 'eclipse' of Desdemona's 'lips' is simultaneously the robbing of the power of speech, speech that may be cut off by doubt before it reaches articulation, burned away in dark smoke, reduced to a shriek that may or may not be interpretable even by the doubt-filled means of augury. The threat here is, among other things, to language; to the possibility of clarity emerging from darkness, and thus the racialist terms of *Othello*, and of the culture it represents and which has preserved it from harm through the conferment of the status of high art, remain visibly at risk from the avatar of a different order of the literary, a hand that burns, a shadow that haunts.

There is, of course, irony here. Of all the major Caribbean poets Walcott, particularly in the earlier work of which these are examples, is the most committed to the importation of a certain repertoire (Shakespeare, Donne, Eliot) of English poets into the colonised scenario.[12] It is not, for him, as though the fossil can be simply exhumed and despatched; the question would be to interrogate it, the ruin as rune, to see what it may be forced to 'give up', in both senses of that term, in the course of its own cultural re-enactment of the 'middle passage'. And so this repeating chaos is at the same time the reminder of a certain precarious order; the adoption of European rhythms becomes a gesture of looking out to see what else may be available, what will happen to the pedagogic tradition when it is turned inside out, when its assumptions of universality are treated to an entirely different climate, a more variable air.[13]

Kunwar Narayan, though, spoke of iron; and it is iron that forms the major substrate of Coetzee's *Age of Iron*, to whose themes of rage, hatred, chaos and ruin we may now turn. *Age of Iron* is structured as a long letter, a letter written by an ageing white South African woman, dying of cancer, to her daughter, who lives in North America. The narrative is self-reflexive and indeed self-undermining: the woman finds herself – in a sense almost somnambulistically – taking under her protection (or is it he who is meant to protect her?) a drunken down-and-out called Vercueil. We are made aware that one of her motives for this potentially dangerous action is that she passionately wishes this letter to be sent; yet although clearly she could, in a sense, send it herself, it is important to her to test whether Vercueil will himself be capable of sending it. The whole reflexive structure is fraught with ambiguities. She continues, it appears, to write while she is already in the grip of death (the 'grip of death' concerned is Vercueil himself – we learn at the end that 'from that embrace there was no warmth to be had'); and she despairs of the possibility that he will send the letter; yet, of course, had he not in some fictional sense done so the letter, and thus the novel, would not be before our eyes ...

She describes with a slow, painstaking finality the fate of the dominated – the frustrated rage, the inexpressible hatred – and she does so, at one point, while watching the television:

> I turned up the sound, enough for, if not the words, then the cadences to reach him, the slow, truculent Afrikaans rhythms with their deadening closes, like a hammer beating a post into the ground. Together, blow after blow, we listened. The disgrace of the life one lives under them: to open a newspaper, to switch on the television, like kneeling and being urinated on. Under them: under their meaty bellies, their full bladders. (Coetzee, 1990, 9)

Rhythm, cadence, the stories language might tell us even before we come, belatedly, upon the scenario of meaning; the tales of the tongue, beating helplessly against all those forces that try to stifle, to throttle. The narrator, Mrs Curren, has been a Latin teacher: she is familiar with dead languages, with the death of languages, with, as the text tells us, Virgil on the unquiet dead; and when Vercueil hears her reciting, he too finds himself in the grip of a certain (dactylic) rhythm, some rhythm, perhaps, to hold up against those other deadening rhythms of murderous apartheid domination.

Yet death for her can only be minutely postponed; her own movement towards the grave is, merely but paradoxically, a more alive version of the gradual sinking of the apartheid state, the most blatant residue of that perverse logic of the foreign body conceived under the sign of slavery: 'life in this country is so much like life aboard a sinking ship, one of those old-time liners with a lugubrious, drunken captain and a surly crew and leaky lifeboats' (20), but there is a sense in which even this seems to serve as an unjustifiably romantic dramatisation of the absolute *stultification* of life in South Africa:

> their message stupidly unchanging, stupidly forever the same. Their feat, after years of etymological meditation on the word, to have raised stupidity to a virtue. To stupefy: to deprive of feeling; to benumb, deaden; to stun with amazement. Stupor: insensibility, apathy, torpor of mind. Stupid: dulled in the faculties, indifferent, destitute of thought or feeling. From *stupere* to be stunned, astounded. A gradient from *stupid* to *stunned* to *astonished*, to be turned to stone. The message: that the message never changes. A message that turns people to stone. (26)

Again, a message written in the only way that messages can be, in language; to be in control of the language, to limit the possibilities for speech, to constrict, sometimes fatally, the throat: these are the means by which colonialism imposes its power on the colonised, and they are also the means – inevitably contaminated by the imposition of a single language upon the many tongues, the tongues of multiplicity – by which these impositions, these devastations, can be made public to a wider world.[14]

But the problem for the narrator is that, for her, there is no wider world. She is destitute of family, reduced to relying (although her reliance is also evidence of a certain complex perversity) on Vercueil (on a (false) memory of Virgil?), fatally alienated from the few black people she knows, at least partly because she knows – or has known – them only as servants. Thus the reduction to the epistolary, paradoxically, and in a sense rather improbably, seen as the only way of getting news out of South Africa; thus also the plight of the white (and in this specific case, English) sympathiser who wants it to be known that she too is 'on fire', that she too can no longer bear the violence and terror of the apartheid state.

But in the midst of her ruin, it is nonetheless not possible for her to get past the hatred. 'These are good children', says Florence, her maid and the mother of a young political activist, 'they are like iron, we are proud of them' (46). Like iron: this is not what Mrs Curren wants to hear, not what she finds conceivable; although she very clearly sees the apocalypse that hovers and waits, and she equally clearly sees that even that apocalypse will not reduce the stultified dogmatism of the Afrikaners:

> A sea of blood, come back together: is that how it will be at the end of days? The blood of all: a Baikal Sea scarlet-black under a wintry blue Siberian sky, ice-cliffs around it, its snow-white shores lapped by blood, viscous, sluggish. The blood of mankind, restored to itself. A body of blood. Of all mankind? No: in a place apart, in a mud-walled dam in the Karoo with barbed wire around it and the sun blazing down, the blood of the Afrikaners and their tribute-bearers, still, stagnant. (58–9)

But in this in-between state, the predicament of the white liberal, there is no salvation to be had, no shielding from hatred. Confronted by the stony image of black comradeship, she has only this to say:

> I fear I know comradeship all too well. The Germans had comradeship, and the Japanese, and the Spartans. Shaka's impis too, I am sure. Comradeship is nothing but a mystique of death, of killing and dying, masquerading as what you call a bond (a bond of what? Love? I doubt it.). I have no sympathy with this comradeship. You are wrong, you and Florence and everyone else, to be taken in by it and, worse, to encourage it in children. It is just another of those icy, exclusive, death-driven male constructions. (137)

Perhaps it is so: perhaps the best way of illustrating the bifurcation that might lie at the bottom of this analysis of resistance, infected though that resistance might be by the thanatic, by rage and hatred, by the reintrojected lust for chaos and ruin, might be by offering two quotations. The first is from Achebe: he uses the example of Graham Greene to suggest how a 'partisan of Rome' might nevertheless be driven by the exigencies of art, the demands of the literary, to exemplify in his fictions the 'ultimate enmity between art and orthodoxy':

> Those who would see no blot of villainy in the beloved oppressed nor grant the faintest glimmer of humanity to the hated oppressor are partisans, patriots and party-liners. In the grand finale of things there will be a mansion also for them where they will be received and lodged in comfort by the single-minded demigods of their devotion. But it will not be in the complex and paradoxical cavern of Mother Idoto. (Achebe, 1987, 100–1)

Here we are returned to multiplicity, to the many selves, to the conflict between the polytheistic and the monotheistic which is at the very heart of colonial and postcolonial history; we are returned also to what might be a site of resistance to the thanatic. Yet, in Robert Young's account of Deleuze and Guattari's *Anti-Oedipus*, we are reminded of the ways in which there is an inescapability about the undifferentiation to which the world is being subjected in the interests of the discourse machine of undifferentiating capitalism:

> [The] description of the operations of capitalism as a territorial writing machine seems not only especially suited to the historical development of industrialisation, but also describes rather exactly the violent physical and ideological procedures of colonisation, deculturation and acculturation, by which the territory and cultural space of an indigenous society must be disrupted, dissolved and then reinscribed according to the needs of the apparatus of the occupying power. (Young, 1995, 169–70)

What, we might nevertheless fairly ask, is an 'indigenous society'? Where might we find a model, or example, of a people or culture which is not angrily haunted by its own phantasms of the past, by the potential uprising of its relics and fossils, by its own fear of reterritorialisation?

# V The Phantomatic, the Transcolonial

> ... he told us to go back to my town where there were only alives living, he said that it was forbidden for alives to come to the Deads' Town. (Amos Tutuola, *The Palm-Wine Drinkard*)

> She filled the sea with fish, drowned ships, mermaids, treasure, kings; and on the land, a cavalcade of local riff-raff – pick-pockets, pimps, fat whores hitching their saris up against the waves – and other figures from history or fantasy or current affairs or nowhere, crowded towards the water like the real-life Bombayites on the beach, taking their evening strolls. At the water's edge strange composite creatures slithered to and fro across the frontier of the elements. (Salman Rushdie, *The Moor's Last Sigh*)

> Will someone come into your room and call your name? Will they come nearer, tap your shoulder to wake you? Is that when you'll start falling to one side? (Ron Butlin, *Night Visits*)

As the great globalising project of modernity, which has its own controlling relation to the postcolonial, rolls on, one of its more curious current effects is that, perhaps against expectation, we live increasingly in a world of ghosts, spirits, phantoms. As an exemplary locus for this phenomenon, we might think of Derrida's 1993 work *Spectres of Marx: The State of the Debt, the Work of Mourning, and the New International*. Spectres, indeed, become the controlling metaphor, in the shape, for instance, of a chapter subtitled an 'impure "impure impure history of ghosts"' (Derrida, 1994, 95–124). We might take as a further example a paragraph near the beginning of the book:

> To be just: beyond the living present in general – and beyond its simple negative reversal. A spectral moment, a moment that no

> longer belongs to time, if one understands by this word the linking of modalised presents (past present, actual present: 'now', future present). We are questioning in this instant, we are asking ourselves about this instant that is not docile to time, at least to what we call time. Furtive and untimely, the apparition of the spectre does not belong to that time, it does not give time, not that one: 'Enter the ghost, exit the ghost, re-enter the ghost' (*Hamlet*). (xx)

Derrida's purpose here, as I see it, is to put into question a whole series of assumptions about time, assumptions which have at all points to do with the 'post' and are perhaps best summarised in what should be referred to as the notion of an 'aftermath'. Among the perceptions that characterise *Spectres of Marx* is the thought of what it might be like to be living after the apparent collapse, perhaps the apparition of the collapse, of the great Enlightenment project of Marxism, to be living in ruins and rubble, to be living a life which cannot but be haunted by the spectres of failed projects, the ghosts of universality fled (see 129ff.). From this, naturally what flows is a question of 'living after' in general; of an afterlife, certainly, but also the conduct of what one might loosely call an enquiry into the 'post': what it is like to live in a world of 'posts' – postmodernism, poststructuralism, and of course postcolonialism. These, as we are well aware, are all formulations of the 'after', of what comes 'after'; at the same time, however, they necessarily conjure up, make uncannily to appear before us, the very phenomena they have, in a different sense, surpassed, they prolong the life of their predecessors – unnaturally, some might say – giving them the status of spirits haunting the apparently purged landscape of the contemporary.[1]

Or we might think instead again of the neo-psychoanalytic work of Abraham and Torok: among their key concepts we can find the whole apparatus of haunting – spectres, ghosts, crucially the phantom and, as we have mentioned before, the crypt. Let us consider, again, an exemplary passage, from Abraham's 'Notes on the Phantom: A Complement to Freud's Metapsychology':

> The belief that the spirits of the dead can return to haunt the living exists either as an accepted tenet or as a marginal conviction in all civilisations, ancient or modern. More often than not, the dead do not return to rejoin the living but rather to lead them into some dreadful snare, entrapping them with disastrous consequences. To be sure, all the departed may return,

> but some are destined to haunt: the dead who were shamed during their lifetime or those who took unspeakable secrets to the grave. From the brucolacs, the errant spirits of outcasts in ancient Greece, to the ghost of Hamlet's vengeful father, and on down to the rapping spirits of modern times, the theme of the dead – who, having suffered repression by their family or society, cannot enjoy, even in death, a state of authenticity – appears to be omnipresent (whether overtly expressed or disguised) on the fringes of religions and, failing that, in rational systems. It is a fact that the 'phantom', whatever its form, is nothing but an invention of the living. Yes, an invention in the sense that the phantom is meant to objectify, even if under the guise of individual or collective hallucinations, the gap produced in us by the concealment of some part of a love object's life. The phantom is therefore also a metapsychological fact: what haunts are not the dead, but the gaps left within us by the secrets of others. (Abraham and Torok, 1994, 171)

'The dead who were shamed during their lifetime or those who took unspeakable secrets to the grave'; that is a thought that it would be useful to hold on to. Abraham here, of course, is not, or at least not overtly, concerned with cultural analysis; the thrust of the argument of *The Wolf Man's Magic Word*, and of the essays collected in *The Shell and the Kernel*, of which 'Notes on the Phantom' is one, is necessarily towards the individual and the familial, towards an analysis of the transgenerational structures of secrecy that provide explanations for the otherwise undiagnosable personal symptom.[2] In other words the realm of the crypt for Abraham and Torok is, in a sense, *below* the unconscious, it is a site of the irredeemably other: in it are locked away secrets that are in no sense our own, and yet we cannot avoid knowing them through their effects, through the unpredictable and apparently inexplicable consequences they have upon our lives.[3] This, then, is a most radical decentring of consciousness, in which the apparently free spirit is revealed as merely the unwitting host to a 'host' of phantoms, spirits of the dead, living on unknown to us as a series of parasitic foreign bodies, lodged inside the psyche, speaking inarticulately with our tongue, looking out through our eyes.

And perhaps the discourse of the foreign body, of host and parasite, developed through Freud and Derrida,[4] is as good a ground as any other on which to turn our attention to the specific relations to the phantom that we find in those literatures that we have become accustomed to referring to, sometimes perhaps without overmuch thought, as 'postcolonial'. We might, for example, think of some of Walcott's reflections on history and the ineradicable, still haunting, presence of slavery as historical residue and psychic contamination:

> I say to the ancestor who sold me [he writes], and to the ancestor who bought me, I have no father, I want no such father, although I can understand you, Black ghost, white ghost, when you both whisper 'history' ... (Walcott, 1974, 67)

Bravery, tragedy, or energetic disavowal are all possible interpretations of these words; here at any rate we have a wrestling with spirits, an apparently unavoidable engagement with a host of phantoms from the past which continue to provide unwanted guests at the banqueting table of modernity, or even that specialised and ethereal feast we characterise as the 'postmodern'. The whisper of history is also the voice of the inevitable, the tragic intoning of 'fate' or 'destiny', the insistence that nothing can be changed. And this, of course, is where the colonisers now find themselves on the world stage; amid a welter of apologies, absurdly saying sorry, years after the fact, in some cases centuries, for slaughters of which their descendants know nothing yet the effects of which continue to reverberate through to the present day. These phantoms are real and terrible; they come, like Beloved in Morrison's emblematic novel of slavery, to remind us of the dead and also to remind us, before the fact, as it were, ahead of the aftermath, of our own death, to assert a terrible continuity between the omnipresent past and the already vanishing present (see Morrison, 1987, e.g., 210).

Voices whisper too in a coruscating passage by Harris on the relation between the world of 'material change', the realm of history, and the other world, of the void, of the spectre; if, he says,

> any real sense is to be made of material change it can only occur with an acceptance of a concurrent void and with a willingness to descend into that 'void' wherein, as it were, one may begin to come into confrontation with a spectre of invocation whose freedom to participate in an alien territory and wilderness has become a necessity for one's reason or salvation. ... I have been stressing a certain 'void' or misgiving attending every assimilation of contraries – I have been stressing this in order to expose what seems to me a fantastic mythological congruence of elements ... (Harris, 1967, 60–1, 62)

This is an extraordinarily dense passage, and many different readings of it are possible. What *is* this 'void' or misgiving of which Harris speaks? In one sense it is a void of history; a point at which it is necessary to accept that the great blank of the past, the great unsaid, is never going to be uttered. It is necessary to stress at this point something which is often assumed, but perhaps too rarely mentioned: namely, that during the last thirty or forty years the West has undergone a process of change that is without precedent. I am not referring now to material change, but to epistemological and archival change; nothing less than a revolution in how the past is viewed. It is only necessary to look back at history school textbooks to see the depth and breadth of the process of unlearning that has had to be addressed; one whole year of an exemplary British child's schooldays, for example, could have been spent in the company of a textbook called *The Age of Discovery*, in whose pages it appeared conclusively proven that most of the lands to which Europeans travelled in the early days of empire were uninhabited, and where there were inhabitants their attitude towards the white man was one of humble respect or open-armed welcome.

These histories have certainly been revised and, as Harris puts it, there has been some assimilation of contraries; nevertheless there remains a gap, a void, a mis-giving, an anxiety or even a turning away of the gift as too little and too late, and in any case a gift that is tainted at root by the giver, by the giver's arrogation of the right of possession. What else, though, might this void be? I suggest a clue in an unlikely source. Iris Murdoch's collection of philosophical essays, *Metaphysics as a Guide to Morals*, contains an essay that is simply called 'Void' (Murdoch, 1992, 498–503). It sits uneasily between the covers of the book, a book which after all, like all of Murdoch's work, is mainly about the quest for 'universal' good and which offers no concessions to positionalist subtlety. But 'Void' is not about a quest at all. It is about that moment when no quest seems possible; it is about an impossible draining of energy; it is about depression and melancholy. It provides a valuable antidote to the sprightly good spirits which, to my mind rather annoyingly, permeate so much of Murdoch's work; but at the same time it is recognisably a writing of extreme pain, a twisted, contorted, half-submerged writing that consumes itself in its own inexpressibility, its location as a foreign body secretly damaging the most hospitable of assumptions; it is the hollowed soul of the husk of idealism.[5]

Melancholy, Julia Kristeva says in *Black Sun* and elsewhere, is the condition of our time.[6] Because, some would say, of the effects of consumer capitalism; because, others would claim, of specific

Oedipal contortions that are endemic to our age, to our politics, to our state.[7] If we descend into that void, go down, perhaps, amid the 'cloudy trophies', what will we find? A spectre, says Harris; a spectre of invocation; a foreign body, a phantomatic inhabitant of one's own psyche whose existence one has not previously suspected. Quite what this 'invocation' might be remains, perhaps, unclear, but it has to do with participation in an 'alien territory', a 'wilderness'. The terms are strikingly reminiscent of the nomadology of Deleuze and Guattari, but their meaning must surely have to do with the position from which one encounters this spectre – for what would it mean to expropriate somebody else's wilderness, just as Europeans have in fact been doing for many hundreds of years?

If we were to go further with this passage, we might want to think again about the crucial relation between mourning and melancholia, a debate revived since Freud by Abraham and Torok, but also by Kristeva and by Judith Butler;[8] but instead I want briefly to mention another phantomatic locus in Harris, which occurs in his remarkable essay on the origins of limbo dancing and its relation to the journeys of slavery and imprisonment. He connects it also to anancy, to spider dancing, and speaks of it as a reaction to the effective amputation of organs that occurs when a person is converted into a slave, a thing, a chattel. This amputation, he says, has its own inevitable aftermath:

> It has taken us [he says] a couple of generations to begin – just *begin* – to perceive, in this phenomenon, an activation of unconscious and sleeping resources in the phantom limb of dismembered slave and god. (Harris, 1981, 26)

The phantom limb; the ghost of feeling; the reminder of loss, the ineradicable certainty, as we understand it from clinical studies, that what has gone is still there, still with us, still looking through our eyes, speaking with our tongue. The story 'Dharma' in Chandra's *Love and Longing in Bombay* begins when Major General Jago Antia feels, for the first time, a twinge of pain in the leg that has been amputated years before. It is this pain that is eventually to lead him to his own phantomatic encounter, his terrifying yet in this case healing meeting with the child-ghost who turns out to be the residue of his former self, reconciliation with whom at last allows the hitherto repressed laughter of the years to be set loose (see Chandra, 1997, 28).

In a paper given by a psychologist on the phenomenon of the phantom limb, which I heard several years ago, he told a peculiarly terrible story about a man who had two misfortunes in one day. In the morning he got a painful splinter under his fingernail, and in the afternoon he caught his arm in a piece of machinery and it was torn off at the elbow. But that was not the terrible thing; the terrible thing was that, for the rest of his life, he suffered constant pain from the non-existent splinter under his non-existent fingernail.[9] Something, then, persists; but in perverse, paradoxical form. The memory of all that has been lost; the impossibility, or in Chandra's terms the extreme challenge, of freeing oneself from the clinging embrace of one's dead twin. In what follows, I want to look at these operations of the phantomatic more closely, in three books: Fred D'Aguiar's *Feeding the Ghosts*, Arundhati Roy's *The God of Small Things* and Seamus Deane's *Reading in the Dark*.

Fred D'Aguiar may be rather better known as a poet than as a novelist.[10] *Feeding the Ghosts* is essentially the story of an infamous journey, the voyage of the slave ship *Zong* in 1783. When it docked, it emerged that the captain had thrown 132 slaves over the side, to save, he claimed, his crew and the other slaves from disease. D'Aguiar's story centres on a particular slave, Mintah, who has been missionary-educated. She, like the others, is thrown over the side of the ship but manages to survive, climb back in and hide in a storeroom, where she is helped by a simple crew member called Simon. In a curiously inconclusive way her survival is represented as giving some heart to the remaining slaves, although it does not succeed in stopping the slaughter. Eventually she is sold in America, but ends up as a free woman in Jamaica.

To tell the story in this way, however, is already to betray the kind of narrative D'Aguiar is trying to construct; for a large part of his effort is devoted to finding ways of saying that in fact such events as these, such personal and historical traumas, can never be recounted in linear narrative fashion, they can never be considered to be 'over', consigned to an untroubled or untroubling past.

> We were all dead [the narrator says near the end]. The ship was full of ghosts. ... There is no fear, nor shame ... There is only the fact of the *Zong* and its unending voyage and those deaths that cannot be undone. Where death has begun but remains unfinished because it recurs. Where there is only the record of the sea. (D'Aguiar, 1997, 229)

This is not a voyage that can be consigned to the sea of history, that can be placed neatly within a sequence of historical facts. It has to be seen more in the uncompromising terms of trauma, as a kind of epicentre from which implications, memories, forgettings, continue to ripple out, to reverberate through the present and, no doubt, the future too.[11] These ghosts, the slaves themselves, the captain and crew, even the participants in the long trial scene that comes towards the end of the book, all of these are reincarnated in the pages of the novel. But there is, again, more to it than that. The ship *continues* to sail; its voyage, like the sea, is unending. Yet this phantomatic life both preserves and erodes reality. Who is to say if those slaves *were* ever real? The factual evidence on which D'Aguiar is relying is scanty, although that of course is hardly the whole of the point; that the Middle Passage was crowded with ships full of ghosts, some still alive, some already drowned, some no doubt passing through those contortions of mind and body that Harris describes as the 'limbo gateway', can scarcely be denied.[12]

And so Mintah is confronted with the task of doing something about those ghosts; and what she does is carve. She does not tell her story directly; if we are right in seeing in the repetitions and inescapabilities of the text an approach to the condition of trauma, then no doubt it would also be true that such a story can in fact never be told because to do so would mean putting in place a narrative structure that has always already been undermined. And so:

> No one knew her story, because she had not bothered to tell it. All her notes were for herself, her failing memory, her recurrent dreams. These used to hurt her once, like a new splinter, but now she did not know they were there. Time had hardened over them.
>
> Ghosts needed to be fed. She carved and wrote to assuage their hunger. Her life of feeding the ghosts had slowed to the Sunday school, the occasional howdy from the parents of a child she taught and the odd errand run for her by one of the children ... (D'Aguiar, 1997, 222)

As the phantom life shows no signs of fading, so Mintah's other life, her life in the material world as Harris would put it, fades instead, becomes attenuated; the feeding of the ghosts is a diversion from her own nourishment, makes it indeed impossible to consider a consolidation, an expansion of life in anything approaching a conventional fashion. These 'recurrent dreams', the ineradicability of memory, are phantoms that suck blood, phantomatic drainings in the night; and as the ship sails on, something needs to be done to placate these hungry spirits. Mintah, then, carves; she carves goblets and other useful items, but she also carves figures.

> If only they could see [she says of those who come to buy the goblets] that what they are laying their hands on is a treasure, that it harbours the past, that it houses the souls of the dead and that the many secrets of the earth are delivered up in it. ... My hut is full of the things I have made and couldn't bear to part with. Objects stacked in corners of my hut making it even more cramped. I call my house my hold. It is crowded with pieces of wood. The shape of each piece is pulled from the sea of my mind and has been shaped by water, with water's contours. People say they see a figure of some kind, man, woman or child reaching up out of the depths. They love what I do with wood but cannot keep such a shape in their homes. Such shapes do not quench a thirst. They unsettle a stomach. Fill the eyes with unease. I keep them in my home like guests who will not leave and whom I eventually cannot bear to part with. ... People will gladly take a goblet from me but not these figures ... (208–9)

'Treasure' again, a harbouring of the past, a housing of the 'souls of the dead': we are returned once more to the multiple connections between treasure, the sea, and colonial exploitation. What kind of artistic process, what kind of dealing with memory, is going on here? It seems to me inevitable that one is reminded of the long argument Leo Bersani has been having through most of his books with the ideas of Melanie Klein – a dialogue, of course, with a ghost (see Bersani, 1990). Klein, to put it very simply, developed a theory of art based on the restoration of primal damage; on the idea that, through Oedipal jealousy, the child fantasises scenarios in which he or she damages the parental body, but then experiences guilt about these fantasies and a desire to put back together that which has been torn apart in Dionysian fury. The outcome of this desire to construct an artificial totality is, according to Klein, art (see Klein, 1988, 306–43); although one may suspect that such outcomes would also include a whole range of monstrosities – from Frankenstein's monster onwards – including some that we shall encounter later, monsters, for example, of shame, blindness and meat.

At all events, Bersani sees this essentially recuperative theory of art as one which fails to recognise the internally and externally subversive forces at work in the creative process, or at least in the process of textualisation, and perhaps this is where *Feeding the Ghosts* leads us, to a place from which we can survey these possibilities of recuperation and, as it were, living amid the ruins, the wreckage. Certainly the very last lines of the novel leave us nervously poised between unresolved possibilities: 'Those spirits are fled into wood. The ghosts feed on the story of themselves. The past is laid to rest when it is told' (D'Aguiar, 1997, 230). The spirits here are the spirits contained in the wooden figures, because a fire, it would seem from a rather ambiguous passage in the text, has just destroyed them and the hut, and possibly Mintah as well, freeing the spirits that were trapped inside them. The ghosts are then, we might presume, free to continue with their own self-consuming, cannibalistic dialogue, a dialogue of the dead which nonetheless – like the voices from Abraham and Torok's crypts – cannot but be known through its effects on the discourse of the living. But is the past laid to rest? In one sense Mintah never did tell her story, although of course in another, on the pages of the text, she did. Would this laying to rest nonetheless permit the endless whisperings to continue? Is this story, we might ask, a story of the past or a story of the future, a recounting of events or an account of the effects, the haunting effects, those colonial events are going to continue to have within the cultures of disavowal of the West?

'I call my house my hold.' The hold of the ship, of the slave ship where there were indeed objects stacked in corners, sick, dying human objects. But also, perhaps, Mintah's hold on the real, on the possibility of a contained space that will continue to hold *her*, that cannot, will not, be invaded as the minds and bodies of the slaves have been invaded, emptied out, turned into ghostly remnants of their previous shapes. 'Such shapes do not quench a thirst': no matter how many times this story is told it can never be sufficient, never enough; there is always to accompany it some misgiving, some void, some absence of explanation, some passage downwards to grave melancholy reflection which is also a reflection of the grave, a passage like the passage of the slave ship but towards a depression of the soul which is indeed unutterable, inexpressible.[13]

We may feel ourselves also returned here to the curious logic of the foreign body, the host and the guest, the para-site. 'Like guests who will not leave': what are the limits of hospitality here? What can we do about phantomatic memories, recurrent dreams, that will not go away? At what point, a point fraught with ambiguity and disaster, do we realise that if these memorials to terror were in fact to leave then the consequence would be unbearable, it would be a sense of loss of all that we have perversely clung to in order to offer explanations of the present state of disaster, and would thus be more than we could stand.

And so, a ghostly impasse. 'They love what I do with wood but cannot keep such a shape in their homes.' Mintah has, in a sense, been 'doing things with wood' all along. The novel is full of the imagery of wood and grain, and of a curious twist whereby that inner grain becomes also the substance of the sea (see 186). The wood is also a link back to Mintah's father, a shadowy presence known only to Mintah – and thus to the reader – in the very moment of their parting. But that parting is also emblematic: it occurred because Mintah's mother was converted to Christianity, and took Mintah with her when she left her village as a consequence. Mintah's father, however, was a carpenter, and was also

> not convinced by the missionaries' insistence that one deity was responsible for everything he saw in the world. Any single thing in all its permutations and manifestations was thought by his people enough of a complexity for one god to worry about. Take wood, for instance. One god would have to devote all his time and energy to keeping up with what wood does, never mind what he, armed with his chisel, did with it. Other gods kept abreast of other things, and all things worked together because the gods cooperated. (57)

If then we connect Mintah's father's beliefs with Mintah's own carvings, what we get is what one might call a dream of polytheism: a dream of the many spirits, which would also be a dream of animism and thus, seen from another angle, a recurrence of what Freud at least saw as a childhood world in which everything is invested with, inhabited by, its own god.[14] In this quite different context, however, these spirits would be spirits of resistance; in their going 'with the grain', so to speak, they would always be in opposition to the violence of the monotheistic, to the imperialist insistence on the single way of right. Iris Murdoch's search for the 'universal' good and the true leads inevitably into the void, gives way to the misgiving, is unseated, unearthed by the impossibility of banishing the phantom of difference, the spirit of the untranslatable. Here, then, there is a significant contradiction: 'convergence' and 'development', those terms beloved of the Western political and economic establishment, stake a claim to be going 'with the grain', but D'Aguiar's position is quite different; such terms, such historical forces, would be inherently aligned with the pressure into unitary form and would be opposed to that kind of respect for the multiple, the divergent, which is the essence of the relation he depicts between the African slaves, the wood and the sea. At stake would be a refusal on the European side to feed the ghosts, a disavowal of the past and the ancestral, a refusal only compounded by later modifications of the imperial stance and all the while producing and perversely nurturing, in Amos Tutuola's words, an army of dead babies (see below, p. 126).

Arundhati Roy's *The God of Small Things* is a large and complex novel, which also plunges us into a world of ghosts. At its heart is a pair of dizygotic twins: a boy, Estha, and a girl, Rahel. In a series of time shifts we are first introduced to the fact that Estha has for many years been entirely silent and that Rahel has in her a kind of emotional emptiness, a vacancy (a void or misgiving); the plot unravels in such a way as to enable us to learn the reasons for these evidently traumatic effects.

Their mother Ammu, already in a dangerous social position because of problems with the identity of Estha and Rahel's father, has a brief affair with an untouchable, Velutha. This begins, as it happens, on the very day when her niece, the twins' cousin Sophie Mol, arrives from England with her white mother for a chance to recover from the recent death of her stepfather. The entire action happens in the next fortnight. The twins and Sophie Mol take to visiting an old house, across the river from their own house – the old house has its own extraordinarily resonant story, to which I will return below. Meanwhile, at night-time the house is being used by Ammu and Velutha for illicit trysts. The affair is revealed by Velutha's father to Ammu's mother and aunt, unthinkingly vicious embodiments of bourgeois correctness who respond by locking her up. Estha and Rahel speak to her through her bedroom door; beside herself with grief and anger, Ammu shouts that she wishes they had never been born, since it is their uncertain birth that is the 'originating' reason for her lack of freedom. The twins, wounded and terrified, decide with Sophie Mol to run away, inevitably to the old house; but on the way across the river the boat capsizes and Sophie Mol drowns. Meanwhile the old women have told the police about the affair, naturally describing Velutha as a despicable rapist; Velutha himself arrives, distraught and exiled, at the old house to sleep; the police come and give him a terrible, and vividly described, beating, which the twins see.

At the old ladies' instigation the police accuse Velutha of abducting the children. It is obvious that he is dying; Ammu's aunt puts it to the children that, even though the notion of abduction is a complete lie, it would be better for everybody if they were to say that it had happened, because that way nobody would be called on in court to give evidence of the affair between Velutha and their mother. Browbeaten by the older women and hysterically shocked by the beating of Velutha and the drowning of Sophie Mol, the children succumb and lie about Velutha, their friend, with the dire and lasting consequences for themselves that we have already seen.

Such an account, of course, can never do much justice to a novel; briefly, though, what can we see here that would effect the connection to the phantom? Most importantly – and this is in any case the only phantomatic aspect of the novel on which I will have space to dwell here – we have the old house itself, the History House, the house to which Estha, Rahel and Sophie Mol try to flee and which proves in the end to be the site of their traumatic encounter with Velutha's fatal beating. What is this house? Interestingly enough it first appears as an imaginary creation, a construct of speech, fantasy and rhetoric, an archetypally *literary* object. Chacko, the twins' uncle and Sophie Mol's natural father, is explaining to them that the whole family is, as he puts it, a family of Anglophiles.

> Pointed in the wrong direction [he continues], trapped outside their own history, and unable to retrace their steps because their footprints had been swept away. He explained to them that history was like an old house at night. With all the lamps lit. And ancestors whispering inside.
>
> 'To understand history', Chacko said, 'we have to go inside and listen to what they're saying. And look at the books and the pictures on the walls. And smell the smells'. (Roy, 1997, 52)

This image of the house from which one is permanently locked out, excluded, has a particular resonance for Chacko, who has had an Oxford education which has done nothing at all for his ability to earn a living, and who is now estranged from his white wife Margaret, Sophie Mol's mother. But it also runs wider than that, spreading in the book to other houses, houses which the twins, for example, have known as home but from which they are now permanently debarred by the depth and bitterness of their knowledge. The footprints swept away will similarly gain a wider textual currency as Sophie Mol, emblem of the attempt – albeit less than conscious – to solder together the separate sides of history, to translate between inside and outside, is swept away by a river which in turn separates two worlds.

What is crucial here though is that the twins, impressed by this image, supply it immediately with a concrete shape:

> Estha and Rahel had no doubt that the house Chacko meant was the house on the other side of the river, in the middle of the abandoned rubber estate where they had never been. Kari Saipu's house. The Black Sahib. The Englishman who had 'gone

> native'. Who spoke Malayalam and wore mundus. Ayemenem's own Kurtz. Ayemenem his private Heart of Darkness. He had shot himself through the head ten years ago when his young lover's parents had taken the boy away from him and sent him to school. ... The History House. (82–3)

So this History House has its own ghost; the ghost of the white man 'gone native', the ghost of a curiously ambiguous figure who obviously, if we look at his suicide, saw himself as guilty of terrible crimes but who, oddly enough, seems to have been blamed little by the boy's parents, who were less concerned with sexual impropriety than with getting the boy a decent education. The point is, however, that the History House is inhabited by the ghost, the phantom, of a feared miscegenation, a perverse hybridity, of precisely the kind that goes on to be revealed in the ensuing conversation.

> '... we can't go in', Chacko explained [still talking about his metaphor], 'because we've been locked out. And when we look in through the windows, all we see are shadows. And when we try and listen, all we hear is a whispering. And we cannot understand the whispering, because our minds have been invaded by a war. A war that we have won and lost. The very worst sort of war. A war that captures dreams and re-dreams them. A war that has made us adore our conquerors and despise ourselves'.
>
> '*Marry* our conquerors, is more like it', Ammu said drily, referring to Margaret Kochamma. (53)

Mixing of this kind then, the attempted reabsorption of shadow by substance, is not possible; it is not possible because it would require real knowledge of the other, and that kind of knowledge on a postcolonial terrain is not available. Knowledge of the other, on this ground, can exist only as an unassimilable foreign body, only according to the logic of host and parasite, a logic that can end only in exile or death. Under these circumstances there can be no dialogue, no real exchange; only whisperings, half-understood glances, intimations that can never be allowed to approach intimacy. Nothing can properly cross the threshold of the History House, because to do so would be to bring into an impossible proximity bodies, metaphors, languages that can be held only in separation. When they come together the only result must be an explosion or a drowning, the explosive beating that destroys Velutha's body, the drowning that sweeps Sophie Mol away even as she is in the very act of crossing the river that separates life from the ghosts of the History House.

It is important to recognise that the logic of the parasite could be read also in the terms offered by the notion of mimicry, developed fictionally by V. S. Naipaul in *The Mimic Men* and critically by Homi Bhabha in his series of essays on colonial mimicry.[15] The policemen who kill Velutha could themselves be regarded as an appalling hybrid, a chimera composed of historic, ancestral prejudice against the untouchables and the further means of violence offered to them by the sanction and authority of an imperial, white-officered police force. The History House is similarly layered, the residue of the 'white gone native' overlain by a furious repetition, a repetition of a love under the sign of taboo in the relationship between Ammu and Velutha, a repetition of death and mourning in Velutha's fate and its own further soundless echo in the emotional and linguistic silencing of the twins.

But hybridity cannot take account of the phantomatic fashion in which this is a book which is born of silence and which seeks to provide a context for that silence. Its very words are inhabited, preyed upon, by a prior history that cannot be verbalised; in the very act of writing, in the further and more complex acts of reading, it repeats its own self-alienation, the 'articulation' of an exiled tongue. The Black Sahib, we hear, spoke Malayalam; but when we come to look at the question – and this is true of many postcolonial texts – of what languages actually take place within the walls of its house, we find ourselves frequently at a loss. Perhaps we ought to pause on that phrase 'at a loss' for a moment; for again loss is clearly, if necessarily paradoxically, the core around which *The God of Small Things* is built, as it also is in the case of *Feeding the Ghosts*. The text we have is haunted, always and forever, by the text that might have been; the language used to recount the story is haunted by the languages in which the protagonists might have told the tale – had they had their own language, or indeed in this case *any* language, at their disposal. Like ghosts they arrive at history too late, in the case of Estha already the victim of a traumatic repetition, for his abuse at the hands of his aunt only repeats and builds corruptly upon the previous abuse he has suffered at the hands of the paedophiliac Orangedrink Lemondrink Man, who has already robbed Estha of his childhood, reduced him to a ghost mourning at the scene of his own lost past, or perhaps a dead baby marching through the wilderness (see Roy, 1997, 103–4).

There are phantoms also in Seamus Deane's *Reading in the Dark*. Deane is an Irish writer; in including *Reading in the Dark* in this chapter, I recall an experience of giving a paper on the postcolonial at a Scottish university in 1999. In that paper I spoke of a Scottish text in a postcolonial context and was promptly challenged by a colleague in the audience who demanded to know why I had not included an Irish text because, as he put it, the Irish have the 'most postcolonial history of all'. I think I became aware at that moment that we are now in an era that should be characterised as one of 'competitive postcolonialisms', and I will return to that thought below when I talk about the 'transcolonial'; but for the moment it seems important to register that the question of who dominates the field of victimhood will be not necessarily he who has suffered most but he who can speak most loudly, and that in turn will depend on ownership of a certain language.

Speaking loudly is, of course, the opposite but also the inevitable companion of that curious whispering, that soft or softened speech which we have already seen to be the perquisite of the phantom. I am not going to try to recount the story of *Reading in the Dark*, but instead will comment on two passages. The story – this nonetheless has to be said – is about a boy discovering his own history, finding his own History House, uncovering secrets of which even his own parents are probably unaware, and at one point the narrator says this:

> Hauntings are, in their way, very specific. Everything has to be exact, even the vaguenesses. My family's history was like that too. It came to me in bits, from people who rarely recognised all they had told. Some of the things I remember, I don't really remember. I've just been told about them so now I feel I remember them, and want to the more because it is so important for others to forget them. Someone told me how my father, the night his parents were buried, was found lying down in the back shed of that house on the High Street where they had lived, among the coal sacks and the chopped wood, crying unstoppably. I imagined it and believed it, but when I looked at him again, I wondered: was that my father? (Deane, 1996, 225)

'I feel I remember them, and want to the more because it is so important for others to forget them.' This is a crucial thought about memory, and also about the particular (perverted) functions memory might assume under colonial circumstances, although it is also worth wondering whether there are, have ever been, any truly non-colonial circumstances, any situations in which the mind has not been already colonised by an other – even if that other is our parent or, in the emblematic case of the imperial/cultural parent, Queen Victoria, that Victoria who was eventually responsible, as he reminds us in a significant context, for Chinua Achebe's birth-name: Albert.[16]

But to remember because others need to forget; to heed to the whisperings, to peer into the grimy windows of the History House – which is perhaps also that same palace where the characters in Poe's 'The Masque of the Red Death' play out their attempted deferral of mourning – and morning – because others will not (see Poe, 1960, 61–7): is this also the story of postcolonial writing and/or, indeed, of postcolonial criticism? Why do hauntings, phantoms, have to be specific? Because, perhaps, they offer a more vivid recollection than does the conscious mind; because for these hauntings there is no advantage in smoothing over, softening the hard edges of a disastrous experience. So while we may wish to suppose that ghosts are vague, that they merely whisper unintelligibly on the fringes of our minds, all the while there is another story going on; ghosts speaking to other ghosts while we are merely the hapless listeners at these oft-repeated tales of rape, violence, murder, suicide; in some cases, perhaps, precisely of those crimes or sins for which ghosts cannot get absolution, for which they are banished to haunting the edge of the cemetery (see Abraham and Torok, 1986, xxxv–xxxvi). Descendants of the colonisers would be merely the overhearers of ghost-gossip.

But that ghost-gossip can also be more real, more vivid, than the shadow-play that passes for 'real life'. In *Reading in the Dark* the boy's mother crumbles into mental illness under the weight of the secrets she carries, but at one point in the novel makes a partial recovery:

> She hugged my head to her breast. She still smelt of medicine and I could feel her older, as though her breath were shallower than it had once been. I held her for a moment, ashamed of the shame I had been feeling. But I never felt less like asking anything. That night, for the first time in weeks, she made dinner and even talked about Hallowe'en and Christmas. By All Souls' Night, she had false teeth, and her smile was white again. But when I saw her smile, then and ever afterwards, I could hear her voice, creased with sorrow, saying, 'Burning, burning', and I would look for the other voice, young and clear, lying in its crypt behind it. But it slept there and remained sleeping, behind her false white smile. (Deane, 1996, 146–7)

A voice behind another voice, a text obliterated, replaced, shadowed, distorted by a 'text instead'; in this trope of the vanished voice, of the voice that could tell secrets yet nevertheless in another sense cannot do so, it is possible to discern an entire problematic of the postcolonial.

At the same time it is precisely on this kind of terrain that the notion of the postcolonial *becomes* most problematic. Not at all on historical grounds: even to contest the point would be to enter into the 'competitive postcolonial', to participate in attempted statistical resolutions, to call in the ambiguous ministry of weights and measures. What is more important is the question of 'what comes after', and it is for that reason that I have preferred in the title of this chapter to use the term 'transcolonial'. The 'transcolonial' might of course – does of course – most transparently signify the importance of recognising that no colonial or postcolonial literature or indeed experience occurs or develops in isolation from others;[17] but more importantly it gestures towards the significance of moments of revelation, and conversely moments of secrecy (if there can be such things) that defy and thwart, bend linear narrative and assert that the 'after' is never 'after', that there is no true 'aftermath' but only twists, skeins, traversings, crossings of terrains that cannot be halted, that continue to ravel and unravel, wind and unwind, in an endless parade of territorialisations from which nothing is lost; in terms of which everything is loss.

# VI Haunting the Secret Site

> For the land has lost the memory of the most secret places.
> We see the moon but cannot remember its meaning.
> A dark skin is a chain but it cannot recall the name
> of its tribe.
>
> (Edward Brathwaite, *The Arrivants*)

> 'It's like I'm in the real Africa'.
>
> He laughed. 'You muzungu are always saying things like that, as if there's some kind of secret to be discovered. We had one man here looking for the site of King Solomon's Mines'. (Giles Foden, *The Last King of Scotland*)

> The Carib flute was hollowed from the bone of an enemy in time of war. Flesh was plucked and consumed and in the process secrets were digested. Spectres arose from, or reposed in, the flute. (Wilson Harris, *The Palace of the Peacock*)

In this chapter I want to keep in mind the rhetoric of haunting which I have been trying to develop in earlier chapters, and to begin by looking at a text I have already mentioned, Naipaul's delicate and bitter *A House for Mr Biswas*. Mr Biswas, pulled this way and that by cultural pressures, and particularly by the power of the family into which he has married, appears on the surface to be a prime example of the kind of mimicry described by Bhabha in the double sense that, on the one hand, he is the victim of a certain emptying out of culture which leaves him with only the poor resource of imitating the culture of others while, on the other, he is capable, at least sometimes, of ironising precisely that culture (see Bhabha, 1984). Much of the knowledge available to him is useless, but this abolishes neither his need to acquire it nor his entrapment in a cultural circle of mistransmission:

> Presently Mr Biswas fell into a Sunday routine. He went to Tara's in the middle of the morning, read for Ajodha all the *That Body of Yours* columns which had been cut out during the week, got his penny, was given lunch, and was then free to explore the *Book of Comprehensive Knowledge*. He read folk tales from various lands; he read, and quickly forgot, how chocolate, matches, ships, buttons and many other things were made; he read articles which answered, with drawings that looked pretty but didn't really help, questions like: Why does ice make water cold? Why does fire burn? Why does sugar sweeten? (Naipaul, 1961, 62)

There is a sense in which Mr Biswas spends the whole of the book struggling for a culture of his own, trying to find out what the truly significant questions would be, but at every step he finds it impossible to escape from the entangling tentacles of his surroundings. He, however, is not in the worst of situations. We hear also about a boy, supposedly brilliant at school, who turns out in the end to have been spending his time simply copying out uncomprehendingly the words in front of him:

> He had impressed his parents by a constant demand for exercise books and by a continuous show of writing. He said he was making notes. In fact, he had copied out every word of *Nelson's West Indian Geography*, by Captain Cutteridge, Director of Education, author of *Nelson's West Indian Readers* and *Nelson's West Indian Arithmetics*. He had completed the *Geography* in more than a dozen exercise books, and was at the moment engaged on the first volume of *Nelson's West Indian History*, by Captain Daniel, Assistant Director of Education. (463)[1]

The crucial phrase here is 'a continuous show of writing', but its ramifications spread far beyond a mere notion of mimicry. We might rather consider the ways in which we are here in the presence of a certain type of uncanny repetition, in the form precisely of a kind of automatic writing.[2]

It is, presumably, not the case that we have here a simple example of the mimicking of a 'high culture' by an exploited subculture, for to make such a claim would be in some sense to fix the 'original' text in place as an unchallengeable authority. Clearly what Naipaul is doing here is pointing instead to a certain problematic circularity, or at the very least an unassignability, surrounding the textuality of these 'common readers'. The fact that these texts are written by military men, by men in positions of colonial authority, has of course its own significance, but what is also raised in the notion of a 'West Indian Reader' is the question of who does the reading, in what sense and with what effects the West Indies have been 'read' (as well as named, inscribed, written, rewritten) by a foreign body, which in turn renders them to all intents and purposes unwritable.

In place of writing as production or as representation what we therefore have is a 'continuous show of writing', a writing 'as if', or a writing 'instead of' a text that can no longer be written because it has been defaced, effaced. The 'copying' activities of Naipaul's unfortunate child could thus be seen as both an unavoidable entering into a world of distorted repetition and at the same time a desperate – and the child is certainly desperate – attempt to make whole that which has been broken, to find a face, an aspect that is free from mutilation, whether this recuperation can be eventually successful or not.[3]

It is these aspects of the uncanny that all the time threaten to undermine the simple notion of mimicry. We might also reflect on a further uncanny doubling that provides a large part of the structure of *A House for Mr Biswas*, a doubling, such as we have come across before in *The God of Small Things*, between two houses. One of these is the 'virtual house', the house that Mr Biswas is always, and against enormous odds, trying to build as a symbol of independence, as a kind of 'housing' for his soul; the other is the sprawling mansion, Hanuman House, which is inhabited by his in-laws. Here is a picture of part of Hanuman House:

> A hammock made from sugarsacks hung across one corner of the room. An old sewingmachine, a baby-chair and a black biscuit-drum occupied another corner. Scattered about were a number of unrelated chairs, stools and benches, one of which, low and carved with rough ornamentation from a solid block of cyp wood, still had the saffron colour which told that it had been used at a wedding ceremony. More elegant pieces – a dresser, a desk, a piano so buried under papers and baskets and other things that it was unlikely that it was ever used – choked the staircase landing. On the other side of the hall there was a loft of curious construction. It was as if an enormous drawer had been pulled out of the top of the wall; the vacated space, dark and dusty, was crammed with all sorts of articles Mr Biswas couldn't distinguish. (Naipaul, 1961, 87)[4]

This and many other descriptions show us Hanuman House to be in some sense a house of dream (see Freud, 1953–74, IV, 85, 225–6);

things are divorced from their functions, they are 'unrelated', in the end they are indistinguishable, they fade off into the blackness. This is, we need to remember, far from what Mr Biswas has expected: the Tulsi family, after all, are, or are said to be, wealthy. But even this is not the whole of the story. For this house, the house the family actually occupies, lies behind another far more modern and imposing edifice which is barely used. Clearly the new house, the 'impressive' mansion, represents the Tulsis' name and status in the community, it acts as a sign for their prominence, even their modernity; but behind this house there lies a further sprawling hinterland full of half-broken antiques and useless toys, a repository of memory which is the only place, to be sure, where the Tulsis can feel 'at home'.[5]

A place to feel at home, a foreign place; these doublings themselves are taken through a further twist when we consider Mr Biswas' own efforts to build, or even find, a place that he can call home. I will cite only one example among many, concerning the shop to which he moves himself and his wife in one of his many attempts to escape Hanuman House. The shop is initially in terrible condition; but even when improvements are made, we are told, Mr Biswas continues to feel that the place is 'temporary and not quite real' (Naipaul, 1961, 147). What might it mean to feel 'not quite real' in this context? The issue here might be bricks and mortar, but it connects to a wider theme of the book, to do with what we might call the 'ghosting' of the immigrant. 'Despite the solidity of their establishment', we learn, even

> the Tulsis had never considered themselves settled in Arwacas or even Trinidad. It was no more than a stage in the journey that had begun when Pundit Tulsi left India. Only the death of Pundit Tulsi had prevented them from going back to India; and ever since they had talked, though less often than the old men who gathered in the arcade every evening, of moving on, to India, Demerara, Surinam. Mr Biswas didn't take such talk seriously. The old men would never see India again. And he could not imagine the Tulsis anywhere else except at Arwacas. Separate from their house, and lands, they would be separate from the labourers, tenants and friends who respected them for their piety and the memory of Pundit Tulsi; their Hindu status would be worthless and, as had happened during their descent on the house in Port of Spain, they would be only exotic. (390)

This is a very rich passage. First of all, of course, we have already seen that the 'solidity of their establishment' is, to an extent, illusory, even schizo: the firmness of the architectural shell that surrounds them is continuously in danger of betrayal by the vulnerability of the past, enshrined in the porous old house that nonetheless has to be 'hidden' from the outside world, held only in secret, in a replica of the equally replicated memories of those who honour them for the memory of their dead ancestor. Similarly the journey itself is illusory, the notion that there are further places to go, the myth of the freedom of the transient who feels he has choices as to how to proceed along the road when all the time, as we saw in the case of Michael K, the fate that awaits comes down to a choice between the ubiquitous camps or a hole in the side of a mountain.[6] And finally, what is threatened, the *reductio ad absurdum*, is the fate of the 'exotic'; the fate, that is to say, of being continuingly misread, being seen 'out of context' or rather in a wholly imposed context, being appropriated as and by a foreign body, so that the narrative the Tulsis – and, by implication, Indian immigrants to Trinidad in general – tell themselves will be falsified in the narrative that is inevitably woven about them and which, because of their ambiguous colonial status, they are powerless to resist or refute.[7]

One of the most often cited aspects of the uncanny according to Freud is that it arises from a conflation of the *heimlich* and the *unheimlich*, often referred to in terms of the 'familiar' and the 'unfamiliar'; but the direct reference in the terms is to that which is 'at home' and that which is 'not at home'.[8] The Tulsis are, at least for certain purposes, disabled from recognising even such 'at-home-ness' as they have come to possess; Mr Biswas is searching throughout, albeit inchoately, for some kind of proof that there is somewhere, anywhere, where he can experience the feeling of being 'at home'. These are not issues that can be summarised in terms of mimicry; they have more to do with an uncanny enactment of the plight of exile, with the internalisation of alienation, foreignness, as the only but ambivalent ground on which a sense of self – in this case, most emblematically Biswas' house – can be painfully constructed.[9]

What, after all, might it take to make one feel at home – in a foreign land, or simply after the sudden, sometimes surprising, recognition that the 'homeland' is indeed foreign? We can turn back again to Coetzee's *Life & Times of Michael K*. Michael is a man who has little sense of where he is in the world, but this serves to make him uniquely privileged in his attention to the curious logic of the host and the parasite, especially at a moment when he is stimulated by a police captain's accusation that the inhabitants of his labour camp (at the aptly named Jakkalsdrif) are so many parasites depending on – indeed, literally *from* – the nearby town.

> Parasite was the word the police captain had used: the camp at Jakkalsdrif, a nest of parasites hanging from the neat sunlit town, eating its substance, giving no nourishment back. Yet to K lying idle in his bed, thinking without passion (What is it to me, after all? he thought), it was no longer obvious which was host and which parasite, camp or town. If the worm devoured the sheep, why did the sheep swallow the worm? What if there were millions, more millions than anyone knew, living in camps, living on alms, living off the land, living by guile, creeping away in corners to escape the times, too canny to put out flags and draw attention to themselves and be counted? What if the hosts were far outnumbered by the parasites, the parasites of idleness and the other secret parasites in the army and the police force and the schools and factories and offices, the parasites of the heart? Could the parasites then still be called parasites? (Coetzee, 1983, 159)

We have already come across another example of the illusory 'neat sunlit town', in the children's reading book of Morrison's *The Bluest Eye*, and we have also already been exposed to an alternative history of sheep, by Banks in *The Wasp Factory*; the rhetoric of 'putting out [more] flags' is also resonant. What would it mean, though, to be a 'secret parasite' – are parasites capable of considering the intricacies of their disclosure strategy? And to complicate matters there are, it would appear, two kinds of parasite being discussed here: those whose parasitism is involuntary and simply assigned to them by state authority, and those whose parasitism might be chosen, might be an act of at least passive political subversion – would it be possible, Coetzee is asking, for these two types of parasite to make common cause, establish, we might say, a concrete solid 'site' (for building development)? 'Parasites of the heart[land]': how would these affect the very definition of the state, how would their continuing reterritorialisations, their postures of continually arrested flight, their paralysing insertion of infectious nomadry into the heart of the well-constituted state machine, pollute and poison the 'health' of the body politic, poison it by the insertion of uncontrollable micro-organisms, tiny points and lines of refusal and distortion – by returning, we might say, the projection of poison onto the very instruments of destruction and exploitation? 'Perhaps in truth', K goes on to muse – without passion, needless to say, for passion is not allowable to those who are already, in every sense of the term, 'arrested' – 'whether the camp was declared a parasite on the town or the town a parasite on the camp depended on no more than on who made his voice heard loudest' (Coetzee, 1983, 160).

Or, we might say, on whose narrative was allowed to supervene, was granted superior status such that that voice and that alone could determine the presumptive truth of the pre-existence of this 'unhostly', this inhospitable host who is figuring as the unyielding, violent, vengeful ground on which the whole apparatus of town, camp, house, home, building is being 'founded'; as if such 'foundation' were possible in a land – whether we are now talking about Trinidad or South Africa – where the borders, the boundaries are no longer determinate, where what happens is responsive to no causal logic but the postcolonial logic of the parasite, the terrible accusation that also surfaces – or rather does not surface – in Coetzee's *Age of Iron* when the protagonist muses on this question of what the 'ground' might be and comes up against a structure of burial, secrecy, the insane persistence of the dead. 'Let me tell you', she says,

> when I walk upon this land, this South Africa, I have a gathering feeling of walking upon black faces. They are dead but their spirit has not left them. They lie there heavy and obdurate, waiting for my feet to pass, waiting for me to go, waiting to be raised up again. Millions of figures of pig-iron floating under the skin of the earth. The age of iron waiting to return. (Coetzee, 1990, 115)

What is dead and what is not dead? On that note we could briefly revisit the mysterious house in Chandra's 'Dharma'. This, as we have noted before, is a ghost story, a story of a phantom limb, and a story also of a revenant who is the earlier self of the protagonist and whose return frustrates the linear attempts of memory and history. It is also, in its account of the house itself in which the events take place (or perhaps only the one whose position as legacy serves as the spur to the recollection of a quite different house – the story is uncannily ambiguous on the point (see Chandra, 1997, 2–3)), the site of a crucial postcolonial narrative. The house is an old one, the only one remaining in a sea of urban 'development'; 'it sat stubbornly in the middle of towering apartment buildings, and it had been empty as far back as anyone could remember'; and so

> the story that explained this waste of golden real estate was one of ghosts and screams in the night.
>
> 'They say it's unsellable', said Ramani. 'They say a Gujarati *seth* bought it and died within the month. Nobody'll buy it. Bad place'.

> 'What nonsense', I said. 'These are all family property disputes. The cases drag on for years and years in courts, and the houses lie vacant because no one will let anyone else live in them'. I spoke at length then, about superstition and ignorance and the state of our benighted nation, in which educated men and women believed in banshees and ghouls. 'Even in the information age we will never be free', I said. (2)

Two modes of explanation, then, the supernatural and the legal, but in fact it may be more difficult than it seems to see the difference. After all, what are 'family property disputes': altercations with the dead, discussions within the crypt, shadowy disagreements that seem destined, like the rooms of Hanuman House, to fade back again into the darkness from which they emerged.[10] But the suggestion here made by the protagonist, however pessimistically, is that somehow the development of information technology might banish the spectre, as though, through a remarkable and improbable paradox, the arrival of a technology designed to inure us to virtual reality will somehow curtail our belief in an alternative and older virtual reality rather than rendering our acts of communication and practices of belief all the more liminal and ghostly.[11]

But the core of the argument extends beyond this: for the house in 'Dharma' (and perhaps this is why the story allows us to continue to believe that there may be not one but two houses after all) is both haunting and haunted, a source of both fear and pride. Another example of such a house, which reminds us like Arundhati Roy's of the terror of history while at the same time representing a past which we dare not slough off for fear of abandoning our historical and geographical coordinates, losing our precarious balance, occurs in R.K. Narayan's *Waiting for the Mahatma*:

> The Circuit House on the edge of the town was an old East India Company building standing on an acre of land, on the Trunk Road. Robert Clive was supposed to have halted there while marching to relieve the siege of Trichinopoly. The citizens of Malgudi were very proud of this building and never missed an opportunity to show it off to anyone visiting the town and it always housed the distinguished visitors who came this way. (Narayan, 1955, 38–9)

Such houses are, obviously, a legacy of empire; at the same time, they are taken as a source of distinction, as representing an unassailable truth about history; they confront us with an extraordinary form of alien intrusion yet at the same time they signify that the 'locality' has been, if only in some uncanny and mysterious sense, important in the eyes of the outside world. They signify, therefore, a curious reversal of the gaze, a de- and re-provincialising. Set up precisely as part of a panoptical encircling of the 'native', as part of the apparatus of imperial control, they pass imperceptibly into being the *object* of the gaze, the preserved – even if also desecrated – relic of a past whose conflicts are rapidly sedimenting into the undifferentiating, slimy texture of 'heritage'.

Other such houses, especially while they still exercise power, might embody strenuous steps to avoid this dangerous fate of the spectacle, as for instance the houses Khalil and Yusuf see in Gurnah's *Paradise*:

> the huge silent houses with blank front walls where the rich Omani families lived. 'They only marry their daughters to their brothers' sons', one of the customers told them. 'In some of those sprawling fortresses are feeble offspring locked away and never spoken about. Sometimes you can see the faces of the poor creatures pressed against the bars of the windows at the top of the houses. (Gurnah, 1994, 49)

As in many other locations the setting itself apart of an elite caste, the isolation of the 'grand family', eventuates in generally accepted accusations of incest:[12] the only interlocking gazes here are those of the curious but ultimately unsatisfied spectator who cannot penetrate the blind front of the house (we might be reminded of the moment in Foden's *Last King of Scotland* when Amin's palace is stormed, or of the strange rooms and apartments the crew see in Harris's *Palace of the Peacock* as they scale their final cliff (see Foden, 1998, 293–4; Harris, 1988, 116))[13] and the presumably idiot gaze that returns – while it does not return – the inspection of the outside. Kwaku Ananse, for Brathwaite, the 'spider' in the ground of all things, is also connected to perception, as he is to language, ghosts, memory:

> he stumps up the stares [sic]
> of our windows, he stares, stares
> he squats on the tips
>
> of our language
> black burr of conundrums
> eye corner of ghosts, ancient his-
> tories ...
>
> (Brathwaite, 1973, 165)

Here it is as though the very act of looking is sufficient to induce the gaze to slide away, to look elsewhere or 'awry' (see Žižek, 1992, 88–106), to find itself staring like Mr Biswas into an impossible gloom, to enter a realm of uncertainties and dreams yet always ones that cannot be separated from the 'origins' of the present plight, here figured in the reference to 'the tips/of our language' and the 'ancient his-/tories', the complexities of expression and memory in a land that can declare itself neither fully homely nor fully foreign.

These complexities of expression and memory also figure very prominently in Keri Hulme's novel *The Bone People*, which is to a large extent structured round dreams and ghosts. Kerewin and Joe drink 'to keep away the ghosts'; she speaks of 'the ghost hour' and the 'ghost-dagger', the demonic 'taipo' (Hulme, 1985, 101, 187, 193, 198). The 'ghost-dagger' is particularly important, because it is one way in which Kerewin speaks – at least to herself – of her pain, of her fear of cancer. It stands therefore as a symptom – and there are plenty of other symptoms in *The Bone People*, including muteness, alcoholism, child abuse – but what are these symptoms of?

Symptoms in this context, perhaps, of a certain ghosting of the self; but if so, then certainly also symptoms of the ghosting of Maori culture. Kerewin asks Joe why Simon, the mysterious silent white child saved from the sea, only to be abused by Joe, his 'foster'-father, sleeps badly:

> The man's smile is crooked.
>
> 'Bad dreams. He doesn't like going to sleep because he'll dream bad dreams'. He twisted round and looked in open wonderment at the still child. 'Spooked, would you believe?'
>
> 'Spooked, I'd believe'.
>
> He wasn't quite joking, nor was he truly serious. There was a strained gaiety in his voice.
>
> 'Scared of ghosts and things in dreams ... if I was proper Maori I'd ...'
>
> Into the following silence,
>
> 'You'd what?'
>
> 'Hah, I don't know'. He laughed quietly. 'Maybe take him to people who'd know what to do, to keep off ghosts in dreams'. (61)

But we are never really certain why Simon sleeps badly. It appears that he has been appallingly treated by whoever was looking after him before the boat they were all on sank; but equally he is frightened of Joe, although the power of the novel lies very much in the ways in which this fear is shown as inextricably intertwined with a heart-rending love. The text sails, as it were, very close to the wind; almost an endorsement of the inevitability of child abuse, it nonetheless continually refers this back to a sense of wider cultural conditions. That is not to say at all that direct or exact parallels are drawn between the strangely abusive 'family' that is the core of the novel and relations between the races in New Zealand: rather the matter is left hanging, ghostly, the symptoms relatively (as it were) unattached. For after all there is no simple binary here, no initial imaginary separation that can be tackled or erased through the sustaining fantasy some theorists, as we have seen, unthinkingly and dangerously refer to as 'hybridity';[14] the question of what is 'proper Maori' can never be answered, the very possibility of an answer lies in 'ancient histories'.

But equally, as the structure of the book tells us by moving as it does into increasingly mystical realms, the possibility of 'erasure of the Maori' is also unthinkable. What seems to lie behind *The Bone People* is an only partially expressed notion of continual *becoming*; it is perhaps not at all that some 'essentiality' of the Maori eludes us merely in the past and in the present, more that Maori belongs to some quite different realm, a realm which lies perhaps in the future or perhaps in some other world of dream from which no awakening has yet come. Certainly this seems to be part of the significance of the kowhai, which is

> a tall thin tree, with greybrown bark. It blooms in the earliest part of spring, with flowers that the tui and korimako love. It likes coastal areas, and lets its seeds fall into rivers and the sea. And they are carried to other beaches so the kowhai blooms through the land. A sea-tree emblem for a sea-people, only the people haven't woken up to the fact they *are* a sea-people yet ... (Hulme, 1985, 125–6)

Which here is the ghost, the tree or the people?

The issue of the debatable status of Maori is portrayed as a condition of waiting, of having no answers, and furthermore of not knowing *why* there are no answers. Kerewin collects 'treasures' the sea brings her, but she has no way of knowing whether she is doing the right thing with them because something intercedes between her and the voices that should instruct, something has always already intercepted the signals:

> I don't know what I should have done ... I argued with myself, for long enough. The sea wouldn't have given it to me if it hadn't

> been meant for me. The ghosts of the old people, or whatever the voices were, didn't say it *wasn't* for me. I asked who it was for, they didn't say. I didn't do anything wrong and nothing bad came of it, so it must have been all right. I just had some strange dreams for a while. (254)

Something in the past is, we might say, no longer responsive. Kerewin, we are told, is cut off from her family, possibly through her own volition, possibly not; she is cut off also from all physical contact, although she is unable to discover why. Something waits in the land before these fractures can be mended. 'I planned to try and unravel the tangle of dream and substance that is me, my family, Moerangi', she says, 'but I am overwhelmed by futility. What use is it to know? What use is it, when I am gutted by the sense of my own uselessness?' (261). The use, perhaps, will be to save Simon from Joe, to save Joe from Joe; or to save, we might say, the gift, the 'treasure' of the sea from the ambiguous corruption of urbanised culture, to preserve something mutely precious from being sucked into the web of drink and violence that here, under the conditions of an over-determined addiction, always threatens to invade and stickily contort any safe place.[15]

Kerewin, in defiance of this threat, has built herself a tower, and it seems to be only in this strange house that conditions can be set aside and the necessary act of waiting performed. Yet the 'absence' of Maori, its banishment or withdrawal while the land is temporarily invaded by the pakeha, has its parallel in the very ghosting of the self, the ghosting of paper, the ghosting of writing:

> I follow the Chinese: on the funeral pyre of our dead selves, I place a paper replica of what is real. Ghost, follow the other ghosts – haere, haere, haere ki te po! Go easy to the Great Lady of the Night, and if we ever meet in the dimension where dreams are real, I shall embrace you and we shall laugh, at last. (437)

And so we see the text itself as a 'paper replica', an attempt to preserve at the same time as banishing memories of a 'time apart', as a haunting and haunted presence/absence inhabiting a dimension which is always provisional; text again, as we have seen it before, as a 'text instead', a mere pale imitation of the text that might have been or the text that is to come; the text that, in this particular case, can be written only when the sea-borne blight of invasion has receded and the gifts of the sea can again be trusted rather than subjected to painful but unavoidable alienation and abuse.[16]

This necessary instability of the postcolonial text is part of the subject of chapter 8 of Derek Walcott's *Another Life* (a title itself resonant with the notion of a 'text instead', a substituted text and a substituted birth), which is called 'West Indian Gothic' and begins by introducing us, perhaps by now unsurprisingly, to a house of history:

> A gaunt, gabled house,
> grey, fretted, soars
> above a verdigris canal which
> sours with moss. A bridge,
> lithe as a schoolboy's leap,
> vaults the canal. Each
> longitudinal window seems
> a vertical sarcophagus, a niche
> in which its family must sleep
> erect, repetitive as saints
> in their cathedral crypt,
> like urgent angels in their fluted stone
> sailing their stone dream.
>
> (Walcott, 1992, 191)

'Gaunt', 'vaults', 'sarcophagus', 'crypt': here are all the materials of a Gothic imagination (see Punter, 1996), a sense of history as an accumulation of relics, as an accumulative relic, an embedding of a notion of mourning that pervades the whole poem but is perhaps particularly focused on the figure of Gregorias, for whom this part of the book is a 'homage'. And what follows this is even more obviously an act of mourning, for Gregorias' soldier father who was 'a Lewis gunner in the First World War' (Walcott, 1992, 192); in a way, it is the sense of pride instilled in him by being part of a 'foreign' army, fighting in a war for aims and lands not his own, that kills him – or rather it is the necessary inverse, an 'inversion' to which we shall return: shame.

But there is a sense in which the incident of his death, any *incident*, is *accidental* compared with the artistic purpose expressed by Walcott on his own behalf as poet and on behalf of Gregorias, the painter. 'Drunkenly, or secretly', he says, 'we swore':

> that we would never leave the island
> until we had put down, in paint, in words,
> as palmists learn the network of a hand,
> all of its sudden, leaf-choked ravines,
> every neglected, self-pitying inlet
> muttering in brackish dialect, the ropes of mangroves

from which old soldier crabs slipped
surrendering to slush,
each ochre track seeking some hilltop and
losing itself in an unfinished phrase . . .

(194)

Which here, then, is more real: the old soldier dead of shame, or the 'old soldier crabs' that are still part of this landscape – a landscape that sets as its task the necessity of being wholly translated into words, a landscape that nevertheless seems already, in a different sense, to consist of words, dialects, phrases, to resist translation into a 'new wor(l)d order'? The task here is to bring back the fleeting, to prevent its flight, to translate it into a 'network' and, in the process of that abstraction, to render it yet more real through the medium of text. Yet behind this apparent but easily corruptible desire for the open, the transparent, the readily available, there is something else hidden; for the promise itself is made 'secretly', in a haunted Gothic half-light, as though to admit it too closely to the light of day would be to risk an inevitable failure.[17]

And the secret returns – in the form, for example, of the 'sanderlings rustily wheeling/the world on its ancient,/invisible axis' (Walcott, 1992, 195), in a sense of ebb and flow that cannot be fully sensed on the surface; yet perhaps there is some uneasy circling here too on the part of the poet in his relation to tradition, for Walcott describes the two of them, himself and Gregorias, when in full creative flood, as 'firm/as conquerors who had discovered home' (195). How, we might ask, does a conqueror discover 'home'? Does he do it, for example, by naming the land that he finds? This would certainly appear, despite the treachery of the Keatsian language in which this part of the poem is couched (as opposed to the Larkinesque of the beginning), to be what Walcott has in mind:

For no one had yet written of this landscape
that it was possible, though there were sounds
given to its varieties of wood;

the *bois-canot* responded to its echo,
when the axe spoke, weeds ran up to the knee
like bastard children, hiding in their names,

whole generations died, unchristened,
growths hidden in green darkness, forests
of history thickening with amnesia . . .

(195)[18]

The act of writing is therefore to stimulate some kind of memory; or perhaps it is to bring something to the threshold of the human, to animate the wild to challenge it with naming; or perhaps, thinking still of the notion of Gothic, it is to tangle in any way available, and at whatever risk of exaggeration or distortion, with the 'forests/of history thickening with amnesia'. For here, Walcott tells us, is 'a life older than geography' (Walcott, 1992, 196), a life that precedes the map-making – and, by implication, the naming and the conquering – but the dilemma would surely be one of how to bring such a pre-cartographic land to the verge of the articulate without violation, and even worse, how to bring it to the verge of an essentially *foreign* articulacy without risking repeating previous violations, without re-invoking the damage of conquest, the theft of language and territory.

Here, certainly, the loss can be felt, the thought of what had previously been trickling away into the slush:

> as the leaves of edible roots opened their pages
> at the heart's last lesson, Africa, heart-shaped,
>
> and the lost Arawak hieroglyphs and signs
> were razed from slates by sponges of the rain,
> their symbols mixed with lichen,
>
> the archipelago like a broken root,
> divided among tribes, while trees and men
> laboured assiduously, silently to become
>
> whatever their given sounds resembled ...
>
> (196)

This last thought is very close to the sense of silent becoming that characterises *The Bone People*; it is also deeply involved with complex questions around the notion of territorialisation. What, we might ask, precedes the 'mark', what secret further back may 'underwrite' even the already 'lost' Arawak signs? The 'root', we presume, is a geological root, but it is also inseparably a linguistic root, the root broken, fractured by the imposition of one language upon another.

The forest we here occupy is, like other forests we come across on postcolonial terrain, a haunted one;[19] but unlike the forests of the West, the ghosts by which it is haunted are in a state of yet further exile, deprived even of the means of making themselves known to the living. But the paradoxical benefit of this further removal is to enable one step farther back; to enable – in a clearer form than would have been possible without the agonising expunging of the 'native' – the observation of the absolute becoming of the 'non-human', the slow growth that will demonstrate the temporary nature of empires, that will keep the 'mark' for ever in a state of incompletion but will simultaneously prevent the foreclosure that is the mark of systems of thought and writing that batten only upon a false sense of achieved cultural superiority.

# VII Hallucination, Dream, the Exotic

> This is a land of fantastic tales. You will hear about a lot of things, but ask for hard evidence and you will get to see nothing. (Satyajit Ray, 'Khagama' in Behl and Nicholls, *The Penguin New Writing in India*)

> I think if time is like a river, the past is on the bed of it like a sunken stone that you know is there only from tangled movements in the water. Or time is like the ice vaults of a waterfall in winter, that melt, that are swept away, to take on new forms in a new winter. (Beverley Farmer, *The Seal Woman*)

> ... the discourse of recognition becomes possible when heterogeneity is valorised by the increasingly routinised metropolis. At this moment, the Third World becomes the place of the unconscious, the rich source of fantasy and legend recycled by the intelligentsia, for which heterogeneity is no longer a ghostly, dragging chain but material that can be loosened from any territorial context and juxtaposed in ways that provide a constant frisson of pleasure. (Jean Franco, 'Beyond Ethnocentrism')

The constancy of hallucination and dream in postcolonial writing is susceptible of a number of explanations, not all of them of the type Franco suggests above. Harris provides some better ones when he speaks of how the 'imagination of the folk involved a crucial inner re-creative response to the violations of slavery and indenture and conquest' (Harris, 1981, 27), and suggests that

> the possibility exists for us to become involved in perspectives of renascence which can bring into play a figurative meaning beyond an apparently real world or prison of history ... I believe a philosophy of history may well lie buried in the arts of the imagination. (Harris, 1970, 8)

The question here, though, would be a dialectical one, about the extent to which these 'new ways of seeing', these potentially quasi-magical responses to the unspeakable conditions of slavery and colonisation, would be impelled by an inevitability of capitulation, thus becoming a further agency of exploitation. The materialist critic San Juan, for example, speaks with commanding passion of how US domination of the Philippines is forwarded by the 'almost hallucinatory spell of the United States fantasised as the land of affluence and immigrant success', and details the sharp contrast between this fantasised 'exoticisation' and the genocidal way in which the USA has historically treated the people of the Philippines (San Juan, 1998, 154).

The question would also be about the 'reality of history', and would therefore touch on the all-important issue – which we have now glimpsed in several contexts – of the relation back to the past, the constant revisiting of the site of trauma, which is inextricably bound to the extending of a historical 'apology' that presupposes some way of 'beginning again'. Here we touch again on the fantasy of a 'new world order', the 'hallucinatory vista' designed to distract from and obscure the prolongation of neocolonialism in the service of global capitalism.[1] Would it be the case that the 'paradise' we have glimpsed in Gurnah's work, in Harris's, in Ondaatje's, and in other contexts can in fact be reduced to an inverted image of the massive disruption of 'native' societies, simply a dream of a lost past or of a putatively separatist future?

In Harris's *Palace of the Peacock*, it seems clear that the matter is more complicated than this, but nevertheless it is dream that is the ground on which the entire narrative precariously stands:

> I dreamt I awoke with one dead seeing eye and one living closed eye. I put my dreaming feet on the ground in a room that oppressed me as though I stood in an operating theatre, or a maternity ward, or I felt suddenly, the glaring cell of a prisoner who had been sentenced to die. (Harris, 1988, 19)

There is a sense in which we can read this remarkable paragraph, regardless of its specific attribution in the text, as an epitome of an entire postcolonial situation. What is being spoken of is a dislocation of vision; the impossibility of putting back together a territory, a field of perception that has been fatally fractured. On this violent and terrifying ground, the epitome of deterritorialisation, not only does the question of vision itself become problematic, the whole situating of life and death trembles through a haze of passivity –

*Palace of the Peacock* is indeed, as has often been said, a 'somnambulistic' text, a slow dancing of sleepwalkers in a land that they can only, fruitfully or otherwise, misrecognise.[2] Perhaps, though, it is this specific misrecognition – or rather series of misrecognitions – that is essential in order to give birth to the 'arts of the imagination'; but if so then, as we see here, that birth (in the 'maternity ward') will always be imbricated with a violent penetration (the 'operating theatre') and over it will inevitably hover the shadow of the panopticon, the blinding gaze before which the colonised are subjected to an incomprehensible sentence for an unknowable crime.[3]

Such metaphors are actualised in, for example, Thomas Keneally's *The Playmaker*, which is specifically about life in the panopticon in the guise of survival after transportation to Australia, and which concludes with four deaths, one birth and one survival, summarised in a concluding sentence that again bifurcates two kinds of vision, coded in this case – though not ineluctably – as fiction and history:

> In the catalogue produced by Sotheby's in another age to advertise the sale of Ralph's erratic journal, it is stated that father and son died on the one day. Neither of them knew that Betsey Alicia herself had suffered a stillbirth and died in the Marine hospital at Chatham. So in a pulse of time the blood and all the complex of dreams and very ordinary fervours of the Playmaker were extinguished, except for his lag-wife Brenham and the new world child Alicia. Of them fiction could make much, though history says nothing. (Keneally, 1987, 364)

The survivor, then, the 'lag-wife', is a convict and she comes here to form the basis of yet another kind of 'new world' order. As the text says, the motif here would most obviously be the birth of a new society from the remains of the old world, remains that are here clearly 'abjected' in the strongest sense of that term (see Kristeva, 1982), yet we are still entitled to wonder how it is that history will say nothing of such matters, just as, in the words quoted from Satyajit Ray, the attempt to search for evidence is doomed also to end in ... nothing. And this too, Ray goes on to tell us in the story from which these words come, is a question of a certain absence, a certain void or misgiving in history itself:

> Consider the *Ramayana* and the *Mahabharata*. They are called histories, but in reality they are just collections of weird tales. Ravana and his ten heads, Hanumana setting fire to Lanka with his burning tail, Bhima's appetite, Ghatotkacha, Hidimba, the

> Pushpaka chariot, Kumbhakarna – what is more nonsensical than all this? (Behl and Nicholls, 1995, 77)

'Collections of weird tales', narratives without validation, visions that can never be brought together: these are in some sense both source and consequence of the effort of finding an account that is less 'nonsensical', an account that might actually provide a version of history that can make some retrospective sense of colonising events that appear from many viewpoints to have been more destructive than all the world's natural disasters put together.[4]

Yet even to say this is to suppose that there is one clear voice that could articulate such a version, and clearly there is not. Each prisoner, according to this cultural narrative, is held in a separate cell: in order to prevent the mutual validation of each other's story, in order to make sure that the stories of subject peoples the world over remain isolated instances rather than 'evidence' of a consistent pattern of imperialism, whether we are talking of East Africa, of North America, of the Philippines, of Australia; a pattern of imperialism, as San Juan among others reminds us, that cannot be separated from the spectre of extermination, genocide and their traumatic aftermath, the reality, we might say, of the 'post' in the 'postcolonial'.[5]

Under such circumstances, as Harris reminds us, the only position we can find may be one in which we are, as it were, 'beside ourselves'. 'I saw him now for the first faceless time as the captain and unnatural soul of heaven's dream; he was myself standing outside of me while I stood inside of him' (Harris, 1988, 26). It is not possible, in this context, to reunify the dislocation of vision; indeed it may even be that the very question of 'location' has become unanswerable.[6] What is happening, among many other things, in this passage may be read as the incredulous confrontation between master and slave, the impossibility of accepting this 'unnatural' distortion of relationship; there is also a hint of different 'possible histories' facing each other for a crucial existential moment before all the possibilities that were foreclosed by the brutality of empire vanish into the hinterland of dream, fade like hallucinations before the blinding glare of the prison floodlights, and yet are doomed to return in a fantastic interplay of further hallucinations – the hallucination of the coloniser which figures an exotic secret that is always tantalisingly beyond reach, the hallucination of the colonised which figures plenitude and reparation on the surface of a murderous body.

Location, indeed, is never stable in Harris's *Palace of the Peacock*. 'It was the first night', we learn at one point, 'I had spent on the soil of Mariella. So it seemed to me in a kind of hallucination drawing me away from the other members of the crew' (42). But what, in this hallucinatory encounter, this dreaming of a unifying force, is Mariella? She is at least as much woman as place, but most importantly encounters with her, encounters that might be in some sense healing, that might provide a place of salvation athwart the exigencies of colonialism, can take place only *under the sign of* hallucination. Yet for Harris, this in itself is doubly equivocal. To fall under the sign of hallucination is not necessarily to surrender to a false escape from the real, it is instead inseparable from a specific political gesture, even if its specificity is deferred, distorted: 'he shrank', we are told, 'from the image of his hallucination that was more radical and disruptive of all material conviction than anything he had ever dreamt to see' (82). Here as throughout Harris's work the curtain between the imaginative and the material sways and ripples. Hallucination, dream, these according to Harris may be precisely the forces to mobilise in order to struggle against a reality that is otherwise too deeply entrenched, too 'unnaturally' entwined within the 'soul', to permit of any softening. This, then, would be part of the force of a famous passage near the ending of the novel:

> The wall that had divided him from his true otherness and possession was a web of dreams. His feet climbed a little and they danced again, and the music of the peacock turned him into a subtle step and waltz like the grace and outspread fan of desire that had once been turned by the captain of the crew into a compulsive design and a blind engine of war. (114–15)

As so often in Harris, there is here something subtle and elusive in the language that raises at least as many questions as it answers, something that is specifically unamenable to the discourse of frameworks and theorisations that has for so long pointlessly preoccupied so many branches of postcolonial criticism. What would it actually be like for a wall to turn into a web of dreams – would that be a reconquest, a reterritorialisation, or would it be an imaginary removal from the scene of the real, an abandonment of an impossible struggle, a final resorting to an oneiric fantasy? What, again, would it be like to be 'turned into' a 'subtle step and waltz' – would it be to join in a hallucinatory celebration at the end of time, or would it be to mark the possibility of a communal return, a recolonisation of the land by the 'folk'?

The design, though, the 'design' in the shape of both the plan and the intention of the colonisers, we indeed need to learn to see as 'compulsive'. On the other side of hallucination, over against this freedom from the conditioned at whatever level of reality it functions, stands the 'compulsive', the visible fragment of the innate obsessive/compulsive disorder of the state machine, a machine which is condemned to – and thrives upon – an unslakeable thirst, a dry repetition, proceeding in the 'same dull round', as Blake puts it, regardless of the ambiguous and already soiled 'beauties' all around.[7] The land has been fatally changed: even where the effects might be for the moment invisible, the drawing of lines on maps, the imposition of systems of regulatory control, the development of forces of law and order, the division of the terrain into governable units, the insertion of military and bureaucratic powers into the heart of the land – all of these factors have built up into a machine, a silent running which at the same time permanently transforms the landscape, replacing imagination with 'compulsion' in all senses of the term.

In Gurnah's *Paradise* Yusuf has a dream, one of many, when he has returned from his journey to the 'interior':

> He told Khalil that so often on the journey he felt he was a soft-fleshed animal which had left its shell and was now caught in the open, a vile and grotesque beast blindly smearing its passage across the rubble and the thorns. That was how he thought they all were, stumbling blindly through the middle of nowhere. The terror he had felt was not the same as fear, he said. It was as if he had no real existence, as if he was living in a dream, over the edge of extinction. It made him wonder what it was that people wanted so much that they could overcome that terror in search of trade. (Gurnah, 1994, 179–80)

The literal reference here – if there can be such a thing – is to the world of the East African Arab trader on the brink of wipe-out, but it is certainly not a European nightmare of 'the interior' that is being described. Rather what is at stake is the dread of a reinscription, a reterritorialisation of the world, in the sense that the old maps the traders had used (though their age, like their accuracy and the lineations that underpin them, is contestable, indeed is the very site and body of contestation) have been torn up and replaced by new ones written by the Europeans. There is on the new maps a space for the African 'native', and it is already inscribed: the inscription reads 'victim'. But there is no space for the Arabs at all: their world is dissolving into dream. This does not in itself make the 'forest' now springing up around us any more dangerous than it had been before, but it does fatally alter the lines of relationship, the sense of belonging or possession. Crucially the dream-body that

Yusuf now senses growing all around him is a foreign body, a body built on the ruins of a sense of 'home', redoubling of course the multiple displacements he has experienced through the ramifications of his indentured (slave) status.[8] A question that now seems to be repeating itself would again be of how this horror relates to Paradise. Khalil too has been bought by Uncle Aziz, but now he is in a sense free although only at the cost of a further, relayed and displaced, dehumanisation, that of his sister:

> your Unce Aziz married her last year. So now he's also my brother as well as your uncle, and we're one happy family in a garden of Paradise. She is the repayment of my Ba's debt. When he took her he forgave the debt. (Gurnah, 1994, 207)

Here Paradise and the trade in human flesh are bound up in the most intimate of ways (they are figured as the two sides of any possible dealing with the female), tied together on the prow of the colonial desiring machine as it penetrates yet further space, gendered and racialised, using an ironised ideal and the realities of trade, that trade on which all others are founded and by which their validity is radically disabled, the trade in human bodies, root of the 'unnaturalness'of soul, as a way of exercising a further colonisation of the realm of possibilities.

Yet we may find too that even this type of power is subject to the logic of the hallucination. Among the many baffling images in Tutuola's *Feather Woman of the Jungle* is one that appears intimately to concern the nature of the 'image' itself. The Feather Woman is herself an ambiguous figure of power, and she is shown to demonstrate that power in baffling fashion by keeping a 'gallery' of images:

> After a while she began to tell us that every one of the images was a person but with her power she had turned him into the form of image for he had trespassed her jungle. She explained furthermore that we too could change into that of images if we disobeyed her. (Tutuola, 1962, 18)

But if this is a fable of power, as it appears to be, then it comes to show too the way in which power has its limitations, and here the reader is in danger of becoming lost in the labyrinthine colonial relations at stake within this apparently fantastic text. For somebody, something, is being beaten: 'she' comes at night to the images – to overcome this loss – with whips:

> She started to flog all of them as she was walking up and down in front of them. She flogged every one of them from head to feet until the whole whips were torn into pieces. As she was flogging them it was so she was snorting and sneezing repeatedly. And with her snappishness, so she was abusing and scorning them despite they were seemed as if they were sobbing as she was flogging them repeatedly. (20)[9]

The images, it would appear, survive this state of terror (it *is* a 'State of Terror', although at whose 'material' command it is not Tutuola's overt purpose to tell us (see Punter, 1998, 82–100)); the whips do not. There is a point adumbrated here, a point of petrifaction beyond which no more terror is possible; there is a condition, the condition of the prisoner, the condition of those from whom their body, their 'land', has been finally expropriated, in which the weapons of oppression are rendered impotent. We might say about this, for example, that it is the *images* that are in themselves 'resistant', the symbols of the folk, nation, entity, although Tutuola is wonderfully evasive about such matters; just so, then, the very images *he* uses are themselves resistant, resistant to classificatory interpretation, resistant as, for instance, an army of dead babies might be resistant, reduced and yet empowered to a condition where all they can do is to reflect terror back into the oppressor, the whips torn up and flung aside, light and destructible as *feathers*. We are again at a point beyond which there is, as we have now seen in other postcolonial contexts, a terrifying yet paralysed 'nothing'.

What, then, is the fictional structure and status of *Feather Woman of the Jungle*? Written in an impossible language, an unthinkable and undecidable English, it appears to deal with the tales told by the narrator in order to establish and consolidate his supreme status in his village (*the* village).[10] Who is meant to believe these tales, what credence, authority, validation, might be on offer? Who, after all, is 'writing back' (long before 'the empire' was thought of as doing so), who is telling these tales to whom? These are travellers' tales, travelling tales, dreams and hallucinations, attempts on the always readily penetrable body of the exotic; they are not attempts seriously to reproduce a vanished 'way of life', they are not assertions of 'African mystery'; they are instead continuous tropes on the notion of the serious and thus of the secret, on the laughable assumption that the (Western) reader will consciously or unconsciously share the hope, or the disavowed terror, that there is something here to be revealed, some heart of darkness, something withheld that will now become open.

But in Tutuola nothing becomes 'open', there is no key provided to the world of the image, unless one might be able to read the 'combination lock' that we might usefully take as the symbol for an improbable matching of languages. The story of his *The Palm-Wine Drinkard* ostensibly concerns the narrator's search for his dead tapster, it is shaped (now and then) as an odyssey to the 'Deads' Town', but the narration obeys the wrong rules. It thereby succumbs to no external narratives of authority or power except to those ironically recognised in the text as inevitable in a world blindly allegiant to the demands and controls of an ultimately foolish 'anthropological' metadiscourse.[11] The 'juju' that produces instant impossible transformations demands to be read on two levels, not merely contentually but also as resistance to a habit of mind, resistance to the imposition of meaning. Thus the transformations grow more intense as the story proceeds, so that instead of moving towards resolution the text moves towards implying the impossibility of a 'narrative outside rules', or perhaps outside *rule*; outside the rule of an imposed language, outside even the conception of what such imposition might be.

Is this freedom? Is it hallucination, or the succumbing to the alternative but fatally compromised rule of the exotic? To mount a purely 'ludic' reading of the text of this novel, or of any of Tutuola's others, one would have to be 'beside oneself', one would have to be ready to be complicit in a betrayal of the depth of resistance; for at the same time the controlling myth of *The Palm-Wine Drinkard*, that of the egg that 'fed the whole world' (Tutuola, 1952, 120), stands as a constructed account of the origins of famine and its imbrication in a regime of power. What is at stake here, more starkly than in Harris, is the nature of complicity and of what might stand against complicity, even if the territory on which that struggle (which has already been lost) must be conducted (and for Tutuola even to name such a struggle would be an unthinkable naiveté) must be – again – the territory of hallucination. For all territories have here become hallucinated, have passed onto a ground of weird concretisations, into a land where to 'sell one's death' and to 'lend one's fear', for example (67), are possibilities among others, feeding terror back into the whirling of the creative process, the hidden 'arts of the imagination' lying encrypted, *lies* that encrypt the imagination's art.

What many of these texts are doing is crucially pre-emptive. We need to allude here again to the debates about how, if at all, to use Eurocentric frameworks – psychoanalysis, Marxism, political progress, economic development – in the context of the 'other'.[12] What is rarely grasped in these debates is that they are, in a crucial sense, not 'overly advanced', as the Eurocentric postcolonial model so frequently has it (in other words, in need of further interminable 'theorisation'); they are instead far too late, deeply beside the point, they have already been anticipated and laid waste – under the sign of hallucination, but a hallucination whose grip on the experience of colonisation is nonetheless of the utmost practical and political power. In the ascription of the 'postcolonial', we find an important but infrequently observed reversibility. In the realm of the 'postal', as San Juan has it (San Juan, 1998, e.g., 54), the question must inevitably be one about what 'succeeds' what, but the worlds portrayed by Harris and Tutuola, among so many others, are ones in which the very notion of succession is under siege. To be 'after' the colonial is inconceivable unless the other side of the dialectic is also grasped: that power only 'runs after' what it is 'before', what it is in the face of. Much is made by postcolonial critics of how to grasp the experience of the colonised; what is more important is to stand 'before' the processes by which the colonised exert a grip on the 'frameworks' imposed, how the bars of the cell are continuingly bent before the very gaze of the prison guards.

What can, to take one example, psychoanalysis learn from Tutuola? Most obviously, it can learn (but it has not yet done so) something about the friability of the concept of the unconscious. It can learn that the 'framework' here, if there is one, is the collective fantasy, the group hallucination. If it is the case, as *The Palm-Wine Drinkard* appears to assert, that learning can only be achieved through a visit to the 'Deads' Town', and if we are tempted to construe this as an attempted return to the forbidden knowledge, the structure of taboo, at the heart of 'development', then we could equally – and better – say that a confrontation with the Deads' Town would be one way of moving psychoanalysis itself forward, of submitting its insights to a regime where the power of authentication lies 'in another sense', where the distinction between host and parasite is quite different and its interpretation is consequently always deferred.[13]

The emphasis within most postcolonial criticism and theory is on establishing a 'ground', on deciding how to describe the many forms of colonialism, on defining what a 'settler/invader' community might be, on establishing the political force of a 'compradore' formation, and so on.[14] In the process of doing that the real, geopolitical processes of territorialisation are, in both senses, 'overwritten', and an inevitable conflict between 'theory' and 'political reality' develops, emblematised again in the opposition – still the only available one although its terms are becoming increasingly stale – between the framework-oriented ideas of Said, Spivak and Bhabha on the one hand, and on the other the conflict-oriented ideas of Ahmad and San Juan. This opposition, however, is, in a crucial sense, 'beside itself'. The facts that, to take one example, US Asians are held up before the Anglo-American world as a 'model minority' while at the same time this effects a concealment of the continuous stream of genocidal impacts of the Atlantic lands on Asian culture[15] (on China, on the Philippines, on Japan, on Vietnam, on Kampuchea – the list is not merely long but literally endless in the sense that the very names used to describe these groupings merely repeat contention, respond only to a Western-imposed 'ordering' of what constitutes a nation, a state, an 'ethnic' grouping) cannot be 'opposed' one to another; rather, they need to be 'translated under the sign of untranslatability', otherwise the truly jammed force of political conflict is lost, frittered away in sterile disquisition. The texts of the 'postcolonial' are, in a partial but crucial sense, *not there*; they are texts written instead of other texts, they are texts unwillingly written under the sign of an 'other' language, they are continuing evidences of the impossibility of visualising the dislocated, they are emblems of all that is unwritten, of all that must now remain unwritten because the very materials for writing are already co-opted, already displayed in the markets of those who sell power, of those who charge unaffordable prices for that which is not theirs to sell.[16]

What is therefore crucial is not to confuse this situation – which is real, and impossible of discourse, and endlessly relayed through the image, all at the same time – with Spivak's deadly supposition that the 'subaltern' cannot *speak*. Of course the subaltern can speak; to suppose otherwise would be to succumb – yet again – to the damagingly simplistic notion that what speaks in a text is the voice of an author, as though we have learned nothing about the complex 'otherings' of textuality. Certainly, if counter-intuitively, texts are composed of silences, as in a sense are dreams; but according to the necessary hallucinatory yet entirely 'material' logic, what fills these silent spaces are voices, continual voices, voices whose sense *we* (by which I mean the 'non-native reader', but it can be argued that that is everybody) cannot grasp. The voices of the colonised drive the colonisers mad, they fill the silences, all the time, but they are always the wrong voices, they do not welcome but neither do they banish; they can do neither because they have already been emptied out, they remain in the unbanishable form, as we are now increasingly seeing, of ghosts, of hauntings.

Is this 'exotic' (other, foreign, a site of unrealisable desire to *become* other, to be 'beside oneself')? Who knows? Who *knows* – this would be the crucial question of the exotic: to capture is to find oneself in the position of flogging dead images, it is to experience the resistance of that which one has oneself turned to stone. Whips and ghosts, words and gods, these would be the magically transformable substances that might appear to us on this terrain; we can find them in Tutuola,[17] or we can find them condensed into a brief passage from Brathwaite's *Arrivants*:

> For on this ground
> trampled with the bull's swathe of whips
> where the slave at the crossroads was a red anthill
> eaten by moonbeams, by the holy ghosts
> of his wounds
>
> the Word becomes
> again a god and walks among us;
> look, here are his rags,
> here is his crutch and his satchel
> of dreams; here is his hoe and his rude implements
>
> on this ground
> on this broken ground.
>
> (Brathwaite, 1973, 265–6)

Let us say that the exotic, the gaze of the other that fixes the text (the sight, the site) into a stony image would be figured in the 'red anthill/eaten by moonbeams'. In what sense, in whose script is this anthill 're(a)d'? What would these moonbeams be but the signal of the transmutation of base, destroyed flesh, bought flesh, slave flesh, into the substance of European interpretation, the 'swathe of whips', the omnipresent *fasces* of power? This, then, is the 'ground' on which the text might walk; but the ground falls away beneath our feet, we are, as we have seen, on the 'edge of extinction', our point of view is fatally coloured (red, like blood). All, then, that we are left with (in the international labour market, for example) is the aftermathic perception of colour.[18]

Who in this passage is speaking of 'rude implements', and in what voice? One of the many voices Brathwaite concentrates into this wordy but unyielding silence would be the voice of the anthropologist, the classifier whose rule is the rule of empire, now transmuted into the rule of development. What would the equivalent, the exchange value be? The farmer dead beside his combine harvester? Would that be the next 'stage of development'? It could only be so, of course, if the ground were not already 'broken', not already the site of an incommensurable confrontation which must resist these simple equivalents, these over-easy relations between the oppressed and the oppressor. We might alternatively figure it as an already potent (if hallucinatory, exotic) resisting, as only the geological can resist, of the mythology of development, improvement, enlightenment – enlightenment even, as it may be, by the transforming (yet not transforming) 'moonbeams'.

There is the 'broken ground'; there is the 'satchel/of dreams'. What, as we always have to ask, perhaps with an undue persistence which is designed to drive secrets from their bed, is the site of the postcolonial? We could consider a further passage from *The Arrivants*:

> So down in thunder from his heaven
> Anokye brought the Golden Stool.
>
> Not since the mighty rule
> of Nana Nyankopong began
>
> had such excitements happened
> in our town. Chiefs' sandalled
>
> feet that never once had known
> the ground, jumped from their palanquins
>
> and ran; stools overturned,
> noon's rule began; women,
>
> moon's servitors, cool water's thoughts,
> songs of before the forest,
>
> dried, vanished underground.
>
> (Brathwaite, 1973, 144)

What, we might continue to ask, is the geopolitical force, the bearing upon territorialisation, of this passage? We might, for example, say that its terrain combines a certain emphasis on ancient ritual with a tendency towards magic realism. What would be saying by that? We would, presumably, be implicitly addressing a question that gestures towards belief structure, and in doing so we would be necessarily coming up against another of the crucial questions about the postcolonial, namely, the question of what truth status to assign to the various discourses which are always there present – unevenly distributed, involved in a complexly ironic yet lethal play. Where, again, is the root and display of the exotic? Who, here, has ever known these 'palanquins'? The chiefs, certainly, can be known as figures of ridicule. A certain conspiracy of power, evidenced in the exile of the women, can be sensed. But the force of the passage does not lie in these details; it lies rather precisely *within* the language, within what can be gained in terms of strength from offering recounted rituals in a language that is not 'owned', that is not one's own; in observing the fireworks, the fallout that comes from seeing these disparate symmetries trying and failing to work in tandem.

The postcolonial, as I have now said several times, is a discourse of loss; what is also important to grasp is that, through the logic of hallucination, dream, the exotic, it is also a discourse of reversal, a reversal beyond the ludic and beyond the satiric, and that it is precisely here, rather than in any exorbitation of the political process, that its genuinely political power lies. Let us put alongside that last passage from *The Arrivants* a passage from Gurnah's *Paradise*:

> In the dusty shadowlands of the snowcapped mountain, where the warrior people lived and where little rain fell, lived a legendary European. He was said to be rich beyond counting. He had learned the language of the animals and could converse with them and command them. His kingdom covered large tracts of land, and he lived in an iron palace on a cliff. The palace was also a powerful magnet, so that whenever enemies approached its fortifications, their weapons were snatched from their scabbards and their clutching hands, and they were thus disarmed and captured. The European had power over the chiefs of the savage tribes, whom he none the less admired for their cruelty and implacability. To him they were noble people, hardy and graceful, even beautiful. It was said that the European possessed a ring with which he could summon the spirits of the land to his service. North of his domain prowled prides of lions which had an unquenchable craving for human flesh, yet they never approached the European unless they were called. (Gurnah, 1994, 62–3)

The most obvious thing to point out about this passage is its reversal of the Western exotic and its dealings with a common group hallucination. All of the attributes assigned here to the European – extraordinary survival, the Kiplingesque control of the 'language of the animals', the invincibility in battle with its associated attribution of supernatural aid, the domination over land, spirits, wild beasts – all of these attributes are ones that were assigned to the 'native' by the Western explorer/anthropologist in his (very occasionally her) quest for 'native customs'. We might, however, try one more time to ask about the voice being used here. Whose voice, for example, is talking about 'implacability'? Is it a voice of exoticisation, or a voice of textbook learning? Would there be much difference for European imperial adventurers, or indeed their 'native' addressees? Again, are there many alternatives for the establishment of a 'native' discourse, essential as it is to the successful and, above all, profitable functioning of the colonial desiring machine (see Young, 1995, 159–82)?

To discuss the passage – like the one from Brathwaite – would, we might say, take an anthropologist. And this is surely the main point; for all of these discourses are functioning without – as we might say in a deliberate pun on that difficult phrase, the 'benefit of clergy' – without the benefit of anthropology, the recourse of those 'scientists' whose historically peculiar and parenthetical task it was to keep hallucination and the exotic at bay in order to allow the imperial work to proceed.

But the last word on this topic, a topic crucial to imperialism and ever returning in the texts of the postcolonial, might justly belong to a writer and a text to which I shall turn at greater length later, Susan Power and *The Grass Dancer*. The character speaking has a serious reputation as a witch, and she is being visited by an anthropologist – a sense-maker, a de-hallucinator, an implicit banisher of dreams – whose relation to hallucination, dream, the exotic, comes under a certain siege:

> The girl who came to me eager to discover a modern mythology had not really believed in it any more than she trusted that Aphrodite would show up at our next powwow wearing nothing but a dance shawl and her magic girdle. I don't know what finally convinced her. Everything that happened in my life could be explained in those bland terms that comfort the faithless. But there was no mistaking the pure fear I saw in her eyes.
>
> 'I am not a bedtime story', I told her now. 'I am not a dream'. (Power, 1994, 168–9)

# VIII Shame and Blindness, Meat and Monsters

> The great white man acquired a new habit: tearing his hair. (Ayi Kwei Armah, *The Healers*)

> The guts of birds are slit and cleaned out, feathers are plucked. The place is spread with bird excrement, blood and innards. A few yards away rises a privet hedge, perfectly trimmed and in excellent condition with a lush green shine. (Louise Ho, 'Apartheid Discourse in Contested Space')

> ... the postcolonial is not that which is opposed to colonialism but, rather, that which seduces colonialism, and the gaze is not that which opposes a set of discourses but, instead, that which seduces discourse, all discourse. (Patrick Fuery, 'Prisoners and Spiders Surrounded by Signs')

In this chapter, I want to pursue previously raised questions of rage, hatred and haunting by showing some ways in which the postcolonial has an implicit connection with the construction and representation of monsters. I shall look at three examples and at the same time offer some thoughts on the relations between monstrosity and power, especially in the contemporary postcolonial context, which will inevitably maintain a dialogue with the realm of the political. There is, of course, nothing new about generally connecting the process of making monsters with the exercise of power in society.[1] To take the emblematic European case of *Frankenstein*, we have there a text that has been read as being about power in all manner of ways and inevitably also, of course, about powerlessness.[2] We might think, for example, about the curious kind of power Victor Frankenstein wields over his creation, the power to bestow and in the end also to withhold life. Or we might think about the monster's frustrated and ultimately futile attempts to wield some kind of power over his own environment and over his creator, attempts that are doomed to come to nothing. Or we might think about recent readings of *Frankenstein* which tend to feminise the monster, to make his namelessness, his helplessness, the chronic misunderstanding with which he is endlessly greeted, symbolic of a specifically female social experience in a particular historical context. And mixed in with all this, of course, there is the enduring relevance of the monster as a representation of childhood experience, as an at least initially uncomprehending victim of a realm that represents the adult world gone mad, crazed with its own power, its own ability to decide who to include and who to exclude in its own excitable continuing production of a 'new world order'.

For power, again very obviously, is all about the ability to include and to exclude; it is about taking on the authority to decide who belongs and who does not belong to the social, the cultural, the national order. It would therefore be the case that one way of tracing the operations of power in a particular culture would be by looking precisely at the ways in which monsters are created. For what do monsters represent? Not, perhaps, total exclusion; that would be too simple an analysis, too inarticulable a possibility. Rather, we might say they represent those genuinely 'hybrid' forms that stand, as it were, at the boundary of what is and what is not acceptable, what is to be allowed to come to the warm hearth of society and what is to be consigned to the outer wilderness. Many early monstrous forms, as we know, take the literal form of hybrids, mixtures of man and animal; in the bird-headed and cat-headed gods and goddesses of Egypt, to take but one example, we would surely be right to see a set of symbols representing the limit of the human species; on the one hand the necessity of frightening oneself with the prospect of a monstrous hybridity, on the other a sense of the power that might come from those – those divine figures, presumably – who are able to take up the challenge of patrolling the boundaries of what is said to be human.[3]

The first monster to which I want to attend was created in 1983; her name is Sufiya Zenobia, and she inhabits the pages of Rushdie's novel *Shame*. To begin with, she figures as a badly retarded girl from a politically powerful family, but her ascension to monstrosity comes up upon her gradually, and that monstrosity is precisely the 'shame' of the novel's title. Rushdie explains it like this:

> Let me voice my suspicion: the brain-fever that made Sufiya Zenobia preternaturally receptive to all sorts of things that float around in the ether enabled her to absorb, like a sponge, a host of unfelt feelings. (Rushdie, 1983, 122)

And these feelings, for Rushdie, are centred on shame. *Shame* is set in Pakistan across the years of independence and at one level it tells the story, only very thinly disguised, of the endless waves of political corruption and nepotism that over many years destroyed, and many would say continue to destroy, Pakistan's hopes of economic or societal success. What this amounts to, according to Rushdie, is a long history of shamelessness: a history of unbelievable actions performed by men – and women too, Benazir Bhutto chief among them – for which, however, they apparently feel no shame. And so, Rushdie asks, where does the shame go when people in power appear uncaring about their own actions? 'Imagine shame', he says,

> as a liquid, let's say a sweet fizzy tooth-rotting drink, stored in a vending machine. Push the right button and a cup plops down under a pissing stream of the fluid. ... [but] what happens to all that unfelt shame? What of the unquaffed cups of pop? Think again of the vending machine. The button is pushed; but then in comes the shameless hand and jerks away the cup! The button-pusher does not drink what was ordered; and the fluid of shame spills, spreading in a frothy lake across the floor. (122)

What indeed does happen? In *Shame*, all of these unfelt feelings collect inside Sufiya Zenobia, and they turn her into a monster. They turn her into a frustrated, violent automaton, a murderer first of chickens and later worse. They turn her also, interestingly, into the victim of a disease that eats away at her own immune system. She becomes the protégé, later the wife, of an immunologist, Omar Khayyam Shakil, who finds in her the ultimate metaphor for political and social contamination: in her body emerge all the crimes and violences of her society, but they have no way out, they are isolated in her, they add up to her own force for self-destruction.

This, then, is part of the image Rushdie offers us of contemporary (postcolonial) Pakistan: as a being made up of shame, reflecting shame back to itself but in a series of reflections which are never recognised. For as Rushdie says, 'there is no place for monsters in civilised society. If such creatures roam the earth, they do so out on its uttermost rim, consigned to peripheries by conventions of disbelief ...' (199). Here, evidently, we may find echoes of *Frankenstein*; what is also interesting, however, is the use of the term 'peripheries'. Whether or not, and in what sense, we might refer to Rushdie as a postcolonial author is, of course, a matter of significant debate,[4] as indeed is the term 'postcolonial' itself; but what is certain is that the term 'peripheries' – and this is not the only time it is used in the novel – belongs very much to a conventional discourse about post-colonial problems, belongs in the by now traditional discourse of margins and centres;[5] and of course one of the political points the book makes concerns the colonial legacy which played such a crucial part in determining the future of the Indian subcontinent.

'Once in a blue moon', Rushdie continues,

> something goes wrong. A Beast is born, a 'wrong miracle', within the citadels of propriety and decorum. This was the danger of Sufiya Zenobia: that she came to pass, not in any wilderness of basilisks and fiends, but in the heart of the respectable world. And as a result that world made a huge effort of the will to ignore the reality of her, to avoid bringing matters to the point at which she, disorder's avatar, would have to be dealt with, expelled – because her expulsion would have laid bare what-must-on-no-account-be-known, namely the impossible verity that barbarism could grow in cultured soil, that savagery could lie concealed beneath decency's well-pressed shirt. (200)

Here we have precisely the dialectic of culture, or civilisation, and the barbaric with which we are no doubt familiar from so many Gothic and monstrous texts, but with an added twist (see Punter, 1996, II, 119–44). It is essential to the continuity of the society in which Sufiya Zenobia lives that she be ignored, for to acknowledge even her existence would be to pay heed to precisely those forces of disorder which are abroad within that society. It would be to acknowledge that dark heart of 'civilisation' which has to be denied, disavowed. Not, that is, that Sufiya Zenobia herself is to blame for her own murderous excesses; on the contrary she is portrayed, again in a way reminiscent of Frankenstein's monster, as a creature of more or less total innocence; she never has any recollection of her own savagery, which she performs, as it were, somnambulistically, as an automaton – we may want to recall at this point that the automaton is one of the key figures Freud invokes when he describes the uncanny.[6]

Sufiya Zenobia is thus in herself an empty vessel. The monstrousness she represents, incarnates, is not her own; it is that of others. When Rushdie speaks of that which would have to be 'expelled', he is talking about a general systemic inclusion and exclusion, about that which has to be denied if the veneer of civilisation is to remain intact. Society, he says, or at least the society of contemporary Pakistan, has a monstrous shape, yet this shape must always be denied, placed elsewhere, so that nobody accepts the blame for shameless actions. And at root what he is describing here is an issue of power. For this monstrous shape, the very body of corruption, is, seen from another angle, precisely a geographical or cartographical shape (see Rushdie, 1983, e.g., 204–5). There is a close equivalence between the distortions of corruption and the distortion that has already been visited on Pakistan, as it were, in the very moment of its birth. Like Frankenstein's monster, Pakistan – and India, and Bangladesh – was born of an exercise of pure colonial power; it derived its existence from lines on a map, lines drawn by a foreign body; and thus there is a sense in which the very country becomes a foreign body to itself, something inorganic, unnatural.[7]

When it comes to laying the blame for this situation, Rushdie is highly circumspect; as indeed he would be later when he wrote *The Satanic Verses*, to discover, to his cost, that power is nevertheless not to be mocked.[8] There are passages in *Shame* where he looks back into history, shows us the grotesque cultural distortions caused throughout the Indian subcontinent by the long years of imperial rule, but the question as to whether one can lay the blame for Pakistan's continuing crisis, and thus Sufiya Zenobia's existence, at the door of specific historical circumstances or whether what he is discussing is a feature of a less easily attributable plight is left unanswered (see Rushdie, 1983, 177–81). What is certain, though, is that his novel serves to reverse some of the easy coordinates of centre and periphery which critics increasingly tend to assume in discussion of the postcolonial. Sufiya Zenobia is not an exile; she is instead monstrously installed at the very centre, the very heart, of her society. She is the fruit of a legacy of that 'mimicry' which should really be described as repetition, such that the behaviour of Pakistan's rulers cannot be easily differentiated from the behaviour of their imperial predecessors.

And these issues of repetition and dominance, of the repetition *of* dominance, of the compulsions of power, bring me to my second monster. This monster was born much more recently, in 1994. His name is Sammy, and he is the hero and virtual narrator of James Kelman's novel *How Late It Was, How Late*, which is probably best known, at least in Britain, because it won the prestigious Booker Prize, although in the process it became something of a *cause célèbre*. It is written in Glaswegian dialect and one result of this is that it is virtually a tissue of swearwords. When it was awarded the prize, one or two of the judges furiously dissented, arguing that the whole novel constituted an impoverishment of the language, and Kelman responded with a fascinating prize acceptance speech, reprinted in *Scotland on Sunday* (16 October 1994), in which he speaks of the necessity of using the language that is actually spoken on the streets, whatever the implications may be.

It is not necessary to recount much of the plot. Essentially Sammy, a working-class Glasgow man, has been jailed for his part in a botched robbery. The book opens with him having just been released and getting again into trouble with the law. He is beaten up, and when he comes round he finds he has gone blind. The whole book is an account of how, blind, he tries to come to terms with his circumstances. This blindness is never fully explained; certainly none of the doctors and bureaucrats whom he encounters believe in the reality of his affliction. There are some appalling scenes where he goes to try to find help – from a family doctor, from a medical specialist, from the social services – but all these encounters are hopeless and fruitless. Nobody believes him; but worse than that, there is an absolute clash between his language and the language of those in authority.

We can turn, for example, to Sammy's encounter with a female official of the Department of Social Security. Her job, it would appear, is to verify the details of Sammy's blindness and its causes, which he has already recounted to a 'Preliminary Officer'. She reads out the version of events he has earlier given, including the phrase 'They gave me a doing'. Sammy, worried about the implications of complaining about the police, says:

> Well I dont like the way it sounds.
>
> I'm only reading out what ye told the Preliminary Officer; he entered the phrase in quotation marks to indicate these were yer own very words. Was he mistaken in this do you feel?
>
> Look I cannay remember what I said exactly; as far as I know I just telt him I lost my sight last Monday or Tuesday, I woke up and it was away.
>
> Are ye denying these were the words used?
>
> I dont know, I cannay remember: I didnay use physical beating but I know that. (Kelman, 1994, 103)

The official, who has already, as it were, 'translated' a 'doing' into 'physical beating', carries on talking in a language which is self-evidently not that of the colonised:

> What's entered here is the phrase 'they gave me a doing', and it's entered expressly as a quotation. But it's a colloquialism and not everyone who deals with yer claim will understand what it means. I felt that it was fair to use physical beating by way of an

> exposition but if you would prefer something else ... is there anything else ye can think of? (103)

Sammy asks if he can change the phrase, but apparently changing it is not possible, only adding explanation to it: 'Yer own words', the official adds in a wonderfully resonant phrase, 'always remain entered anyway Mister Samuels', before going on to explain to him the mechanics of the situation:

> Now there are two bands of dysfunction; those with a cause that is available to verification, and those that remain under the heading pseudo-spontaneous. The former band may entitle the customer to Dysfunctional Benefit but those in the latter may not. But both bands entitle the customer to a reassessment of his or her physical criteria in respect of full-function job registration, given the dysfunction is established. (104)

The clash between the two languages is made even more apparent here, but of course it is, as always, far from a simple binary of the kind beloved by postcolonial theorists. Rather, the relation between the languages is one of phantoms, of shadows; although in a sense we hear the words of the official, it is also as though we hear them through Sammy's ears; and yet not so, for the perfect spelling of terms like 'dysfunctional' can have a relation to Sammy's literacy that is only ironic. Again, to use the word 'colloquialism' of Sammy's expression would be not only to suggest that his is a restricted form of speech, it would be simultaneously to confess that those dealing with his claim will not understand (or will 'claim' not to comprehend) street language, and at the same time to summarise in the very word 'colloquialism' the elaborated imperialism of linguistic control.

What are 'quotation marks', what is a quotation, what is translatable? These questions are at the core of this passage, and of many others in *How Late It Was, How Late*, and they are questions that cannot be separated from postcolonial uses of language. Let us consider, for example, a comment by Sara Suleri:

> The telling of colonial and postcolonial stories ... demands a more naked relation to the ambivalence represented by the greater mobility of disempowerment. To tell the history of another is to be pressed against the limits of one's own – thus culture learns that terror has a local habitation and a name. ... the story of culture eschews the formal category of allegory to become a

painstaking study of how the idioms of ignorance and terror construct a mutual narrative of complicities. (Suleri, 1992, 2)

She is talking, in fact, about Indian fiction in English but much of the argument would also hold good for the narrative of *How Late It Was, How Late*. Specifically, it is a text which is indeed about the idioms of ignorance and terror, and which finds a startlingly vivid metaphor for disempowerment. More to the point, however, it is also a text which takes arguments about 'a local habitation and a name' through a further twist. For what Sammy learns during the novel is that even his relation to his own neighbourhood is contingent; that although street cultures may appear rooted in their own traditions, when confronted with the naked exercise of power this cosy version of the 'homeliness' (the *heimlich*) of the colonised reveals itself as a mere sentimental fiction, a way of saving face on the part of those who hold the reins, those who are able – with the stroke of a pen – to determine lines of access, points of control, whole geographies and trajectories that shape the mind (see Kelman, 1994, e.g., 297).

Deleuze and Guattari have something to say which might seem to add to our previous discussion of maps; they are concerned with maps as sources of empowerment:

> The map is open and connectable in all of its dimensions, it is detachable, reversible, susceptible to constant modification. It can be torn, reversed, adapted to any kind of mounting, reworked by an individual, group, or social formation. It can be drawn on a wall, conceived of as a work of art, constructed as a political action or as a meditation. (Deleuze and Guattari, 1988, 12)

But what *How Late It Was, How Late* shows us is that Deleuze and Guattari are, in this respect, deeply and bitterly wrong. This is Sammy's best attempt at a map after he has managed, with tremendous difficulty and some help, to cross a street:

> Sammy was on the pavement and he didnay stop till he made it to the tenement wall; it was a shop window, his hand on the glass; he was breathing fast; fuckt, drained, knackt, totally, felt like he had run a marathon. Fucking tension, tension. When ye done something. Every fucking time. Strain into the muscles; everything, every time; just so fucking tense, every part of yer fucking body. And he needed across the new street, he knew where he was, he thought he did, and there was another street now round

> the corner round this corner, where he was standing jesus christ alfuckingmighty. The traffic was roaring. Oh my my my my, fuck sake, my fucking ... (Kelman, 1994, 54)

This is a type of knowledge, or absence of knowledge, an 'information' to which Deleuze and Guattari have and provide no access. How, though, might any of this connect with what I have said about Sufiya Zenobia and *Shame*, and furthermore what might one mean by referring to Sammy as a monster? I will address the second question first. Sammy is unemployed, a petty criminal, a drinker; all his attempts at relationships have failed, he has just emerged from a term in prison, his language is, as we have seen, crammed with violence and anger. But this, of course, is not in itself sufficient to make a monster. The way in which Sammy becomes a monster, very much again in the manner of Frankenstein's monster, is in the perceptions of others, and here we get to the heart of the construction of monstrosity. For Sammy is seen as a monster precisely because of his postcolonial disenfranchisement, his disability, his pain.[9]

The whole history of monstrosity cannot be separated from the histories of disability and pain, although such a separation has structured most criticism to date. Frankenstein's monster, after all, is in a sense disabled; he has been given life but not granted the full equipment necessary to deal with that life. He is disabled by his lack of knowledge; he is disabled also by his ugliness; he becomes that which nobody wants to see. Similarly, Sammy becomes 'that which nobody wants to see', and here is where Kelman's portrayal strikes at the heart of the plight of the monster and at the same time of the crucial invisibility of the colonial subject. For just as Sufiya Zenobia's shamefulness is a projection of the shamefulness of the society around her, so Sammy's blindness is a projection of the wilful blindness of the society around him. Essentially, Kelman's book is a book about culture itself; it probes the boundary beyond which it is not possible to go without entering the wilderness. And just as with Sufiya Zenobia, that wilderness is not in the far places of the earth, those spots on the map which are simply marked as *terra incognita* or 'Here be Dragons', but right in the heart of social life, in this case on the streets of Glasgow, streets on which Sammy used to feel at home but where he now becomes a permanent exile, a victim whose condition nobody can dare to acknowledge.

I have thus already broached the other of my questions, about the connection between Sammy and Sufiya Zenobia. Both of them incarnate the monster as martyr; in both cases too they serve as mechanisms for the demonstration, not of their own monstrosity, but of the monstrosity of the culture in which they live. And this brings me back to questions of power, politics and the postcolonial, about which it is now necessary to be a little more explicit. For *How Late It Was, How Late* has to be seen as a postcolonial text. One thing we can say about the postcolonial condition is that it is the outcome of a sustained and catastrophic imposition of power. In the case of Rushdie's Pakistan, that power has been exercised through a malevolent imperial history whose reverberations continue through to the present day; in the case of Kelman's Glasgow, the essential division is represented through the conflict between the holders and speakers of different languages.

In *How Late It Was, How Late*, and also in Kelman's reaction to the award of the Booker Prize, we can see precisely the same issues being aired as those which have formed the substance of debate within African writing and criticism over the last fifty years: namely, what language the writer can use.[10] The necessary hypothesis would be this: language makes monsters. Sammy appeared as a monster (and no doubt so did Kelman) to those prize judges who regarded the English language as something sacred or, to put it in another way, something within which it is desirable to be included. But Sammy's discourse is decisively not included within the dominant language; he is forever outside it – because of his (Scottish) nationality, because of his education or lack of it, because of his endless and unthought conflicts with authority. The book documents, through the admittedly – and indeed determinedly – melodramatic means of his blindness, what it is like to be outside the dominant culture. Is this the same as a question of being colonised? Clearly the history and the circumstances are very different, but the fact remains that the ruling class in Scotland speaks a language, or a set of languages, very different from the language spoken on the streets. To what extent this is an effect of domination by the English, or of other differences and divisions within Scottish culture and society, is the subject of an anguished contemporary debate;[11] but whatever the result of that debate, if there ever is one, what is clear is that Sammy is 'outside culture', he is outside the circles of power and, at its most extreme, his very existence has to be denied.

So who is the monster here? Is it Sammy, or is it for example the official who, when Sammy tells him he is blind, insists blandly that he will need to fill in a whole sheaf of forms to prove it – Sammy, who is not only blind but effectively illiterate? What is it that society will not see, in terms of shame, inequality, injustice, that provokes the endless formation of monsters? Another interpretation of *Frankenstein*, which I did not mention before, has it that the monster represents the emerging working class (see, e.g., Mellor, 1995, 133–5). I am not sure how much there is in that, or how much Mary Shelley can be supposed to have known or sensed of the 'unwashed masses', but certainly Sammy represents those people who slip through the net of the State, those for whom no membership in the social or national body is available, those for whose apparent benefit the present government in the UK has set up its amusingly misnamed 'Social Exclusion Unit'; perhaps indeed such a unit will serve only to perpetuate and legitimate the existence of precisely the socially excluded, a class, or group, or caste which, some theorists of imperialism would say, is essential if the operation of power is to go through its usual motions – those of inclusion and exclusion (see Harvey, 1985, especially 47–61). Sammy, we might further say, is a 'native', with all the disability and disenfranchisement that term has come to imply.

On the basis of Sufiya Zenobia and Sammy, we can venture a further hypothesis about the monster and its relation to the postcolonial; which is that the monster's primary function is frequently as a grotesque representation of the colonised body. In the case of Sufiya Zenobia, she is inarticulate, she has no words in which to express or explain her plight. In the case of Sammy, he has no ownership of language; the rest of the world comes to him in disembodied voices which have no conception of his physical condition. And this again is an exercise of power. For, according to theorists from Foucault to Judith Butler and others, what the State cannot take account of is bodies; because bodies represent difference.[12] Power exerts itself through processes of standardisation and control: but all bodies are different, and thus their existence cannot be recognised except in the most abstract and violent forms of domination – the prison, the clinic, the asylum, the means for the purging of unwelcome class or ethnic difference; and, of course, the colony. Where power needs pure forms to deal with, pure abstractions, bodies are always in some real sense 'hybrid' between the human and the animal – and yet, of course, what is lost in this analysis is the stark fact that, in this sense, there is nothing *but* hybridity; that is the human condition, and any attempt fully to separate the human from the animal is necessarily an act of violence – on the body – that society must then proceed to disavow (see Young, 1995, 17–19).

Let me introduce my third monster. His name is McCoy Pauley, and he is dead. He occurs in William Gibson's novel *Neuromancer*, first published in 1984. Gibson, Canadian by affiliation, is the doyen of cyberfiction; *Neuromancer* concerns the adventures of a character called Case, and puts the reader through a plot of Byzantine complexity. The crucial point here is that this plot works on two levels at once: one set of actions goes on in virtual reality, the world of cyberspace, while the other happens in what we still loosely, I suppose, refer to as the real world, a world which Case and other characters in the novel refer to as the world of 'meat'.

The fantasy behind this division is, it seems to me, easy to detect; it is that somehow the world of cyberspace will provide a further, and perhaps cumulative, way of disavowing the body. Very few of the characters in *Neuromancer* are, as it were, entirely organic; they are full of artificial implants, pumped up on drugs, hard-wired into their computers, semi-automatically exchanging sensory impressions with each other through the ether. Even by these standards, McCoy Pauley – who, I should say, does not play a large part in the novel – is a bizarre construction – because, as I have said, he is dead. But while he was alive, according to the text, he was the greatest 'console cowboy' around. His great claim to fame, in other words, in a world where the kinds of defence system inserted into computers to protect sensitive information can, by means undisclosed, kill the operator who tries to break in, is that as a computer operator he 'died braindeath three times' (Gibson, 1984, 65). The 'three times' is, of course, resonant; like Christ on the cross McCoy Pauley suffered for his mission, and also like Christ he returned to tell the tale. But not the last time; and this is why, when Case receives an especially tough assignment, he finds that his employer – whoever that is – has made for him a virtual McCoy Pauley, a reconstruction of the brain and expertise of the so-called 'Dixie Flatline' (thus named because he was from the south, and because 'flatline' refers to the encephalogram of braindeath) to help him with his task.

It is not necessary to go into too much detail about McCoy Pauley – after all, what is there to say about a construct? But the point that does need to be made is that what we have here in *Neuromancer* is a character – if character is still a word one can use in connection with cyberfiction – who is at the farthest remove from the bodily, who represents something about an exercise that will finally effect one of the key projects of colonialism, namely, the disappearance of the body and its replacement by an entirely man-made psychogeography.[13] Pauley consists, presumably, of a reconstructed brain pattern, a replacement map which refers to no living reality, a cartography of death; like many of Gibson's visions of the possibilities of the future, there is a shortage of detail about precisely how this might be achieved, but that is not the point. What Gibson writes is not coterminous with science fiction in the sense of trying to show what real future possibilities there may be; rather what he is exploring in *Neuromancer, Burning Chrome, Mona Lisa Overdrive, Count Zero, Virtual Light,* and elsewhere is a particular stock of contemporary fantasies which strain at the borderline of what we may be able to do with our bodies and also, necessarily, what we may be able to do without them, and which, necessarily and at the same time, probe the maps of the world we are constructing around us, maps that have less to do with the conventional geography of mountains, rivers and so on but are based instead on the consuming virtual reality of economic and financial power, a 'new world order' – versions of a new colonisation, the 'colonisation of indifference'.[14]

Let me try to relate these concerns back to the topics which have, I hope, emerged as the themes of this chapter. First, of course, the monster. The way Gibson portrays most of his characters is in terms of the accommodation they have reached, or not, with their bodies. For them the body is not a given but a kind of schema, a template that can be improved upon, changed; bits can be discarded and replaced, nothing is given as unalterable. There is clearly a sense in which this is a liberating perspective, and it is obvious that it has been widely seen as such by Gibson's fans; but there are other, less optimistic considerations we might think of.

For example, if what Gibson is representing is, as I believe it must be, a set of contemporary hopes, fears, anxieties, aspirations about the body, bearing thus on the relation between the human and the animal and on the relation between the powerful and the powerless, then it is clear that he sees salvation as coming not from what one might call a kind of 'at-home-ness' (the *heimlich*) in our bodies but rather from a scenario in which we wave our bodies goodbye, consign them to the fate of all 'meat'. But, as I have said, the body is in one sense the guardian of our political differentiation: no such differentiation is truly possible within the abstract lines or shapes of computer simulations – even the Dixie Flatline's accent is, it appears, but a poor reproduction of his lifetime Southern drawl. And in this particular dealing with monstrosity, in this will to do away with differentiation, we return to the contemporary problematic of the postcolonial and its location in the 'new world order' by a different route.

For we now need to see that the difficulties of postcolonialism, the difficulties of living in and with a geography that has been violently disrupted, can be seen from one perspective as a subset of a wider global difficulty, which has been expressed by recent political thinkers like John Gray in terms of what he calls de-localisation

(Gray, 1998, 57). In other words, and put very crudely, the global necessities of free trade are currently serving to abolish difference altogether; against the force of the apparently unalterable facts of geography and history, the two great putative salvations of our national and regional differences, free trade needs a world in which all is essentially the same, a terrain from which bodies have been conveniently removed. And this, evidently, is where Gibson's fiction tends: towards a world where the bodily becomes merely the realm of meat, a product, a consignment, a resource with no connection with the world of the spirit – and a world also of standardised accents, a world where voice, language, discourse are no longer guarantors of untranslatable difference but have instead been reduced to a lowest common denominator of terse intelligibility.

In this radically purified world – we need to refer to it as a world in which total ethnic cleansing, in the sense of the expulsion of difference and thus the completion of the task of the colonial desiring machine, has already been accomplished – we need to ask, where and what is the monster? *Neuromancer* can be seen as, in a sense, a postcolonial book; or at least, it encourages us to ask again what the postcolonial might mean. In Gibson's near future the whole planet – and various other nearby bits of the solar system – have been effectively recolonised, not by imperial powers or nation-states but by multinational corporations, the colonial powers, as he sees it even if somewhat short-sightedly, of the future. As nationality has declined, allegiance to one corporation or another has assumed similarly obsessional dimensions. We may agree with Gray and disagree with Gibson in suggesting that these so-called all-powerful corporations are really as flimsy as the national structures they are replacing; nevertheless within the fantasy for these all-powerful entities nothing is impossible, although what we in fact have here is gang warfare writ large – as of course we see all around us, especially in the collapsing nation states of the ex-Soviet Union and in the appalling and continuing disaster of Kosovo and its implications for the destabilisation of Macedonia, Montenegro, Albania, and potentially indeed for Europe in general.

If we were to think farther in that direction we would begin – and quite rightly – to question the entire notion of the postcolonial and dwell instead on the repetitive power structures of a worldwide neocolonialism. Anne McClintock's extremely revealing essay 'The Angel of Progress' provides a wealth of examples, and a rejoinder to the conventional binary division between a 'colonial' and a 'postcolonial' world:

> orienting theory around the temporal axis colonial/postcolonial makes it easier *not* to see, and therefore harder to theorise, the continuities in international imbalances in *imperial* power. Since the 1940s, the United States' imperialism-without-colonies has taken a number of distinct forms (military, political, economic and cultural), some concealed, some half-concealed. The power of US finance capital and huge multi-nationals to direct the flows of capital, commodities, armaments and media information around the world can have an impact as massive as any colonial regime. It is precisely the greater subtlety, innovation and variety of these forms of imperialism that makes the historical rupture implied by the term 'post-colonial' especially unwarranted. (McClintock, 1992, 89)

I should like in particular here to hold on to the phrase 'easier *not* to see', and to take this rather further than McClintock. For the question that needs to be put is precisely this: to what extent is the postcolonial, as a heuristic category, as the name for a set of cultural phenomena, as an object of intellectual enquiry, in fact not merely vague, or obscurantist, but actually an *alibi* for not looking at what else lies before us in terms of distributions and flows of power?[15]

'Without a renewed will to intervene in the unacceptable', McClintock warns us at the end of her essay, 'we face being becalmed in an historically empty space in which our sole direction is found by gazing back, spellbound, at the epoch behind us, in a perpetual present marked only as "post"' (McClintock, 1992, 97); Gibson's world, we might fairly say, is indeed becalmed, bereft of movement and inflected by difference only in respect of the particular niche market in the international community of capitalism that might be found for, for example, Chinese cigarettes or indeed Dixie brain constructs. This 'historically empty space', we might suspect, is also a *hysterically* empty space: a space in which such difference – difference beyond moral or political recommendation or disapproval – as might be modelled on enduring patterns of dependence and maturation has been sucked dry, in which there is no possibility of new birth; precisely, and paradoxically, because the memory of loss has been further repressed. What has been emptied from the historically empty space, I would say, is its own loss and therewith its own ground of being, leaving us, as McClintock aptly reminds us, alone with Walter Benjamin's terrifying and terrified angel of history (see Benjamin, 1992, 249).

Bhabha speaks of the colonised foreign body, and also of the body of the 'mother country' as it is hallucinatorily constructed from the perspective of the colony (see Bhabha, 1994, 107–8). *This* body, he claims, is the mother's body, and this is the root of the distinction between 'mother culture and alien cultures', between 'the mother culture and its bastards, the self and its doubles' (111). But this is typically muddled thinking. The relation between mother and child is not reducible to the relation between doubles. Gibson's world, the world of continuing neocolonialism in which the place of an aristocracy has simply been taken over by corporate dynasties, is full of doubles – and indeed triples, clones, sets, series, all the vast apparatus of repetition, of replication which is at the service of the multiplication of indifference, the force of delocalisation; but this is necessarily accompanied by an emptying out of dependence relations, such that we might suggest that the attempt to preserve postcolonialism as a category has more to do with a fantasy of retaining Europe as a mother, no doubt how deserted and reviled, than with recognition of 'independence' in any of its useful senses.

However, it is also possible to go back to the monster; perhaps, in some sense, it is impossible not to. What these three fictions – Rushdie's, Kelman's, Gibson's – might suggest to us is that on the postcolonial terrain we confront a bifurcation of monstrosity. We are in a sense accustomed already to this bifurcation: in traditional terms we might think of, on the one hand, the ghost as a spirit without a body and, on the other, of the zombie as a body without a spirit. Anne Rice's *Interview with the Vampire* provides us with an encounter between two types of vampire which represent precisely this bifurcation, located, interestingly, in stereotypically New and Old Worlds – one kind of vampire certainly represents a 'new world order' (Rice, 1976, 205–12).

For Gibson, this is the available dialectic: towards a site of power which seeks to purify, to disavow the body and to reside entirely in the technologised spirit, and conversely towards a place of bodies, of meat, which has no purchase on the conditions of power – this latter world, we might think, is Sammy's world, the world of the streets, the world of the 'native', in any realm where power has been removed, by another twist of bureaucratic mystification, to a virtual plane. We can come back again, then, to the real issues behind the notion of hybridity, and perhaps we can now discern two kinds of monster lurking on the contemporary scene: on the one hand monsters of hybridity, man/machine chimeras, human/animal crossovers; on the other monsters of purity, monsters that deny the mixed human state, monsters that claim to have dispensed with the body entirely, to have relegated physicality and thus any concern for the inviolability of the flesh to the realm of meat.

But as in, for example, Chitra Divakaruni's 'Tiger Mask Ritual', we need to keep in mind that these hybridities, these chimeras, also have a local habitation and a name:

> Once you locate the ears the drums begin.
> Your fur stiffens. A roar from the distant left,
> like monsoon water. The air
> is hotter now and moving. You swivel
> your sightless head.
> Under your sheathed paw the ground shifts, wet.
>
> A small wild sound is sheltering
> in your skull
> against the circle that always closes in
> just before dawn.
>
> (Behl and Nicholls, 1995, 92–3)

The question would then be one of separating the creation of the monster from the process of 'becoming-animal' of which Deleuze and Guattari speak and which serves precisely the function of breaking through the constitutive human disavowal of animality (see Deleuze and Guattari, 1988, 232–309). Perhaps one lesson that can be drawn from postcolonial encounters with monsters is that monsters are not what they seem; that their very 'difference' serves also to underscore the crucial 'differences' in the worlds within which they are created.

I want to conclude this chapter by looking briefly at a text that can be fairly regarded as one of the most startling and provocative, as well as one of the most politically revealing, in African literature in English. It is from Tutuola's *The Palm-Wine Drinkard*:

> We met about 400 dead babies on that road who were singing the song of mourning and marching to Deads' Town at about two o'clock in the mid-night and marching towards the town like soldiers, but these dead babies did not branch into the bush as the adult-deads were doing if they met us, all of them held sticks in their hands. But when we saw that these dead babies did not care to branch for us then we stopped at the side for them to pass peacefully, but instead of that, they started to beat us with the sticks in their hands, then we began to run away inside the bush from these babies ... (Tutuola, 1952, 102)

It is in the silences, in what is not said, Macherey reminds us, that the story gets told (Macherey, 1978, 85ff.). What story gets told here in this ghastly surreal world of mourning and marching, where here is the 'literary'? It seems to me impossible to 'read' this set of images without being reminded of a whole world of displaced populations, of sites and regions made monstrous by death. The 'adult-deads' may be forgiving, even resigned to their fate – even, in fact, absurdly deferential. But a baby has no such qualms; what one senses here is omnipotence defeated, a howl of outrage, vengeance for a final injustice. What is the relation between baby and soldier? It is offered as one of metaphor, but what is also suggested is both a relation of antagonism and also, perhaps more importantly, a relation of succession: this ragged army of the weak and dispossessed will in time become a real army, continuing to wreak havoc on a land from which it has been wrenched, continuing to mourn being made into a foreign body on its own terrain. Crying and killing, mourning and beating, this army of potential child-soldiers will proceed along its lines of reterritorialisation sweeping all before it, driving the remnants of opposition deeper into the bush in a savage parody of the monstrous force that has previously rendered it powerless, reduced it to a condition of weeping in the night. The question again appears to be: who is the monster? Is it this horrifyingly distorted postcolonial army, or is it rather whatever web of violences has driven it into the world of death?

There is again here a dialectic of shame and shamelessness, and the question also of blindness, of what it is that is unbearable to see. There is also meat, the reduction to mere (dead) bodies of a different kind of vitality and hope. Above all there is loss, babies singing a song of mourning as though the cycle of the generations has always been already forestalled, as though foreknowledge, a premonition of doom, is the only available birthright, the natural consequence of the global culture of indifference, the outcome of a maddening deracination.

'One night', says Tutuola elsewhere in *The Palm-Wine Drinkard*, 'we met a "hungry-creature" who was always crying "hungry" and as soon as that he saw us, he was coming to us directly …' (Tutuola, 1952, 107). When we think of the way in which Jameson outraged postcolonial critics with his suggestion that all postcolonial narratives were in some sense national narratives – a position with which, as I have said, I disagree because it demonstrates no understanding of the literary – nevertheless in Tutuola's extraordinary images, in his portrayals of beings that are totally driven by some inescapably preordained fate, we have also to recognise that it is difficult not to see at least a plight for Africa, a conjuring of a territory inhabited by monsters, a land where death and hunger have achieved a blithe supremacy, the supremacy of loss.

# IX Mourning and Melancholy, Trauma and Loss

> ... storytellers are a threat. They threaten all champions of control, they frighten usurpers of the right-to-freedom of the human spirit – in state, in church or mosque, in party congress, in the university or wherever. (Chinua Achebe, *Anthills of the Savannah*)

> Was it possible that one's memory and apprehension of a tragic event would strike one's spirit before the actual happening had been digested? Could a memory spring from nowhere into one's belly and experience? (Wilson Harris, *The Palace of the Peacock*)

> ... an archaeology of silences, a slow brushing away of some of the cobwebs of modern Indian memory, a repeated return to those absences and fissures that mark the sites of personal and national trauma. (Suvir Kaul, 'Separation Anxiety')

Story-tellers are a threat, as Achebe says; they challenge the boundaries of what it is possible to remember. Furthermore, because we are dealing in the 'literary', the very nature of remembering, of 'remembrance' – which is bound on one side to memory and on the other to mourning – is itself a challenge and a potential terror, an activity that will be perceived and codified, as required by the state machine, under the heading of the 'terroristic'; terrorists are those, we might say specifically in a postcolonial era, who will not call a close to history, those who continue to be inspired by past configurations and conflagrations, who refuse to accept that the past moment can be surpassed, those whose desperation, although it tells and signifies a story, will not be bought off by the alternative narratives so readily on offer from the consensus of the neocolonisers.

It is time, then, to collect together some images of postcolonial loss, to attempt a temporary re-collection of that which has been scattered. There is, for example, loss as a somnambulistic succumbing to an irresistible invasion whose success has always already been accomplished, has preceded the awareness of absence, of emptying out. This is the loss that pervades Atwood's *Surfacing*, for example at the moment when the US visitors turn out to be Canadians instead:

> But they'd killed the heron anyway. It doesn't matter what country they're from, my head said, they're still Americans, they're what's in store for us, what we are turning into. They spread themselves like a virus, they get into the brain and take over the cells and the cells change from inside and the ones that have the disease can't tell the difference. Like the late show sci-fi movies, creatures from outer space, body snatchers injecting themselves into you dispossessing your brain, their eyes blank eggshells behind the dark glasses. If you look like them and talk like them and think like them then you are them, I was saying, you speak their language, a language is everything you do. (Atwood, 1973, 123)

There is also the registration of loss as the fate of an annihilated childhood; in Chandra's 'Dharma', for example, it is the loss of Jago Antia's childhood, lost beneath the pall of a tragic event, certainly, but equally lost beneath the shroud of imitative and repetitive actions, the only actions possible in a colonised society where even the compulsion to repeat is infected, 'body-snatched' at the root (see Chandra, 1997, 28). Again in Chandra's 'Shanti' we see a curiously somnambulistic meeting between two people who have, it turns out, suffered loss in similar fashion, and this is in some sense a 'strange meeting', a war story in a traditional mould; but what bears down upon it is the nature of the war, the question of for whom it was fought, on behalf of what dominating power, the colonial expulsions of truth that result in the incommunicable silences that continue to separate the protagonists (219–57).

Or we could look at a rather different text:

> Since I was a young man, my cherished aim has been to restore the Stuarts. I believe in a fully independent Scotland with its own history, culture and industry – a country with its own natural genius, a country able to make choices according to its own spirit. Scotland did not choose the closure of coal mines, Scotland did not choose the closure of shipyards, Scotland did not choose nuclear power stations and the leukaemia that they bring. That is why I have done what I have done. (Foden, 1998, 327)

An unexceptionable programme for national self-determination; but the 'origin' of these words is undecidable, for they are uttered by Major Weir, the British intelligence officer in Kampala in Foden's *Last King of Scotland*, and the text ends without the reader knowing whether he was a patriot or an *agent provocateur*. And this undecidability is repeated in his very words: what could it mean for a nation to have 'its own history'? Would this be a history that could somehow be recuperated, decrypted from the past, dug up in pristine form from the vaults? Or would it be a wholly constructed version in which, in this example, the depredations wrought by English domination would somehow be magically undone, as though the past four hundred years had never existed? And what, we might ask in the context of the text overall, might the relation be between these acts of magic nationalism, these fantasised replacements of loss, and the alternative form of magic nationalism practised by Idi Amin himself, for instance when *all* is lost and he sits in the ruins of his torture chambers, seeking magical help from the head of his decapitated archbishop (295–7)?

What lies behind many of these senses of loss, as we might expect, is the loss of the land and the endlessly repeating questions about who is to blame for destruction and ruin. This is what Joe, for example, is forced to hear in Hulme's *The Bone People* after he discovers the existence of the talismanic 'mauriora' and his role in its guardianship:

> I was taught that it was the old people's belief that this country, and our people, are different and special. That something very great had allied itself with some of us, had given itself to us. But we changed. We ceased to nurture the land. We fought among ourselves. We were overcome by those white people in their hordes. We were broken and diminished. We forgot what we could have been, that Aotearoa was the shining land. Maybe it will be again ... (Hulme, 1985, 364)

In this particular lost world, the lost world of the place now most usually known as New Zealand but which could be named quite 'otherwise', we see one moment of a repeating scenario: the need to attribute misfortune, the need to locate the source of disruption. In fact the waters in which the mauriora lies are 'milky': they have to do, perhaps, with a vision of nurture, but at the same time and indissolubly they prevent vision, history is lost in a cloud of pain.

In postcolonial writing, loss is ubiquitous (a dream of ubiquity is loss). It is (not) there, for example, in the dream of a Jamaican

Independence Day parade that begins Joan Riley's *The Unbelonging*, a dream that rapidly turns into a rude awakening, a painful and violent account of bed-wetting and punishment, 'independence' reduced to its opposite, the lineaments of an agonised dependence (see Riley, 1985, 9–10). It is there in Arundhati Roy's 'God of Small Things', that highly particular god who is also, she tells us, the 'God of Loss' (see Roy, 1997, e.g., 265). It is there in the writings of Amitav Ghosh, in the context of whose *The Shadow Lines* Suvir Kaul poses an essential question, which is also a question *about* a question:

> Do you remember? – in *The Shadow Lines*, this is the insistent question that brings together the personal and the public. It shapes the narrator's search for connections, for the recovery of lost information or repressed experiences, for the details of great trauma or joy that have receded into the archives of public or private memory. ... This remembering is often tinted with the sepia-tones of nostalgia, often darkened by the dull shades of grief, but in each case it is fundamentally a search for meaning, for explanations and reasons, for the elusive formal and causal logic that will allow the narrator's autobiography (and equally, the national biography that is interwoven with it in the novel) to cohere, to make sense. (Kaul, 1994, 125)

As an account of *The Shadow Lines*, this is persuasive; but if we look at some of the terms Kaul uses we run into difficulties. For what underpins his approach to the text is a notion, one that we have come across before, of a potential recuperation, an idea that somehow traumatised material can by mere processes of introspection or self-expression be rearranged into the stuff of causality and linear history. This is not so, and here is another location in which the whole issue of the connection between the postcolonial and the literary – so often taken for granted – requires further exploration. The literary, we may say, can be defined – among many other ways – as the major site on which that crucial question – 'Do you remember?' – is insistently asked. But this does not convert or reduce the literary into a 'search for meaning'. Rather, the literary begins at that point where we realise that such a search for meaning is a rationalist illusion, a turning, a veering away from the realm of symbols and images in which power lies – both the power of enforcement and the power of resistance. These symbols and images, as Harris above all insists, do not 'cohere' or 'make sense'; if they did so there would be an end to the literary, an end to the need repeatedly to ask the crucial questions. But this, indeed, is true of the literary in general; the question remains of what marks its 'special relationship' with the postcolonial. I suggest that this is at least partly a matter of the mutual connection with trauma, and thus inevitably with mourning and melancholy.

Susan Power's *The Grass Dancer* is an emblematic narrative of cultural and personal trauma in a native American context. There are any number of figures – tropes, incidents, characters – in the text on which we could concentrate; we will begin with the mother of Harley Wind Soldier, the novel's protagonist, a woman who is what would be clinically defined, in a common phrase but one of extraordinary insouciance, as an elective mute:[1]

> Ever since the accident that had claimed her husband, Calvin, and Harley's brother, Duane, she refused to speak to anyone, refused to form even a single word. Had it not been her choice to remain mute, Harley was convinced she would have discovered some other means of communication, such as sign language. But she expressed herself only minimally, with nudges and shrugs, leaving an empty space between herself and her son, a deep cavity Harley had internalised. (Power, 1994, 25)

But the 'accident', of course, was no accident; perhaps no accident is ever an accident, but in this case what we might more accurately refer to as the 'founding event' is the result of an act of white racism. In this context, as in others, the notion of the 'choice to remain silent' and its relation to trauma becomes deeply complicated. What *kind* of choice is Harley's mother exercising, on behalf of others among the bereft and traumatised? If a choice is really being exercised, then we might reasonably say that there must be other available alternatives. What, in this case, might they be? The madness of the endlessly prolonged shriek, perhaps; or the manifestation of a deadly but ultimately self-defeating vengeance, self-defeating precisely because of the surrounding cultural circumstances, the ever-present and only thinly disguised exterminatory impulses that have killed her husband and son. Neither option, perhaps, is particularly appealing, certainly not sufficiently so to prevent the ego's own defences from coming into play. The only way in which body and mind can survive this traumatic event is by closing down, in an act of refusal whose 'origins' are entirely 'foreign' to the will; here we see the foreign body itself acting, the parasite interfering to ensure the survival of the host but only at an appalling cost, the cost of an inner fragmentation and the passing down of that fragmentation – and of the crypt that lies at the base of the cleft – through the generations – to Harley and, no doubt, so on down the line. The possibilities of a 'post-traumatic' healing or cohesion are here – as they always are – remote indeed.[2]

What the literary might here stand for, then, the mark of the specific way in which the literary 'becomes' the postcolonial, in which the literary and the postcolonial are implicated in a series of acts of mutual becoming that makes nonsense of the endless 'theoretical' arguments about centre and periphery, hinges on the question of language and silence; for here the mother's mutism (the emptiness where nurture might be) becomes additionally inflected by the issue of language and theft. What language precisely is it that she is refusing? Any language, we may assume, that would bear upon, or be borne upon by (or might be born from) the language of the persecutor; but perhaps it is also true that even the so-called 'native' language has become fatally inflected, such that any prospect of a 'nativity' that might occur within language has fallen foul of the rule of exile, which is also the law of the orphan, the certainty that exiles have, the knowledge that one's words, like one's babies, are to be taken away in the moment of their 'conception'; this is the law of the colony, brutally enacted in, for example, the Australian 'lost generation', which signifies also the process of generation of loss, an impossible genealogy of the lost. The elements of a prior language may remain but they are already dispersed before they are spoken, they are set aside, stamped and relegated; rather like, in *The Grass Dancer*, the face of Chester Brush Horns, an 'Indian' whose traumatic 'founding accident' has left him alive, but only just:

> he was pliant, his mind a crushed bird. I don't remember what the damage was – a car accident, a beating, or a drunken fall from a window. It didn't really matter. He was handsome in pieces, but the placement was all wrong. His features were crowded around the centre of his face, orbiting his nose the way darts cluster around the target. But he was strong ... (Power, 1994, 160)

Let us 'repeat' the discourse. 'Do you remember?' No, 'I don't remember'. 'An empty space'; 'the placement was all wrong'. This is in no way a recuperative discourse, a discourse about putting back together what has been broken, a discourse that can found or sanction a 'new world order'; to claim that would be to put all such claims 'out of court', it would be to create a 'reservation' on which such cases cannot be put. It is instead a discourse about haunting and the echo; it is about false memories of dim pasts, about the impossibility of taking on the pain of memory, about the unassuageable symptom whose force has lost all relation to its apparent 'origin', about the unreality of the hope – as *The Grass Dancer* brilliantly illustrates – even of putting the available narratives themselves into any kind of recognisable order, of sorting through them so that they might make a humanised assemblage of features, a faciality that might be recognisable in the sense of effecting any connection between the inner and the outer (see Deleuze and Guattari, 1988, 179–80).

Here is another account in *The Grass Dancer*, from the 'inner', of mutism: 'And so I have become another person, the one who sits on her tongue. I answer to Lydia, but when I think of myself, I use another name: Ini Naon Win. Silent Woman' (Power, 1994, 197). This has, of course, a great deal to do with what, for want of a more complex analysis, we might have for the moment to call the plight of 'women in general';[3] but it is also a mark, a symptom, of the postcolonial condition. That symptom inheres not only in the silence, but also in the crucial bifurcation of naming, the gap, the 'empty space' between the naming that signifies 'you' from the outside world and the naming that signifies 'I' in the interior self, which itself we might consider to be the after-effect, the aftermath, of the 'founding accident', the continuing legacy of a specific *méconnaissance*. And it should surely be obvious in any context (but equally obviously has not been, and continues not to be, in the colonial and neocolonial mind) that if these two possibilities of identification are forced too far apart, if they are driven 'from home', rendered foreign by a whole sociocultural apparatus whose very purpose and *raison d'être is* indeed to drive them apart, then we are no longer in a world where the simple panaceas of cause and effect, cohesion and closure, can have very much impact. We are in a world instead where a profound melancholy may be the only response to a set of disabling impositions (see Kristeva, 1991, 9–10).

Melancholy, perhaps, of such a kind as we find in Brathwaite. This is a dead man talking:

Bring me now where the warm wind
blows, where the grasses
sigh, where the sweet
tongue'd blossom flowers

where the showers
fan soft like a fisherman's
net thrown through the sweet–
ened air

Bring me now where the workers
rest, where the cotton drifts,
where the rivers are
and the minstrel sits

on the logwood stump
with the dreams of his slow guitar.
(Brathwaite, 1973, 23)

What we have here, again, is haunting and exile. It runs through *The Arrivants*, it is the ground, one might say, on which the melody rests. And yet it is a ground which is no ground, since as we inspect it – checking it, we might say, for evidence of burials, inhumations, crypts – or as, more compellingly, we try to find our way back to it in search of a lost genealogy that might serve as a focus for mourning, all we find – as perhaps we have already known – is a gaping hole (the whole of a gap), an absence; a silence. Or worse. What we find, in sharp contradistinction to the 'dreams' of the 'slow guitar', is not so much a silence or a muted space as one which is quietly crowded with insult, a space where the interiorities of one's naming drop away before the pressure to rename, to derogate and slander, to refuse to entertain the possibility of a dignified other.

Yet, of course, we should all be familiar with the political danger here, the danger of *responding with dignity*: the danger of acculturation, the danger of submitting, for example, to the fakery of Eurocentric multiculturalism when most of the cultures concerned have already been invaded, distorted, reduced to the status of an already ignored client.[4] What, for example, is the message Chandra is conveying when he speaks of

> Ranjitsinhji, who was really a prince, who went to England where they called him nigger and wog, but he showed them, he was the most beautiful batsman, like a dancer he turned their bouncers to the boundaries with his wrists, he drove with clean elegance, he had good manners, and he said nothing to their insults, and he showed them all he was the best of them all, he was the Prince, he was lovely. (Chandra, 1997, 23)

This, of course, is not Chandra's own voice, whatever in a literary context that might mean; but regardless of the complexities of such a putative 'origin', it begs many questions. 'The best of them all': the best of what group? The best of that supposedly international group of cricket-players whose boast might be of a 'level playing-field' (despite the multiple ambiguities of 'bouncers to the boundaries')? Or the best of a different group, a group of stereotyped 'subcontinentals' (resounding, echoing term) from whom no such manners and style are conventionally to be expected? The melancholy content here would consist in the implacability of long historical process, the inability to fight one's way out from the centuries of prejudicial fantasy. Perhaps this is also the weighty and destructive body of fantasy that Harris is talking about when he alludes in *Palace of the Peacock* to 'the enormous ancestral and twin fantasy of death-in-life and life-in-death' (Harris, 1988, 327).[5] These would indeed be two sides of the same coin: on the one hand, the 'death-in-life' to which so many millions, 'native' and diasporic, have been consigned by the operations of the colonial desiring machine; on the other, the 'life-in-death' that may be the only 'form of life' available as the racially abused and denigrated try to force their way out of the coffin, the site of burial. But at the end of the day, as we might appropriately put it, the melancholy which is becoming more evident text by text necessarily manifests itself also in a grinding repetitiveness: the futility of trying to comprehend that which is fundamentally alien, of trying to 'make sense' of one's own banishment, one's own conferred and magical status as an exile.[6]

At one point in Naipaul's *House for Mr Biswas*, Mr Biswas decides to indulge in a little 'native genealogy', to write down some available names for his promised son, and he uses the only material means available to do so, which results in a reinscription of books that have already been written, archived, canonised:

> on the back endpaper of the *Collins Clear-Type Shakespeare*, a work of fatiguing illegibility, he wrote the names in large letters, as though his succession had already been settled. He would have used *Bell's Standard Elocutionist*, still his favourite reading, if it had not suffered so much from the kick he had given it in the long room at Hanuman House; the covers hung loose and the endpapers had been torn, exposing the khaki-coloured boards. He had bought the *Collins Clear-Type Shakespeare* for the sake of *Julius Caesar*, parts of which he had declaimed at Lal's school. Every other play defeated him; the volume remained virtually unread and now, as a repository of the family records, proved to be a mistake. The endpaper blotted atrociously. (Naipaul, 1961, 161)

'[F]atiguing illegibility': this, then, is a melancholy effect, the effect of the imposition of another culture, one whose irrelevance to

Biswas's life would be laughable in its absurdity were it not for the emphasis on the hollowing effect, the emptying out of whatever clarity and ambition he might have had, its reduction to the scramble to 'build a house', however inadequate, to find a location in an absurd society. Naipaul's strength, frequently derided,[7] is nevertheless in this absurdity and in the seriousness with which he takes it, and in his recognition of the compromised position in which this means his texts must be 'found', or founded. This absurdity is, for example, what is emphasised in the insistence on the full titles of these 'weapons' of cultural imperialism – in the case of the Shakespeare, the significantly repeated title. And what of *Julius Caesar*? A text, we might say, floating down a different cultural stream, but a text of empire if ever there was one; but then Biswas's relation to it has only been one of 'declamation', a repetition of a repetition, a minor ebb in a gradual draining of meaning. Small wonder, then, that when the artefacts of this cultural conjuncture are torn apart, what is exposed is ... what else but 'khaki', the military impulse thinly concealed inside the ridiculously pristine detritus of empire, but also the 'foreign' term reused in the service of invasion and expropriation.[8] And so we see that the effect of the conquerors' culture in this context can be only twofold: empty declamation or melancholy defeat.

Brathwaite powerfully details the relation between this specific melancholia and a mourning that infuses the history of colonised peoples:

> So for my hacked
> heart, veins' mem-
> ories, I wear this
>
> past I borrowed; his-
> tory bleeds
> behind my hollowed eyes;
>
> on my wet back
> tomorrow's sunlight dries ...
>
> (Brathwaite, 1973, 148)

'[T]omorrow's sunlight': is it possible, Harris asks in the epigraph above, to apprehend tragedy before the digestion of the relevant experience? Is it possible under conditions of trauma, one might respond, to do anything else; for trauma is that which inverts linear history, that which forever inserts a wedge into history's doors, keeping them permanently open, preventing closure but permitting the seepage of the heart's blood of which Brathwaite here speaks. Borrowing, hollowing, attempting to fill in and bridge gaps that are themselves not to be plumbed; what, in this context, might we make of the use of the word 'wear'? This borrowed past is 'worn', in the sense that clothes are worn. But it is also ambivalently worn in this context in the sense that something in this historical conjuncture traversed by trauma might indeed get 'worn' – worn out, worn down – but how will this happen, where will this 'wearing' sense of history be most felt?

Not, we may fairly assume, in the realm of the conqueror, whose clothes, khaki or not, are pristine and well pressed, whose means of preservation are endlessly at hand. These means of preservation include the maintenance of the archive; the activities of historians and post-imperial anthropologists; the constant reworking of the imagined past; the suppression of diasporic identities; the international exploitation of the resources – animal, vegetable and mineral to name but three – of those states, those 'conditions of being', that have passed under the thrall, that have been forced into the 'wearing' of others' ill-fitting clothes. What is at stake here, again, is mourning: mourning wear, the wearing of the symptoms of mourning on the sleeve, as even the racially ambiguous Simon in Hulme's *The Bone People* wears his inner silence inside out – another so-called 'elective' mute whose silence has been thrust upon him and is about to be repeated, confirmed, even at the hands of 'subject' peoples, reduced as they have been to the violence of the desperate. Joe, seeing the mauriora in its milky pool, may see this – or we as readers may be encouraged to see this – as a dream of nurturing, but it falls apart before his eyes; just as his own fantasies of a nurturing self continuously fall apart as he recognises his abusive treatment of Simon yet, because of his mixed genealogy, his complexly inadmissible ancestry, remains 'at a loss' in his apprehension of the symptom.

What, Hulme keeps also asking in *The Bone People*, is responsible for Kerewin's 'condition': for her vocal fragmentation, her physical evasions, the 'uneven development', to use a resonant phrase in the realm of postcolonial manipulations, of her body and mind?

> 'I haven't been raped or jilted or abused in any fashion. There's nothing in my background to explain the way I am'. She steadies her voice, taking the impatience out of it. 'I'm the odd one out, the peculiarity in my family, because they're all normal and demonstrative physically. But ever since I can remember, I've disliked close contact ... charged contact, emotional contact, as

> well as any overtly sexual contact. I veer away from it, because it always feels like the other person is draining something out of me. (Hulme, 1985, 265–6)

How or where, then, to look for an 'explanation'? In confronting such a passage it is clearly necessary to avoid two dangers: one is the reduction of a cultural condition to an individual psychopathology, the other, exemplified by Jameson, is the treatment of all narratives from the 'ex-colonies' as 'national narratives'. *Something*, it is evident, has been abused here. Perhaps, as Kerewin says, it is not 'I'; but then, the 'I' of the mixed white and Maori background from which Kerewin comes is in any case under interrogation, under erasure. If there is nothing in 'my' background to 'explain', then it is these terms, the controversial 'I' and the impossibility of explanation, that need to come under scrutiny. What should not be possible – in the face of the vast ignorings of colonial and postcolonial history – is further to ignore the symptom, which is at least partly a 'symptom of mourning', unrecognised because linear history is here contorted, wrapped around itself in an unending cycle of repetitions of abuse.[9] The whole of *The Bone People*, indeed, is a catalogue – an index would be the more fashionable but less accurate term – of inexplicable symptoms, all revolving around the fracture, death and rebirth, in this instance, of Kerewin's relation to her family and to her 'background'.

I want to take this discussion forward on what might at first appear to be an unlikely terrain, namely Irvine Welsh's novel *Marabou Stork Nightmares*, which is by far the most significant book he has thus far written and which is a book about trauma, melancholy, loss and mourning. What is the trauma that underpins the text? Welsh offers us various alternatives. One we might find in the text's epigraph (which I shall myself repeat as an epigraph later): 'Scepticism was formed in Edinburgh two hundred years ago by David Hume and Adam Smith. They said: "Let's take religion to the black man, but we won't really believe it". It's the cutting edge of trade' (Welsh, 1995, xi). It needs immediately to be said that the relation between this epigraph and the text is by no means obvious. *Marabou Stork Nightmares* does have a clear engagement with the postcolonial, but it is not along these lines. Instead the engagement takes its place *within* one of the complex of discourses that make up the text. Roy Strang, the protagonist, is one of a group of Edinburgh youths who, amid other 'anti-social' activities, have committed a group rape of the most obscene and violent kind. The text details, for the most part, Roy's time in hospital, recovering from a suicide attempt he has made in the aftermath of the event (the 'founding accident'). During this recovery his main concern (although to call it a 'concern' is to assume too much volition in a text whose strength is to explore the actual fantasy content of structural disavowal) is to keep the 'remembrance' of the event at bay; in the course of doing so what gets elaborated is a further fantasy, a mythic life taken direct from imperialist comics where he figures as an 'explorer' and developer, a colonialist with all the positive connotations that come from *Boys' Own* magazines.

What is the relation between this fantasy scenario and the location of Roy Strang's life? That life has in itself been, if not a response to trauma, at least an experience of living with the continuing possibility of trauma: his mother, when drunk, appears maddened by Japanese war fantasies, and more generally

> I grew up in what was not so much a family as a genetic disaster. While people always seem under the impression that their household is normal, I, from an early age, almost as soon as I was aware, was embarrassed and ashamed of my family. (Welsh, 1995, 19)

He has every reason to be, given the extraordinary violence of his father and his associates; but the point is that under circumstances of the utmost gravity (and that gravity is catastrophically underlined by the castration that, in more senses than one, concludes the text) what becomes necessary is to replace this narrative by another one. *Marabou Stork Nightmares* is thus a crucial example of the relation between disavowal and 'the text instead', and what it places before the reader is the way in which that supervening text, the one that will 'make everything alright', is a text of empire.

But the 'third term' in this complex of discourses is supplied by Roy's 'remembrance' of a specific episode in his life, an episode of abuse. By now, perhaps, this is becoming an all too familiar narreme. Cholly Breedlove; Joe in *The Bone People*; any number of other abusers, all of whom place before us the direct connection between abuse and deprivation. About this, perhaps, we need to be quite stark. Child abuse is the great unwritten narrative of the twentieth century. By this I do not mean at all to suggest that such abuse has been more prevalent in recent times; what I mean is almost the opposite, it is that the pressure of the secret, the pressure of the unspoken and unwritten, has become more evident, and I suggest that one of the points made repeatedly by the postcolonial is that this constellation of suppression, this 'open secret', is directly related to the dehumanisation attendant upon deprivation and, in the final analysis, on the relation between deprivation, slavery and colonialism.

This, certainly, would be the message of Riley's *The Unbelonging*, to which we shall shortly return; in *Marabou Stork Nightmares* it figures in the attempted displacement of abuse, which is also the conjuring of a scene in which Roy is repeatedly abused by his uncle. The scenario is South Africa, during a brief interlude the family spends there as the uncle's guests; he is an 'unreconstructed pro-apartheid white supremacist' (Welsh, 1995, 62). Uncle Gordon takes Roy to visit the Museum of the Republick Van Suid-Afrika, and here he discovers an interesting text, which goes in part as follows:

> South Africa is the only country in the world where a dominant community has followed a definite policy of maintaining the purity of its race in the midst of overwhelming numbers of non-European inhabitants – in most not still administered as colonies or protectorates either the non-whites have been exterminated or there has been some form of assimilation, resulting in a more or less coloured population. Indeed, far from the extermination of non-whites, the advent of the European in South Africa has meant that whole native communities have been saved from exterminating each other. It is not generally realised that scarcely a century ago Chaka, chief of the Zulus, destroyed 300 tribes and wiped out thousands upon thousands of his fellows. (81)

The text is reticent about the connection between this apparent but unvalidated evidence of disregard for human life and human dignity and Roy's own actions; on the whole, and in an interesting symmetry with Hulme's treatment of Joe in *The Bone People*, Welsh, while not condoning Roy's behaviour, seems more concerned that we 'understand' it than that we see things from the side of the victim. Nevertheless, textually, what such passages do is to set off for us a necessary chain of connection between South Africa, the home of apartheid, and Edinburgh, where, we presume from the text, the 'equivalent', the exchange value, that is being advanced must have to do with subjugation, with the emptying out of a 'national capital' that has no State to command (is in no state to command).[10]

Roy (within his imperial fantasy) comments ironically to Lochart

Dawson, who is among other things a fantasised 'cod sociologist' with a significantly Scottish name:

> Extremely visionary stuff, Lochart, not at all the type of questioning based on perpetuating the narrow economic interests of an already wealthy but spiritually impoverished elite at the expense of their more financially disadvantaged bretheren. Truly the type of questioning which will help enable mankind as a species to self-actualise and fulfil its cosmic destiny. There's a real sense of destiny underpinning it all. (Welsh, 1995, 93)

Every word of this, of course, needs to be taken ironically; what is at stake here is a vision of 'development' based on extermination, and this is also the overall theme of the fantasy world Roy tries to inhabit while 'estranged' from the world that is too frightening for him to acknowledge. The extermination in question is the extermination – a not infrequent general theme in colonialist travel writing – of the marabou stork, a bird whose habits – unprepossessing yet oddly resonant in human terms – clearly leave it open to a wide variety of identifications; what becomes clear in *Marabou Stork Nightmares* is that it has been Roy himself, and perhaps his 'colleagues',[11] who have been the marabou storks, the hunter/scavengers, that Roy's hatreds and loathings are self-hatreds and self-loathings, that his problem is to find a ground between the remembrance of abuse and the presence of self-pity on which to found some apprehension of the tragedy that has already happened, some ground on which to rest the ruins of his life, short-lived as even those ruins turn out to be.

*Marabou Stork Nightmares* ties the issues of the postcolonial, here figured in the triple guise of Edinburgh as the 'absented capital', South Africa as the terrain of horror, and the empire at large as the site of a fantasised potential recuperation, very closely to the figuring of trauma, and within that traumatised discourse to the issues of melancholy, mourning, loss. Brathwaite, perhaps unsurprisingly, achieves a similar yet more devastating effect in fewer words:

> so let me sing
> nothing
> now
>
> let me remember
> nothing
> now

let me suffer
nothing
to remind me now

of my lost children

(Brathwaite, 1973, 13)

Perhaps this effects an essential postcolonial move from epigraph to epitaph.

# X Becoming-Animal, Becoming-Woman

> Dangerous animals became even more sinister and uncanny in the dark. A snake was never called by its name at night, because it would hear. It was called a string. (Chinua Achebe, *Things Fall Apart*)

> ... they were only Sweet Home men at Sweet Home. One step off that ground and they were trespassers among the human race. Watchdogs without teeth; steer bulls without horns; gelded workhorses whose neigh and whinny could not be translated into a language responsible humans spoke. (Toni Morrison, *Beloved*)

> ... of the endless chain for the summons of the god and the phallus of unorigin pointed at the sky-hole past divination ... (Wole Soyinka, *The Interpreters*)

In Morrison's *Beloved,* the character known only by the dehumanised name 'Stamp Paid' reflects at length on race relations, and in particular on what has been, and is still being, done to blacks. 'Very few', he recalls, 'had died in bed ... and none that he knew of ... had lived a livable life':

> Even the educated coloured: the long-school people, the doctors, the teachers, the paper-writers and businessmen had a hard row to hoe. In addition to having to use their heads to get ahead, they had the weight of the whole race sitting there. You needed two heads for that. (Morrison, 1987, 198)

You would need, in short, to be a monster; you would need to be able to obey the imperative of stepping outside the human condition, since that condition was every day withheld from you. But one of the legacies left to postcolonial writing, one of the bodies of fantasy still active and still undefeated – just as slavery, despite its apparent banishing, still continues[1] – is the specific connection between these prejudices and an assignation to the animal. Deleuze and Guattari talk constantly in *A Thousand Plateaus* of a 'becoming-animal', and place a positive value on this as a way of working with the decentring of consciousness, a way of spreading outward from the merely human and achieving some wider contact with the world beyond consciousness on which terrain, according to them, things actually happen, governing territorialisations take place (see Deleuze and Guattari, 1988, 255). But a reading of the postcolonial suggests that, in this respect at least, Deleuze and Guattari are caught in a conceptual trap of their own devising.

'Whitepeople believed', Stamp Paid continues, 'that whatever the manners' (and we have seen this question of manners aired already in Chandra's tale of the cricketing prince) 'under every dark skin was a jungle':

> Swift unnavigable waters, swinging screaming baboons, sleeping snakes, red gums ready for their sweet white blood. In a way, he thought, they were right. The more colouredpeople spent their strength trying to convince them how gentle they were, how clever and loving, how human, the more they used themselves up to persuade whites of something Negroes believed could not be questioned, the deeper and more tangled the jungle grew inside. But it wasn't the jungle blacks brought with them to this place from the other (livable) place. It was the jungle whitefolks planted in them. And it grew. It spread. In, through and after life, it spread, until it invaded the whites who had made it. Touched them every one. Changed and altered them. Made them bloody, silly, worse than even they wanted to be, so scared were they of the jungle they had made. The screaming baboon lived under their own white skin; the red gums were their own. (Morrison, 1987, 198–9)

This body of fantasy takes as one of its points of origin precisely the world through which Welsh's Roy Strang travels when he is trying to evade the memories and consequences of his own violence. It is again the world of *Boys' Own* adventure stories, the world of rapid rivers and tormented jungles where there are impossible dangers to overcome; a world in which, of course, from the very start the fantasised threat posed by the wild animal is indistinguishable from the danger posed by the hidden 'native'. We can find precise equivalents across the entire imperial realm, in the America, for example, of Fenimore Cooper, and thus already the terms are set up for an apparently unthinking equivalence between the 'native' and the animal.[2]

Except that to call it 'unthinking' is to shift the question, the crucial question of 'what thinks what'. For to place the 'native' in the position of the animal, although from one perspective it may look like an inevitable blurring consequent upon deep-rooted fears, from another perspective fulfils an important goal. That is one of the goals of the colonial desiring machine, namely to pretend that the land that is so obviously and ubiquitously populated is in fact empty of human life. To assimilate the 'native' to the animal is, as it were, to 'clear the ground'; and thus we see one of the ways in which an imperial 'logic' of extermination and genocide is preceded and accompanied at all points by a cultural logic – ultimately derived, if vicariously, from Darwin[3] – that sequesters the notion of the 'human', places its definition at the service of the colonial administrator just as, in other but related contexts, the notion of 'eugenics' provided a cultural fig-leaf for the destruction of (usually prior) races.[4]

But in Stamp Paid's reflections we can see a great deal more than this. We might want to enquire, for example, into the tone of 'how gentle they were, how clever and loving'. This, surely, is not meant to be taken 'straight', it is *already* a measure of the way in which, when a dehumanising identity is thrust upon a group, of whatever kind, the most frequent response is to try to take up the terms offered by the rulers and invert them. This, of course, neither helps the argument nor alleviates the consequences of domination. All it does is reinforce the crucial assumption behind the fantasy, namely that there are no individuals out there in the jungle, the ghetto, the enclave, merely a 'mass', and that in itself is sufficient to provide further 'evidence' to justify the fulfilment of the dehumanising function.[5]

But even more crucially what we have here is a diagnosis of a certain kind of projection and reintrojection,[6] although we need to insist that it is not merely fear that is the motivating force but rather the will, the will to exclude, dominate, exterminate. This 'jungle' is one of the 'whitefolks'' creation, but Stamp Paid's assumption that it produces fear, that it 'scares' them, is surely not the whole of the story for it seems perfectly evident from recent history that, if anything, it does not scare 'them' enough. The point, surely, is that *this* 'becoming-animal' is, always and everywhere, functional; it serves the purpose of extending dominion, and in turn it reinforces the dominators' claim to be extending civilisation through the slaughter of the very people who, from another perspective, are supposed to be benefiting from it.

We would need, also, to look again at the contrast the passage draws between the 'livable' place and the 'unlivable' place, between the fantasy of a prior Africa and the reality of a brutalised and brutalising America, between the fantasised Paradise of the old world and the grimness of the 'new world' order. For the essential point is that this contrast has in fact no meaning at the level of the real; rather, both poles are implanted, constructed, necessary accompaniments to the documentation of slavery. What is stolen from the slave, the exile, is not merely the present but also the past, just as in Rastafarianism the twin poles of Caribbean exile and Ethiopian elysium can all too often serve simply to prop up the failing edifice of white rule.[7] From this system, from this machine, there would be no escape; and it is in this context that we need to view the complex dealings between the postcolonial and the animistic.

Animism, Freud says, represents a primitive level of belief, prior to the acceptance of a fully-fledged distinction between the human and that which is 'less' than human (see Freud, 1953–74, XIII, 64–99). This distinction, ecological thinkers now welcomely assert, needs to be rolled back as we reassess the relations between human and animal, whether we conceive these as being *within* the 'human animal' or more broadly spread across the supposedly 'natural' spectrum.[8] But to go back to Banks's analogy of the sheep, it could be said that just as there are no longer any 'natives', just so there are no longer any animals; the very nature of the animal has for so long been intimately bound up with, has been through the grinding mill of, human systems of inclusion and exclusion that the animal has become emptied, invisible. Thus we may see the desiring machine of the colonial as conducing to and forwarding an emptying not merely of the 'native' but of the so-called 'natural world' in general, an extermination that would be so far-reaching that it would abolish the other entirely, prevent all possibility of competition;[9] just as, indeed, that machine in its new global capitalist guise is continuing to behave as an agent of extermination. And at this point, we cannot ignore the further frightening fact that recent theories of the decentring of consciousness, far from being radical in their assumptions about human identity, are in fact the very emblem of complicity. In their extreme questioning of the human, in their exaltation of the 'inhuman', they are in fact repeating precisely the 'colonising' gambit, emptying the world of all inhabitants who do not conform to the central structure of prejudice that keeps the Western tradition in being.[10]

Yet animism is ubiquitous within the postcolonial. In Atwood, for example:

> I lie down on the bottom of the canoe and wait. The still water gathers the heat; birds, off in the forest a woodpecker, somewhere a thrush. Through the trees the sun glances; the swamp around me smoulders, energy of decay turning to growth, green fire. I remember the heron; by now it will be insects, frogs, fish, other herons. My body also changes, the creature in me, plant-animal, sends out filaments in me; I ferry it secure between life and death, I multiply. (Atwood, 1973, 161–2 )

The important question is not an ethical one of whether it might be 'good' to feel this kind of mystical affinity with plants and animals, neither is it a cultural one about how such an affinity might promote societal health and serve to dam up violent impulses. The question is rather – must *always* be rather, but particularly in the postcolonial context – a political one: what will the effect be of this reassumption of the attributes of the animal, in what context, and for what interpreter?[11]

For a white Canadian writer such effects will differ from those felt by a black African; but even for the particular white Canadian that is Margaret Atwood and/or her character, the most obvious consequence is that the visiting US hunters – only fantasised in *Surfacing*, but we can be in no doubt that they are, or will be, there – will simply regard this curious becoming-animal as a signal to shoot; this 'security' is an optical illusion, a supposition that 'waiting it out' will suffice. This did not work, as we have seen, in the case of Coetzee's Michael K and neither does it appear to be working in the world at large; but perhaps more importantly, what it shows us is that even the myths of animism – and they do, of course, have a great deal of instructive potential – will always be contaminated at root by the power system within which they live and move and have their being.

The prospect of a joining of archaic forces that will effect resistance, while attractive to the dissident Western intellectual, is always subject to a lethal 'encircling', as Divakaruni appears to realise if we look again, and in a different context, at 'Tiger Mask Ritual':

> Once you locate the ears the drums begin.
> Your fur stiffens. A roar from the distant left,
> like monsoon water. The air
> is hotter now and moving. You swivel
> your sightless head.
> Under your sheathed paw the ground shifts, wet.

A small wild sound is sheltering
in your skull
against the circle that always closes in
just before dawn.

(Behl and Nicholls, 1995, 92–3)

What we might now see in this emblematic poem is that the apparent donning of power signified in a ritual of totemic animalism is revealed as a diminution, a failure of senses, of hearing and of 'sightless' eyes; the mask is merely a constraint, the only sound that can still be made is 'small' and its 'shelter' is ambiguous. The paw remains 'sheathed' while the circle closes in – the circle of hunters, the circle of (Eurocentric) interpretation and 'high' quasi-anthropological 'theory'. What might, in some now unimaginable time 'before', have signified the acquisition and ritual confirmation of power now signifies only victimhood; after all, there are almost no tigers left.

One of the most astonishing recent texts that deals in this animistic is Cormac McCarthy's trilogy about the 'borderlands' between Mexico and Texas, which in *The Crossing* in particular focuses around the wolf, around the image of the wolf, the perceptions of the wolf, the relation between wolf and man, but what is most crucial in this extraordinary work is the elegiac tone (see McCarthy, 1994). This is not a putting on of power, it is a doomed attempt at rescue and salvation, and it is this elegiac that we have to keep in mind when we look at ambitious and in many ways entirely admirable attempts to 're-animate' the animistic. In Maori literature, for example, what Ken Arvidson refers to as 'extreme animism' (Arvidson, 1991, 121) (although with no particular justification for the term 'extreme' – what would a mild animism be?) is, as most critics would agree, everywhere; the important thing would be to recognise that although from one perspective this might be seen as a healthy revivification of the archaic, a remaking of broken connections, from another it represents a culminative turning of the face away from power, an abjection into the world of the animal *as it has been reformulated* by the colonisers.

The emphasis, though – and Deleuze and Guattari are right to insist on this – must remain upon the 'becoming'. Let us consider a remark made by Jean Franco in her influential article 'Beyond Ethnocentrism', a remark that takes us over the boundary from 'becoming-animal' to the even more problematic category of 'becoming-woman':

> the mother can only (literally) *embody* certainty because of her immobility, because she is related to physical territory. Indeed, it was the female territory of the house that allowed private and family memory to be stored; there, archaic values, quite alien to the modern world, continued to flourish. (Franco, 1988, 508)

This construction of an immobilised matriarch, which owes more to the myth of the 'queen bee' than to any known society, is bizarre on many counts. First, it ignores processes of transition and becoming, it re-enshrines the notion of the 'immobile primitive' which was a cornerstone of imperial discourse. Second, it supposes a continuing version of male/female relations which inhabits only a paradisal fantasy of Western imposition. Third, it ignores the rhetoric of damage and weakness which is in fact what we more frequently find when we turn to the literature itself, the anxiety of becoming-woman precisely coded as the destruction of relations attendant on the masculist, phallic power of the Western imperialist. This is the real story behind one of the most fatal moments in African literature, Okonkwo's complicity in the killing of his 'son' in Achebe's *Things Fall Apart*:

> As the man who had cleared his throat drew up and raised his matchet, Okonkwo looked away. He heard the blow. The pot fell and broke in the sand. He heard Ikemefuna cry, 'My father, they have killed me!' as he ran towards him. Dazed with fear, Okonkwo drew his matchet and cut him down. He was afraid of being thought weak. (Achebe, 1996, 43)

It is evident from his own treatment of Ikemefuna that what Okonkwo most fears is a 'becoming-woman', considered as a reduction of status – his own father has been referred to as a woman – or we might think of the fate of 'Mahmoud the Woman' in Rushdie's *Shame* (see Rushdie, 1983, e.g., 62). What we do not find in this literature is a celebration of these traditional roles, roles which, like cannibalism, were largely called into being by the West's rage for explanation; what we need to attend to instead is the broken pot, the pot which, as Aruna Dhere tells us in 'The Night Has Come to an End', comes under the rule of empire to signify not plenitude or nurture but death:

> At dusk, waterpot braced by her hand, the mother
> Bears the burden of children and menfolk on her head.

One waterpot, one *dudi* above the other, the woman comes
 toward the water.
Not toward the water, but comes to her childhood home.

The water gently sways, the dream enters the water, drowns.
When the moon enters the song, every day she asks for death,
 The woman asks for death.

(Behl and Nicholls, 1995, 101)

The point of Deleuze and Guattari's dwelling on the notion of 'becoming-woman', and the reason, I take it – although they explain this very poorly – why there is no room in their system for a comparable 'becoming-man' is that this 'becoming', like the 'becoming-animal', is the only alternative to masculinist reinterpretation.[12] In other words the point about the female, the trap into which Franco so neatly falls, is the way in which 'she' succumbs to becoming a site for interpretation, explanation, her role guaranteed, her force supposed to conduce to stability; and the reason for making these points here is that on this terrain we have one of the starkest mismatches between postcolonial writing and postcolonial 'theory' – and it is of course because of this that relations between woman writers and woman critics on the postcolonial site remain, as in the emblematic case of Donna Haraway, so strained.[13]

*Marabou Stork Nightmares*, which, while it does not run the risk of condoning rape to quite the same extent as *The Bone People* runs the very real risk of condoning child abuse, nonetheless reverberates with elements of masculinist self-pity, is however also pithy on the relations between conventional interpretations of psychoanalysis, the use of psychoanalysis as framework and the reinscription of the female. The lawyer who represents the rapists anticipates the success of their defence when he advises them on the mind-set of the judge before whom they are to appear:

> Judge Hermiston's attitudes are very much influenced by his practising of criminal law in the fifties where the dominant school of criminology was the Freudian model. This essentially does away with the concept of the crime of rape by proving that there are no victims. Female sexuality is deemed by nature to be masochistic, hence rape cannot logistically take place since it directly encounters the argument that all women want it anyway. (Welsh, 1995, 207)[14]

It is not clear to whom we should attribute the mistaken use of terms like 'proving' and 'logistically', but the point is that we are again looking at a reinscription, and there can be little doubt in *Marabou Stork Nightmares* that, as in *Things Fall Apart* – and as also in Morrison, and in Tutuola, among many others – this reinscription is the direct result of a reassignment of victimhood, of a vicious fallout from the becoming-woman that occurs under conditions of persecution and slavery.

We can look at these matters in more detail by turning to Tsitsi Dangarembga's *Nervous Conditions*, a text that hovers around the edges of fiction, biography, autobiography and which derives its title from a sentence in an introduction to Fanon's *The Wretched of the Earth*: 'The condition of native is a nervous condition' (Dangarembga, 1988, iv).[15] The controlling absence in *Nervous Conditions* is that of the father, and his absence is caused by his situation at the confluence of two opposing forces. On the one hand he is a staunch traditionalist, much to the exasperation of his daughter ('My father's idea of what was natural had begun to irritate me a long time ago' (33)); on the other his laziness and ability to 'swing both ways' mean that he has neither the courage nor the means to carry out his many threats to prevent his daughter from having an education or thus to consign her to a 'female' role:

> He did not like to see me over-absorbed in intellectual pursuits. He became very agitated after he had found me several times reading the sheet of newspaper in which the bread from *magrosa* had been wrapped as I waited for the *sadza* to thicken. ... In frustration he resorted to absolutes. ... he threatened to take me out of school again. It was a thoughtless threat: how could he have done that? Not having the power, he left me alone. We co-existed in peaceful detachment. (33–4)

Here we see one way in which the issue of becoming-woman is inextricably linked to writing. Dangarembga's protagonist Tambu speaks of the past: 'how could he have done that?' For her, therefore, paternal power is over, but of course the evidence for that is the book itself, and behind that lie the spreading fields of silence, the realm of these girls and women whose ambitions – writerly or otherwise – were indeed thwarted by the figure of the father.[16]

The point, however, is that these roles are not stable, they are always in the process of becoming, but this 'becoming' in a post-colonial situation is inevitably thwarted, damaged. The specific damage in *Nervous Conditions* is represented by colonial rule and especially by the English language, and they are tied together both characterologically and at the level of the symptom. The reason for Tambu's father's plight, for example, can be explored at a further level than that of character defects, rather in terms of an implanted system of dependence. His brother Babamukuru has had an English education and has become a teacher; since in this exalted position he earns, in the colonial service, far more than it would ever be possible for his brother to make even if he were a successful subsistence farmer, Tambu's family is reduced to awaiting handouts from Babamukuru which, although they are naturally helpful to the family, nevertheless require an engagement, however modest, with the colonising power.

But that engagement turns out in the end not to be modest at all. Tambu's brother Nhamo, not obviously more clever than her but, of course, male, is given opportunities for study by Babamukuru which culminate when he goes off to his school; but there he dies, at the age of thirteen. He dies of a medically 'explicable' illness, but that is not what the text makes of it: the illness, the disease, as it is seen from other perspectives, is precisely the disease of Englishness, a disease (or unease) carried in the language; or, perhaps, the disease of being *between*, of being in a condition of 'thwarted becoming', of being stretched over No Man's Land where neither tradition nor ambition can help him. Babamukuru's daughter Nyasha, Tambu's sophisticated friend, suffers an equally dreadful fate: brilliant and energetic, she finds the traditional elements of her home life intolerable and the symptom mutates into anorexia, emblematic of an impossible force-feeding, a rejection of a model of nurture which she has outgrown.

How is it possible in these circumstances to 'become'? What indeed is it that one might become without in the very process severing one's own roots or relapsing into the passivity and somnambulism that, in the shape of Tambu's father, constitute one response to what I want to refer to as *the continuing crisis of control in a colonised state*? What the text clearly recounts is a becoming-woman as the only resort under circumstances of duress. In the first paragraph Dangarembga/Tambu tells us that

> my story is not after all about [my brother's] death, but about my escape and Lucia's; about my mother's and Maiguru's entrapment; and about Nyasha's rebellion – Nyasha, far-minded and isolated, my uncle's daughter, whose rebellion may not in the end have been successful. (Dangarembga, 1988, 1)

Lucia is the 'loose woman' of the village, who in the end enrols successfully for the education she has previously been denied; Maiguru is Babamukuru's wife, with a British education far more successful than his own, who tries to leave him but fails. By the final paragraph of the book Dangarembga/Tambu is even clearer that this is 'the story of four women whom I loved' – her mother, Nyasha, Maiguru, Lucia – 'and our men, this story is how it all began' (204).

In that phrase 'and our men', and in the parody of the originary story of the Bible implied in the phrase 'how it all began', lies the epitome, the kernel of the text, which is a 'becoming-woman', an abandonment of the already empty site of the male, and an account of the various trajectories, the various lines of flight, that women might take if they are to flee from the ruins. Some of those lines of flight may lead to successful outcomes, some not; but the option of remaining unaffected, of remaining stable and untouched amid the scenario of damage and ruin being enacted all round under colonial conditions does not, despite the various romanticisations of literary critics and theorists, exist.[17]

And these considerations of becoming-animal and becoming-woman can lead us further into the question of 'becoming' in general, onto the terrain of transformations and multiplicities, which I want to pursue in the context of Wole Soyinka's *The Interpreters*. I shall adopt here a dual focus: first, a focus on the way in which *The Interpreters* is crucially not a novel about individuals, about an 'ideally individuated' in the Western mode but instead tends always towards a multiplicitous becoming that will set the individuated in a different context, in a context of the 'different'; second, a focus on a particular passage, one small part of which has been quoted epigraphically above, but which begins to run more largely as follows:

> And of these floods of the beginning, of the fevered fogs of the beginning, of the first messenger, the thimble of earth, a fowl and an ear of corn, seeking the spot where a scratch would become a peopled island; of the first apostate rolling the boulder down the back of the unsuspecting deity – for they must learn the first stab in the back and keep inferiors harmless within sight – and shattering him in fragments, which were picked up and pieced together with devotion; shell of the tortoise around divine breath; of the endless chain for the summons of the god and the phallus of unorigin pointed at the sky-hole past divination; of the lover of purity, the unblemished one whose large compassion embraced the cripples and the dumb, the dwarf, the epileptic –

> and why not, indeed, for they were creations of his drunken hand and what does it avail, the eternal penance of favouritism and abstinence? (Soyinka, 1970, 224–5)

Perhaps at this point it would be as well to take a break in the middle of this sentence, so much longer than 'Of man's first disobedience, and the fruit/Of that forbidden tree' (Milton, 1980, 159), and yet in another sense also a reply to it, or a swerving aside from it. For the novel *The Interpreters* is one that raises, of course, the whole question of who the interpreters are, and of what their sanction or authority is, and of what power they can achieve. The problem of the text is of how to gather together this vast scenario of variety and difference into coherence, of how to 'band' it together (the character Bandele is the focus of the text), of how to create within this spreading field of impossibility a site of interpretation; to put it in the more political terms which are obviously Soyinka's own, it is of how to bend this religious rhetoric into the service of present action, although this problem is, as we might expect, not entirely solved within the text.

The novel is a meditation on the site, purpose and possibility of interpretation, and it thus raises the crucial questions of the postcolonial and gives us a new opportunity to break the term 'postcolonial' apart again for inspection. Does the 'postcolonial', we might now – perhaps belatedly – ask, refer to a literature, or to a mode of 'interpretation'? To put it another way, to what extent and in what way are there literary effects that we might refer to as postcolonial, or are we in using the term referring to an after-effect, an aftermath, of a way of classification that is contingent upon Eurocentric domination? Many writings, many literatures, exist in the aftermath of empire; among them are the entire literatures of, for example, the United States and of 'Latin' America, as well as those writings in nations whose 'freedom' from European rule has been achieved more recently.

*The Interpreters* is concerned with questioning these issues – what can survive, the text asks, under conditions where such imposition has been considered absolute? But the real question here, the one that Soyinka is raising in this key passage and which he continues to raise throughout the text and in the specific shape of the character Bandele's emergence and shaping, is about the way in which a 'native' imagery can survive the depredations of colonisation (see Soyinka, 1970, e.g., 233). Four fates, we might say, await such survival, such impertinent continuation under the regime of a 'new world order'. One is silence, of which no more can be said. The second is exile, which is the destiny perpetuated by the positioning of postcolonial writing on the acceptable fringes and margins of the Western canon. The third is absorption, which is the fate to which writers such as Achebe are so alive as they ironically rebut the West's ludicrous criteria of universalism.[18] The fourth is exoticisation, which has to do with having to stand permanently in the place of the other, having to accept the role of that against which all forces have been ranged but which has somehow still survived – and which, worse, achieves its readership on the back of publishers' lists which are dedicated to the distant, the foreign body.

But we need to be clear about this, as we do about our readerly existence as 'the interpreters'. For it is important to realise – and the very rhythms of Soyinka's writing in this passage attest to this, if with a supreme irony – that the very existence and promulgation of postcolonial literature is inseparable from the sign of the exotic. There is no pure reading act; there is no way in which the increased publication and reception of texts from what we may now perhaps call the post-colonies will alter *in itself* without concomitant social but more importantly economic change. Only such change could alter the first terms on which a Western readership will 'take' texts written in the former colonies; to see that one has only to look at the dust-jackets (dust-jackets are so crucial for Naipaul's characters) of the Heinemann African Writers series, with their standardised versions of jungles, palm-trees, cubist natives.[19]

The force of this passage from *The Interpreters* is to restage a notion of origin in 'unorigin'; it is to insist that the problematic presence of a notion of 'origin' on the literary scene (a presence, of course, hardly perceived in the West as problematic until Derrida, although the groundwork for that problematisation had already been laid, as Derrida repeatedly says, by Freud (see Derrida, 1978, 203)) is not some kind of transcultural value, it has a specific resonance for the West. In effect, what is being said here is that the very 'act of empire' was what permanently contorted the notion of origin for the West – and therefore for the whole of the rest of the world. For we need again to be clear here: the imperial West set in motion, over several centuries, a huge series of disavowals about where the 'origin' might be found. How can we begin to list the evidence? We would have to look, first, at massively entrenched denials of the very existence of not only millions of people, but also of whole 'peoples' themselves. In the case of these peoples, not only their contemporary existence was denied but also their historical claim to credibility; they were reduced to the status of mythical inhabitants of empty lands.[20]

We would have to look, second, at the massive transportation of peoples from one land to another. The Middle Passage, the slave trade, is of course the most obvious; but in terms of a geopolitical view we would also have to take into account the whole long history of settlers, who may appear to have chosen their fate but who now appear to us also as transplanted figures, whose part in the ruse of history was again to obscure origins. We would have to look, third, at the backwash, at the impact of these developments on 'home' societies, and at what then happened to the sense of 'home'; for example, although few households in the West had slaves this makes in a sense no difference: when you consider the general impact of the concept of 'slave', its location within a general discursive economy, the question in for example eighteenth-century England of how one might treat a servant becomes fatally inflected by the question of how one might if only notionally treat someone according to a quite different concept and procedure, that of slavery, and how that expanded the limits of what kind of domination over another body one might have.[21]

These considerations, if they still appear reasonably close to questions raised by Soyinka's 'phallus of unorigin', might nonetheless appear rather distant from the other terms raised in the passage, but really they are not; for what the passage suggests is the idea of a Godhead, perhaps a destroyed Godhead, that has to do with a sense of inclusion and exclusion, and wherever inclusion and exclusion are now debated within the Western tradition this debate is inseparable from the history of slavery and empire. There is no such thing as pure difference, any more than there is such a thing as Derrida's fantasised abstraction of 'différance'. What there is instead is a complex opposition between the unilateral or monotheistic and the multiplicitous, an opposition which Soyinka goes on to detail:

> Of the lover of gore, invincible in battle, insatiable in love and carnage, the explorer, path-finder, protector of the forge and the creative hands, companion of the gourd whose crimson-misted sight of debauchery set him upon his own and he butchered them until the bitter cry pierced his fog of wine, stayed his hand and hung the sword, foolish like his dropped jaw; of the one who hanged and did not hang, who ascended on the llana to sky vaults and mastered the snake-tongued lightning and the stone of incandescence, long arms of the divine sling playing the random game of children, plucking houses trees and children like the unripe mango ... (Soyinka, 1970, 225)

What this discourse principally details is the multiplicitous and the 'becoming'; the important self-imposed task that Western criticism would appear to set itself would be the distinguishing within this discourse between the 'native' and the 'postcolonial'. In attempting to make that distinction, of course, a huge amount is at stake within the Western literary establishment, whom we may refer to, for the moment, and using what I suggest to be the displacement of Soyinka's terms, as 'the interpreters'.[22] Their relation to the 'native interpreters' who are the subject of Soyinka's book, however, will remain an ironic one, in which respect that relation exactly replicates (as Soyinka intends) the relation between the Western 'expert' (whose expertise hung closely with his amateurism) and the 'native guide' on whom he depended – for the necessary language to ground his anthropological speculation; for his attempt to simulate the act of 'tracking' in inhospitable terrain of which he understood nothing; in his attempt, for example, to conquer the far peaks of the world's mountain ranges, whereupon he would always find his 'tracks' already 'pre-tracked', already in a sense foreclosed by those for whom such 'adventures' were in fact 'habitats', with all the recourse that that implies.

It may appear that my speculations have now run a little wild of Soyinka's passage, but I think not for the whole question he is raising is of the nature of interpretation, and this is the gauntlet he is here throwing down; whether the Western critic or reader might be able to 'interpret' (in the sense of following references, dictionaries, encyclopaedias) or to regard the passage, the genealogy, the 'bible' as a spur to considering the question of interpretation in a new light. Because I believe the latter to be the more important, I will conclude this chapter with the rest of the passage:

> of the bi-sexed one that split himself into the river; of the parting of the fog and the retreat of the beginning, and the eternal war of the divining eyes, of the hundred and one eyes of lore, fore- and after-vision, of the eternal war of the first procedure with the long sickle head of chance, eternally mocking the pretensions of the bowl of plan, mocking lines of order in the ring of chaos; of the repulsive Scourge riding prurient on noontides of silent heat selective of victims, the avaricious one; of the one who stayed to tend the first fruits of the ginger of earth with passages of the wind around him and of the heat and the rain, and the marks of the moulting seasons ... (Soyinka, 1970, 225)

# XI Diaspora and Exile, Arrival Addicted

> ... it was best to concentrate on getting to Jamaica, away from the threats and madness of England. (Joan Riley, *The Unbelonging*)

> [Mother] refused to allow the word 'immigrant' to be used about Father, since in her eyes it applied only to illiterate tiny men with downcast eyes and mismatched clothes. (Hanif Kureishi, *Love in a Blue Time*)

> Praise had bled my lines white of any more anger,
> and snow had inducted me into white fellowships,
> while Calibans howled down the barred streets of an empire
> that began with Caedmon's raceless dew, and is ending
> in the alleys of Brixton, burning like Turner's ships.
> (Derek Walcott, *Midsummer*, in *Collected Poems 1948–1984*)

Chelva Kanaganayakam, in an influential essay called 'Exiles and Expatriates', claims that 'to be an expatriate or an exile is not to inhabit a void. It is not ... to choose the artistic freedom and anonymity afforded by the metropolis. It is, rather, to be granted a special insight, a vision not available to the insider' (Kanaganayakam, 1996, 213), and then quotes – wildly out of context – a passage from Nuruddin Farah's 'Homing in on the Pigeon':

> Indeed, somewhere between fleeing and arriving a refugee is born, who lives in a country too amorphous to be favoured with a name but which, for the sake of convenience, we may label as one delivered out of the womb of sublime hope, a country whose language is imbued with the rhetoric of future visions. (Farah, 1994, 5)

Alongside these optimistic comments, this valorisation of a 'special insight', perhaps we might place the official estimate of the world's refugee population in a typical year in the late twentieth century (1980). That figure is 15,105,000.[1] I wonder whether all of them then – or now in 1999, starving on Albanian mountainsides or dying of dysentery in Zairean camps – feel that they have been granted a 'special insight', or what they might have to say, if granted a voice by permission of their captors/rescuers, about 'sublime hope' or the 'rhetoric of future visions'.

Such critical crassness, of course, not only dismantles the real world of pain and dislocation; it similarly crucially misjudges and misrecognises the fictions produced on the huge terrain encompassed by the refugee, the exile, the diasporic. I am not going to attempt to provide artificial boundaries to this field, nor am I going to try to effect distinctions between the key terms, since through an inalienable historical necessity they overlap at all points.[2] I shall most usually use the term 'diasporic' rather than its semi-cognates in what follows simply because it covers a broader variety of experience and text and does not attempt the impossible task of distinguishing between, for example, the refugee and the exile, or (the bane of immigration officials the world over) between the political and the economic migrant.

Hanif Kureishi's *The Black Album* is a novel that, in spite of its own 'hip' bleakness, provides a rich compendium of diasporic themes. From the very beginning, in conversation between the protagonist Shahid and the spokesman for Islamic purity, Riaz, the issue is of 'losing oneself in England' and the various meanings that might come to have (Kureishi, 1995, 7). This is further mediated through the text's engagement with other diasporic texts, and particularly those of Rushdie. The plot hinges on the role that Rushdie's *Satanic Verses* comes to play in defining political correctness; as Riaz says at the beginning, *Midnight's Children* might be seen as politically acceptable – 'I found it accurate about Bombay', he comments, although on quite what this judgement is based remains obscure – but with *The Satanic Verses* 'he has gone too far' (9).

There is the possibility in *The Black Album* of everybody having gone, as it were, 'too far': too far from home (Shahid's family are, with a nice flourish, travel agents), too far in revolutionary zeal, too far, in the case of Shahid's elder brother Chili, into a realm of addiction that bears heavily also, as we shall see, on the fate of the diasporic. Or, as we also see, there is the possibility of going too far in a different direction: Shahid has surprising fantasies of joining the British National Party and becoming a 'swaggering racist':

> I argued ... why can't I be a racist like everyone else? Why do I have to miss out on that privilege? Why is it only me who has to be good? Why can't I swagger around pissing on others for being inferior? I began to turn into one of them. I was becoming a monster. (11)

His cultural heritage is, after all, curiously skewed. From his Uncle Asif (of all names – and one that recurs elsewhere in Kureishi) he has inherited a small library of classics of European thought and literature – 'Joad, Laski and Popper, and studies of Freud, along with fiction by Maupassant, Henry James, and the Russians' (20) – while the institution of 'higher learning' he attends reflects the uncertainties and ambiguities of assimilation:

> The college was a cramped Victorian building, an old secondary school, twenty minutes' walk away. It was sixty per cent black and Asian, with an ineffective library and no sports facilities. Its reputation was less in the academic area but more for gang rivalries, drugs, thieving and political violence. It was said that college reunions were held in Wandsworth Prison. (24)

The condition of exile resonates throughout the text. The white lecturer Andrew Brownlow (again, Kureishi is interested in a complexly Dickensian habit of naming) is from the British upper class but, according to one astonished student, 'he tol' them to get lost. He hated them all, his own class, his parents – everything. He come to this college to help us, the underprivileged niggers and wogs an' margin people' (32). Chili, with his smart cars and smarter suits, never reads, but for a bet has embarked on a classic text of internal exile, *One Hundred Years of Solitude*.[3] There is an uncle, Tipoo, who lurks in the shadows and is probably schizophrenic (we might remember that in Dangarembga's *Nervous Conditions*, we are told that blacks are incapable of suffering from mental illness (see Dangarembga, 1988, 201)). Shahid, who is trying to write, completes a first story, called 'Paki Wog Fuck Off Home', but it is destroyed by his mother, who incarnates the fearful disavowal of the immigrant:

> More than anything she hated any talk of race or racism. Probably she had suffered some abuse and contempt. But her father had been a doctor; everyone – politicians, generals, journalists, police chiefs – came to their house in Karachi. The idea that anyone might treat her with disrespect was insupportable. Even

> when Shahid vomited and defecated with fear before going to school, or when he returned with cuts, bruises and his bag slashed with knives, she behaved as if so appalling an insult couldn't exist. And so she turned away from him. What she knew was too much for her. (Kureishi, 1995, 73)

It is perhaps this diagnosis before which the reader of *The Black Album* is principally arrested: the intensity of the fragmentation of family and 'community' in the face of unrelenting, insensate hatred, and the consequent resistance to an insupportable knowledge. What kind of knowledge can be obtained, and to whom might it be relayed, under diasporic conditions? A knowledge, one might say, that is forever under pressure; one that is forced through the coils of self-consciousness, certainly, but whose processes must always be intertwined with disavowal, with an abiding incredulity about the extent to which the 'self' must remain 'not known' – not known by the outside world, of course, but also in the end not known even on the inner screen, forever screened out in order to survive.

Later in the book a character points out that there is no respite from these kinds of prejudice to knowledge to be afforded by the contemplation of 'home'; in Pakistan, in the subcontinent in general, 'the lunatics are running the asylum' (Kureishi, 1995, 251). And here we touch on the heart of the diasporic, which is that there is, in the end, no heart at all. As Stuart Hall puts it, there is no 'fixed origin to which we can make some final and absolute Return':

> The past continues to speak to us..But it no longer addresses us as a simple, factual 'past', since our relation to it, like the child's relation to the mother, is always-already 'after the break'. It is always constructed through memory, fantasy, narrative and myth. Cultural identities are the points of identification, the unstable points of identification or suture, which are made, within the discourses of history and culture. Not an essence but a *positioning*. Hence, there is always a politics of identity, a politics of position, which has no absolute guarantee in an unproblematic, transcendental 'law of origin'. (Hall, 1990, 226)

Hall is clearly right about the importance of establishing this discourse of 'positionality' in any consideration of the diasporic, but in other respects his analysis does not really go far enough. The 'child's relation to the mother', for example, cannot be fully revealed by treating it as 'after the break', as though it were again an aftermathic effect, a question of the 'postal'; on the contrary it is a matter of constant pressing urgency, and recurs principally in the form of the 'mother-of-separation',[4] the figure here for a culture that continues actively to patrol its boundaries, to resist appeals for nurture or tolerance, that time after time confronts the 'child-as-parasite' with a redoubled withdrawal and absence, one that empties the selfhood, that destroys history, genealogy and the body. Similarly the absence of a 'law of origin' needs to be recast in more active mode; what is confronted in the diasporic is a new, a replacement law, the 'law of the orphan' as I have been outlining it in this book and elsewhere: the certainty that all that has made this condition possible is now dead, that there can indeed be no return but also that even the fantasy of return only serves to highlight the terrors of the present. For Chili in particular, both 'sides' are damned:

> You see them, our people, the Pakis, in their dirty shops, surly, humourless, their fat sons and ugly daughters watching you, taking the money. The prices are extortionate, because they open all hours. The new Jews, everyone hates them. In a few years the kids will kick their parents in the teeth. Sitting in some crummy shop, it won't be enough for them. (Kureishi, 1995, 201)

Chili's response to this refusal of nurture, this impossibility of succour in a conflicted 'state', is what that reaction will always be in one shape or another: addiction.

But the most consummately appalling of British texts of the diasporic still remains Joan Riley's agonising masterpiece, *The Unbelonging*, a novel that has never received its due share of praise or criticism because, I am certain, the materials in which it deals are too painful for the reader, whatever his or her cultural positioning. The protagonist Hyacinth has been sent from Jamaica to live with her father and his new wife in England. Her 'unbelonging' has already begun – there has never been any 'alter-native', any other subject positioning, any other home – and it filters into and colours her memories in particular of Jamaica and her early childhood, memories that she uses as a refuge from the cold, grey, violent world in which she now finds – or rather, loses – herself. The victim of racist insult and injury at school and on the streets, she is also the victim of abuse – verbal, physical and sexual – by her father, so she clings to these 'memories' – like lianas:

> Lianas trailing in sparkling green pools
> tempted our childish minds to adventure,

> Gullies stretching forbidden and deep
> calling us to delve in their mysteries,
> Sky blue and smiling beckoning forward
> unclouded minds to reach for perfection ...
>
> Unclouded minds saw unclouded visions
> then we were young, in a land of our own.
> (Riley, 1985, 7)

But for Hyacinth the only question for the present is of how to choose between two different kinds of rejection, how to find a self that can emerge from between the crushing rocks of insult and abuse, although to call this a 'choice' would be to succumb to a volitional logic which is far indeed from Riley's text. The matter is crystallised when, removed at last from her father's 'care', she ends up temporarily in a reception centre:

> 'They don't like neaga here'. Her father's words came unbidden and unwelcome to her ears. She would have liked to blot them out, but in her heart she knew the truth of it. She had been in England over four years and always she had seen it and now, at the reception centre, she was forced to live with it. 'All these white people trying so hard to hide their hate', she thought sadly. 'Yet they could kill you because you are different from them'. She always had to remind herself that they had not hurt her yet. Of course, they let her know she was not wanted, did not belong, but at least they were not violent like black people. (69)

Yes, her father does have knowledge. He has precisely the kind of diasporic knowledge that is combined with incredulity and that, in his case at least – or so the text suggests to us – has meant that he has internalised lack of worth, absence of dignity to the point where, like Cholly Breedlove in *The Bluest Eye*, an ultimate abjection constantly beckons. Where then, *is* the 'heart'? Held here, it would seem, only in absence, as Hyacinth's later history suggests. It is here at the ambiguously named 'reception centre' that she learns a lesson that she will be unable to forget, a lesson instilled under conditions of trauma, namely that there will indeed be no 'reception'. There will be no ceremony of welcome to institution, family or state, there will be no 'reception' of the signals she is trying to transmit – or at least tries to transmit until she finally and even more deeply understands that their transmission is pointless. There will in the end be no 'centre' of any kind, only a hopeless whirling between devalorised points of the compass, an oscillation on a map whose geographics have been already erased, overwritten with a new and more violent text. 'They had not hurt her yet': in this deferral of harm the fate of the diasporic is summarised. Of course the rejection and exclusion by the host culture may be deferred, withheld; but that withholding only makes it the more effective as a weapon for subjugation, as a device for scooping out the heart, for replacing it with a trembling absence, an absence of self – and it is this very absence of self that Hyacinth also finally realises in the phrase 'like black people', a phrase in which she signifies her inability to resist summing up an entire people – in a sense her people – under a single stereotyping banner.

Without succumbing to the delusory and damaging Eurocentric logic of the 'theoretical framework', we can nonetheless continue to think about the series of parallels between the diasporic condition and the problematic of maturation suggested by Hall, but in order to develop further the notion of the 'law of the orphan'. What might this law be, how might it operate – we might add, at whose service?, but the answer is too obvious. This law, as I would try further to delineate it, is based on the impossibility of return and thus, more importantly, on the impossibility of secure knowledge. It spreads into an absence of grounds for self-definition; and it embraces a wide emptying of the heart, such that unwelcome fantasies will take root there and begin, in their turn, a rhizomatic spread. The law of the orphan forbids resistance, for there is no ground on which resistance might take its stance; within this law there is no way of transcending dependence, only of finding a different footing for it as each successive foothold proves untrustworthy. 'A parent who is able to formulate and discuss a coherent narrative of the past and hence become in touch with pain', says Caroline Case in an important unpublished lecture on child abuse, 'will be able to stop the past repeating itself'. There can be no doubt that this is true, or in fact that it depicts, in its assignation of narrative purpose, one of the major functions of the literary, which is to do with a dealing with repetition that brings it immediately and inevitably into contact with trauma and aftermath; but it also depicts the very structure that the 'postcolonial literary', especially in the form of the diasporic, comes to doubt.

For who or what would the parent be who, under these conditions, could formulate a 'coherent narrative of the past'? Notice that such a narrative would not need to be 'true', whatever that might mean; it would need only to be coherent. But this possibility of coherence is fractured in the diasporic condition at every moment:

it is fractured, perhaps most emblematically, by the *name* – not merely the naming of individuals, crucial though we have already seen that to be in various contexts, but the naming of streets, of cities, of emblems, of heroes, of brands, the whole apparatus and panoply of the environing culture whose deep imbrication with the practices and profits of slavery and empire constantly surround, across a whole range of transnational and transcolonial situations, the exile in the 'host' nation.[5] The imperial narrative of history relied, to be sure, upon a certain kind of coherence, but it was a coherence based on rewriting and eradication; it was essentially complicit in an exercise of global power and one of its principal means of supporting and enforcing that power was through the stereotyping of ethnic groups. Hyacinth comes across this again when she attempts to find herself a 'reading position' in British culture, a position that would in some way address both her maturation and her racial position. She discovers

> romance, found it between the pages of a stack of old Mills and Boon books that Auntie Susan had been about to throw away. Hyacinth loved the stories from the start, reading them from cover to cover, finding it hard to put them down, to concentrate on anything else. Now her lonely nights were peopled with tall, dark, handsome strangers, Spanish caballeros with warm brown eyes, romantic and intense Frenchmen. Sometimes in her secret fantasies she would be swept off her feet by a rich, passionate stranger and taken to live in his wild, remote castle. Always her hair would be blonde and flowing, her skin pale and white. (Riley, 1985, 78)

Maybe it is only a petty parapraxis, but the notion of a finding 'between the pages' is nonetheless significant – not 'in the pages' or 'between the covers', we notice, but 'between the pages', as though Hyacinth's reading position has to be always 'between', the position of the 'margin people', of somebody who cannot look at the pages, the lines, direct but is forever caught in a 'floating world', a world not of privilege or 'special insight' but of terror, unable to alight, unable to occupy any position that could be sanctioned by the dominant culture, unable to achieve free access even – or perhaps especially – to the materiality of the book.[6] The diasporic terrain, which we may also ally to the territorialisation of the exile, or the geography of the refugee, is also and inevitably one that cannot be fully written or read, it is a land of 'secrets', of the uncanny, where any reading is curiously doubled, falls again under the rule of the 'text instead'.

The whole of Britain, for Hyacinth, is a 'text instead', bracketed and bound by her fantasies of Jamaica, and what makes *The Unbelonging* so extraordinary is, after Hyacinth's entry into adult life has been destroyed by the psychological residue of her abused 'orphanage', the brief and searing account of her return 'home':

> She would have liked to deny that she was in the right place, but the familiarity of weathered wood and corroded zinc refused to be dismissed. Her breakfast churned alarmingly inside her stomach, the bumpy ride and the shock pouring the salt of sickness into her mouth. The smell was like a physical blow, dredging up smells and tastes from long, half-buried memories; and she did not know whether heat or fear caused the sweat to trickle between her shoulder blades. (Riley, 1985, 136)

This, then, is a crisis of denial, as it is indistinguishably a moment of trauma; the odour of death is in the air, the death of half-buried memories, the death of fantasy, the new death of the self whose structure has been founded on this unstable, and now destroyed, site. At this point the recurrent phrase around which the entire novel – and Hyacinth's life – has been structured floods back into her mind, a phrase, ironically, from Laurie Lee's *Cider with Rosie*: 'Incest flourished where the roads were bad' (see, e.g., 49). In that phrase and its specific provenance is summarised a whole history of the postcolonial. Hyacinth too has roads – or rather paths – on her mind as she continues with her disastrous journey into the place that cannot own to her, or any other, name, a place that challenges memory and the safe construction of the self:

> This was not the place she remembered. ... She could never remember a path so long, so choked with dust and rubbish. Every time the wind stirred a piece of faded newspaper, or rustled one of the dry pathetic bushes, she would tense. Her whole body shook, the shivers starting deep inside and spreading everywhere. (137)

This traumatised reaction, the text tells us, evidently parodies Hyacinth's exile of her own sexual nature, her own orgasm: in her condition of removal from her own body, her 'location', this further removal of fantasy triggers an inverted reaction which leaves her with nowhere to go except, as the very ending of the novel confirms, back into her 'cave', back into a fantasy that now runs directly counter to the appalling knowledge she has gained. Although the ending of the text does not say as much, the most likely interpretation would be to see this as a psychotic reaction, as a decisive move away from the real into a realm where all 'knowledge' is suspended, the necessary consequence of a fractured and ruined personal and cultural history, the *débâcle* as Jamaica Kincaid puts it, or the *reductio ad absurdum* always inherent in the diasporic.[7]

In *The Black Album* the diasporic fantasy, or rather collection of fantasies, is already sidelined, reduced to a series of tantalisingly glimpsed sideshows but never entertained as an enveloping whole. In *The Unbelonging* the fantasy is all too present, indeed it frames the text, but its relation to the real undergoes a disastrous and traumatic transformation. In Meera Syal's *Anita and Me*, the fantasy actually appears to go through a process of realisation, for this is a 'comic' novel in the broadest sense of the term, with a 'happy ending'. Meena, the first-person narrator, ends up in a position of transcendence, floating above the English Midlands village of her 'home' and observing other lives from a position of presumed superiority, after which 'it was time to let go and I floated back down into my body which, for the first time ever, fitted me to perfection and was all mine' (Syal, 1996, 326).

As a consequence of this achievement of integration, so apparently different from Hyacinth's experience, she is able to break the envious dependence on her white friend Anita that has been the linchpin of the narrative; but we need, I suggest, to look more closely at what this fantasised transcendence of the diasporic condition truly implies, and here the text reveals itself to be more complex. As a preliminary example, Meena's entry into her own body is undercut a mere two pages later in the context of a remark she makes *apropos* of her relations' stereotypical wish for her to become a doctor: 'I already knew', she says, 'I wanted nothing to do with bodies and breakdowns' (328). The trauma that disrupts Hyacinth's life is also somewhere here in Meena's, albeit disavowed – as such material so frequently is – by the author: the immediate occasion of her break-up with Anita has centred on a scenario in which Meena sees her in a sexual encounter, and although the connection is never drawn the signs of her 'entry' into her physical body, stimulated but disavowed in this perilous context, remain deeply ambiguous (see 310–11).

Most of all, the account of Meena's experiences of racial inferiority and insult is subjugated to a fairy-tale version of the structure of life in the village of Tollington where, for almost the whole novel, the reader is meant to think that her family are the only non-whites in the village. There is, to be sure, a semi-derelict 'Big House' whose inhabitants nobody has ever seen; the myth has grown around it, as we might expect to be the case, that it is inhabited by a witch, and on the night of the disaster that precipitates the end of the narrative Meena finds herself unavoidably investigating this myth in the attempt to find help for a supposedly drowned child.

The house, we are not surprised to discover, turns out to be a Gothic relic, 'a veritable time warp; old, clumsy wooden furniture cluttered every available bit of floor space, ancient oil paintings and tapestries adorned the walls and the floors were dull wooden parquet which gave off a faint lavender smell' (Syal, 1996, 316). Shades here of Naipaul's Hanuman House; but the Mills and Boon flavour of mystery is deepened when the 'man of the house' appears:

> He must have been the former mine owner, he must have owned a lot of something as he walked erect and slowly, exuding an air of authority and gravitas, but the crags and jowls of his face showed he was also connected to the earth, a miner made good perhaps. He had a workman's face and philosopher's eyes, and in his shovel-sized hands he held the lead of a jumping spaniel. But all of this became secondary when he finally spoke. '*Chup Kar Kure, Thahar Jao Ik Minut!* Get me a torch, Mireille'. (317)

As the narrator aptly says, 'my miracle was complete' (317). All is signified in the name: Harinder P. Singh is also 'Arry, the Sikh is also a thoroughly English mine-owner, albeit – like all the others – a failed one. But this fantasy sealing of contradictions spreads much further than that. Meena has known already that her family's small house can be viewed from the 'Big House', but here the fear of surveillance is conveniently neutralised as it emerges that the gaze that has been fixed on her family for so long has in fact been a benevolently Indian gaze. If social climbing is in the air, why, the figure of Harinder/'Arry neatly solves it with his 'air of authority' and his 'workman's face', a man who unites in his curiously Lawrentian person all the attributes of wealth and power and of contact with the earth. If we are thinking of the language issue that fractures Meena's family, again the problem is solved: 'The Big House boss was an Indian man, as Indian as my father, and he spoke Punjabi with a village twang to his dog' (317).

The fact, of course, that it is his *dog* to whom he speaks Punjabi might, among other signals, alert us to the extraordinarily shaky foundations of this vision of plenitude, but the text will have none of such political doubts; instead it seeks to resolve them in a superfluity, an excess of the word that would be designed to allay any diasporic fears. For as Meena is seated to recover from her shock, she finds that she can

> make out that we were in some kind of study as a vast mahogany desk sat in a corner, piled high with papers and letters, some of them air mail blue, and an ancient typewriter sat in the middle of the mess, a half-finished memo in its jaws. And then I saw the books, thousands of them lining the walls from top to bottom, an armoury of paperbacks, hard covers, some leather-bound with cracked spines, others cheap and cheerful off an airport stand. Every one of them wore their dog ears and thumbed covers with pride because this was proof that they had all been read and appreciated. (317–18)

Once again, all the relevant diasporic contradictions are sealed. Here we have (reasonably) up-to-date technology (the airmail letters) and ancient tradition (the archaic typewriter) neatly cohabiting, privacy and seclusion no longer in conflict with international communication, the contradictions between the domesticated world of 'small things' and the vast world of intercontinental communication resolved as though no gulf separated them. Neither is there any longer any problem with cultural or class difference: ancient leather-bound tomes sit happily alongside paperbacks, all of culture is sealed into one big happy family, equivalent in use value. Mahogany, a 'transported' wood, sets the final seal of approval;[8] here the world of the 'native' and the world of the host culture are no longer separated, and all coexists under the sign of an expansive wealth. It is, finally, Mireille ('wonder'? 'mirror'?) who tells the story of how she and her husband came to be here, a story of extraordinary improbability but involving all the necessary signals of exemption and privilege (Cambridge, Paris, 'his mad uncle, some maharajah type' (319)), but the significant thing is not the story itself but the fact that it is told by somebody who – being French – is magically outside the conflicts, quite athwart the ancient prejudices and deprivations of Tollington, somebody who, if not quite a witch, certainly fulfils the fairy godmother's role in relation to Meena and her wish to be 'discovered' and rescued from a life of silence.

Such a rescue would be, obviously, a freeing from a life marked and marred by external incomprehension; it would also be a life freed from whatever it is in the novel that is represented by Anita, and here we come upon some confusions. To cut through these, I suggest that what Anita represents in the novel is addiction, and that brings us again, though by a different route, to the addicted 'heart' of the diasporic. This is not to say that the character of Anita is practically 'addicted' to any of the more obvious substances, but rather that her life bids fair – because of her deprived childhood, because of the limitation of her expectations – to be, as it were, 'naturally addicted' in the sense that she will be unable to break loose of 'controls' that are well beyond her own will to change. In this respect too one might see *Anita and Me* as a novel enshrining a peculiar bad faith, as a text of displacement and projection, the figure of Anita as an aspect of Meena herself, the aspect that would remain bound down by the diasporic condition, that would be unable to achieve the ('nervous') condition of dreamlike transcendence that characterises Meena's own final apotheosis.

What wider evidence might we find textually of the connection between these conditions of addiction and the postcolonial – beyond, that is, the blindingly obvious correlations that afflict First Nation people the world over? There are, for example, John Banville's protagonists in *Mefisto* and *The Book of Evidence*, addicted to hard drugs or alcohol, emblematically if ambivalently responsive to the 'Irish question', answering it with the pure symptom. There is the anorexia that characterises Dangarembga's *Nervous Conditions* – addiction is indeed in a sense, or perhaps in two senses, a 'nervous condition' – and that relates closely to the 'disease of Englishness' that kills at least one of her characters and threatens the lives of all the others. In Gurnah's *Paradise* Mohammed the mendicant, admittedly a bit-part character but nonetheless one with an important role, lives a life that has been ruined by 'the weed' (see Gurnah, 1994, 10). The fate of Simon, and hence of Joe and Kerewin in Hulme's *The Bone People*, is already determined by the heroin addict who has been Simon's previous – and perhaps murderous – 'carer', and in *The Bone People* this has a curious connection with the theme of the 'last of the cannibals'. In Kureishi's *The Black Album*, as we have seen, the major alternative to the regime of purity preached by Riaz and uncertainly embraced by Shahid is the addiction which destroys Chili: 'Maybe addict's my name now' (Kureishi, 1995, 255), he says, in a supreme trope on the realm of the diasporic, dependent on an alien blood system, deprived of nurture, deprived of the 'name of nature', renamed in a desperate search for an alternative identity – for addiction is always in an intimate relation with naming, as it also forms itself as the only alternative to a '(m)oral law' in turn dependent on a history perceived as unreliable, the soul of prejudice.

What does addiction produce? The sense of an unassailable alternative world, but also the terror of the fading of that world. Shahid has this experience too, in contact with Riaz's addictive politics:

> The problem was, when he was with his friends their story compelled him. But when he walked out, like someone leaving a cinema, he found the world to be more subtle and inexplicable. He knew, too, that stories were made up by men and women; they could not be true or false, for they were exercises in that most magnificent but unreliable capacity, the imagination, which William Blake called 'the divine body in every man'. Yet his friends would admit no splinter of imagination into their body of belief, for that would poison all, rendering their conviction human, aesthetic, fallible. (Kureishi, 1995, 133)

The addictive conflictual regime of Blake's 'Poison Tree' would seem apposite here (see Blake, 1966, 218), as would the whole history of the means by which an imperial regime made other people dependent upon – addicted them to – a 'different' textuality – as Naipaul tells us of Mr Biswas:

> He bought elementary manuals of science and read them; nothing happened; he only became addicted to elementary manuals of science. He bought the seven expensive volumes of *Hawkins' Electrical Guide*, made rudimentary compasses, buzzers and door-bells, and learned to wind an armature. Beyond that he could not go. Experiments became more complex, and he didn't know where in Trinidad he could find the equipment mentioned so casually by Hawkins. (Naipaul, 1961, 79)

Addiction prohibits satisfaction; or rather, it is that which is born from the impossibility of satisfaction. We are dealing here in a ceaseless disappointment, a limitation of hopes and expectations, as we are in the drug narratives of Irvine Welsh – in *Marabou Stork Nightmares* even salvation, such as it is, comes in the form of 'another' drug, ecstasy, which is supposed to offer magical relief from its more evidently malign counterparts (see Welsh, 1995, 236ff.). What is important to establish here is how and in what terms dealings with the diasporic and dealings with addiction meet: in terms, for example, of what Kenneth Ramchand has notably described as the 'terrified consciousness' (Ramchand, 1969, 9). They meet on the deterritorialised terrain of the displaced self.

But this is not to say that these meetings will always be under the sign of deprivation. We might also consider the relation between diaspora and addiction in the figure of Zulma, Chili's wife in *The Black Album*:

> She came from a prominent, land-owning Karachi family and, like other such types, lived part of the year in Pakistan and the rest in England. In Karachi she zipped around the camel-carts and pot-holes in an imported red Fiat Uno, a Hermès scarf knotted around her head. In London she went to her friends' houses and pursued the shopping, gossiping and general trouble-making-in-other-families she enjoyed so much. She was light-skinned, beautiful, Zulma, but never beautiful enough: it took her two days to prepare for a party. She brushed her hair, of which she had sufficient for three people, with a hundred strokes and washed it only in rain-water. At the first hint of a shower Zulma would shake Tipoo awake and have him dash into the garden with bowls and saucepans. (Kureishi, 1995, 85)

'Never beautiful enough'; 'light-skinned'. These terms, obviously, are not racially innocent. What would it mean to be addicted to a fantasy of a body that can never be 'achieved' (although admittedly Zulma's feelings about that would undoubtedly be different from those of Riley's Hyacinth)? What does it mean to live in or with a culture that 'lays down the law' and in the context of which one has the choice of assimilation or rejection or, in the bitter interstices of that rarely willed decision, of a psychopathy of addiction? One thing it might mean would be that one could attain to a knowledge (albeit inevitably flawed) of what Gray refers to as global 'narco-democracy',[9] and it is the implications of such a global regime of addiction which can lead us into the issues of global politics in general that I will talk about in the next, and last, chapter.

# XII Delocalisation and the Alibi

Scepticism was formed in Edinburgh two hundred years ago by David Hume and Adam Smith. They said: 'Let's take religion to the black man, but we won't really believe it'. It's the cutting edge of trade. (Irvine Welsh, *Marabou Stork Nightmares*)

In the late twentieth century there is no shelter – for corporations or for governments – from the global gale of creative destruction. (John Gray, *False Dawn*)

the Chrysler stirs but does not produce cotton
the Jupiter purrs but does not produce bread
(Edward Brathwaite, *The Arrivants*)

To begin in what may seem an unlikely place: R.K. Narayan's *Waiting for the Mahatma* is a comic novel, a limpid novel that charts the somnambulistic progress of an anomic young man both towards marriage with his object of desire and towards involvement with Gandhi's peace movement; the two are entwined, and their relation puts humorous questions against people's motives for involving themselves in political action. The novel ends at the point where Gandhi is killed, with the marriage still not consummated; the postponement and deferral signified by this ending that is not quite an ending evidently encourage the reader to look again at what and what has not been achieved along the road to independence in the subcontinent.

Behind this, however, another text looks out; a text that has much more to do with the passionate anger of a colony involved in a war that is not of its own making, an essentially 'non-Indian' war which nevertheless has results of the direst kind:

'There is no food left in these villages', he cried passionately. 'There is no one to look after them; who cares for them? Who is

> there to help them out of their difficulties? Everyone is engaged in this war. The profiteer has hoarded all the grain beyond the reach of these growers. The war machine buys it at any price. It's too big a competitor for these poor folk'. (Narayan, 1955, 89)

The analysis is perhaps a familiar one, but that does not mean it is unworthy of repetition. The meagre resources of the peasant grower, valued highly though they are by the international market – here in time of war, but the point is a more general one – fail constantly to deliver any dividend; they are expropriated by the 'profiteer', who is intimately and suspiciously allied with the 'war machine', and the benefits fall to him, resulting in yet further destitution for the poorest of the poor, for the agricultural masses, for the 'folk'.[1] The story, I suggest, repeats itself time and time again through the literature we call 'postcolonial'; it is a subtext, a 'text instead' craving for our attention, always on the verge of obliteration by more 'heroic' narratives, by stories that form themselves into redemptive patterns, by plots that will be valorised by the West.

We can recognise in Narayan, despite the comic tone, something of an ironic version of the epic sweep of Brecht; we can also hear the clanking of the Deleuzian war machine.[2] But this is, of course, coming through the grid of a different economic positioning:

> [The trees] are going into the making of ships and rifles and bridges and whatnot, all of which are to be used for the destruction of this world. They are going into a war which we are being forced to fight because Britain chose to drag us into it. We shouldn't have to strip our forests for this task. It's going far away, to far off countries, and the money you are getting is a puffed up, illusory currency, which will lose its value soon. Don't supply these materials for the war, it will take centuries for us to grow all this timber again. (Narayan, 1955, 107)

Evidence suggests that the timber can never be grown again; it suggests that the destruction of the forests in the name of 'far off countries' continues apace; and it suggests that we have wildly underestimated the knock-on effects of deforestation.[3] It is perhaps also worth contemplating again, with mixed feelings, the shortage of paper that will no doubt in due course accompany the destruction of paper's source.

What is lost here in the loss of the trees can also be assimilated to the loss of a language, the loss of a signature, the loss of a material resource that is also the guarantee of a certain *habitus*. Postcolonial writing, which in many cases necessarily manifests a specific awareness of its own material means of production and dissemination, is particularly aware of the *precariousness* of writing, and still more of naming in a realm where 're-naming' in the service of the other (the re-naming of the orphan for a 'different' family) is the law. In Keneally's *The Playmaker* we are told that the purpose of a particular bush expedition is 'to vivify and transform – perhaps with a new name – one of these beings *ab origine*' (Keneally, 1987, 162). The 'being *ab origine*', of course, is the native Australian; but it can be seen to refer also to a general move to 're-naming from the origin', the removal, for example, of children from their 'aboriginal' parents, and also to the re-naming of the 'location' in the service of imperial expansion and control.

There would, of course, be those who would see in this series of acts of re-naming a positive hope for the future. Bhabha writes – sliding as elsewhere from 'location' to 'locution' – of a 'space of translation' (Bhabha, 1994, 25), but I would argue that this is precisely a space the exorbitation of which would merely allow the movements of global undifferentiation free range. More important to me seems the securing of a specific notion of *untranslatability*; the fixing of a boundary beyond which the strange, the uncanny remains, not only unconquered but also free to haunt the colonisers' illusions of coherence. It is in this fashion, I suggest, that George Lamming's famous announcement that English 'is a West Indian language' (Lamming, 1960, 36) needs to be read: not as a simple linear counter-imperialism but as a move deliberately to 'unsettle', in all senses of that term, to force expropriation into a question – not a question it is capable of asking about itself, but a question that might nonetheless return to haunt it even after it thinks that all resistance has been crushed. Would it be possible to *empty*, to drain the centre, in the way that so many former colonies are now menaced by threats of draining, of emptying, of 'cleansing'?

Theorists of various kinds have been in the business for quite a long time of trying to finesse the economic and linguistic robbery that lies at the root of these phenomena; for example, Chantal Zabus argues at some length that notions of 'translation' need to be replaced by the concept of 'relexification' (Zabus, 1991, 101–55), but her argument falls at the first hurdle because it supposes, rather like Bakhtinian theory, two discrete languages as the poles between which such a process might operate; one has only to look at the relation between, for instance, Scots and English to see that such a polarisation is impossible. More to the point are Achebe's reflections on the power of the word and its relation to the processes of globalisation in *Anthills of the Savannah*. There is a sense in which the whole novel is structured around the conflict between languages: between, for example, the power of the traditional proverb and the power of westernised language ('I don't quite get you, Professor. Please cut out the proverbs, if you don't mind' (Achebe, 1987, 19)), or around the power/impotence of the journalist and of the newspaper in a controlled and censored state. But what is crucial in Achebe is that this is at all points linked directly to the wider exercise of economic power, as in the case of the Western 'visitor' who

> began reading His Excellency and his subjects a lecture on the need for the country to maintain its present (quite unpopular, needless to say) levels of foreign debt servicing currently running at slightly more than fifty-one per-cent of total national export earnings. Why? As a *quid pro quo* for increased American aid in surplus grains for our drought provinces! (Achebe, 1987, 78)

At this point we can begin to realise that *Anthills of the Savannah* is an uncanny, a secret book, a text with a crypt; it consists of what we might call a 'cover story', a 'text instead', and a deeper narrative that cannot find its way into the light of day, and yet the two are linked in the most intimate of ways. The outer story, the carapace, has crucially to do with the notion of the 'rain-maker'; but all the while as discussions about the feasibility and cultural and political status of such activities continue a quite different story of drought, a story in which it is allied to foreign expropriation, to the economic ruination of the state, is being told. The moment at which we are offered various versions of the 'origin of the present crisis' gives us an opportunity to inspect a number of diagnoses of what is hidden behind the symptom:

> The prime failure of this government began also to take on a clearer meaning for him. It can't be the massive corruption though its scale and pervasiveness are truly intolerable; it isn't the subservience to foreign manipulation, degrading as it is; it isn't even this second-class, hand-me-down capitalism, ludicrous and doomed; nor is it the damnable shooting of striking railway-workers and demonstrating students and the destruction and banning thereafter of independent unions and cooperatives. It is the failure of our rulers to re-establish vital inner links with the poor and dispossessed of this country, with the bruised heart that throbs painfully at the core of the nation's being. (Achebe, 1987, 141)

That 'failure', certainly, is central to Achebe's diagnosis of the condition of the postcolonial African state; but the reader may also be permitted to continue to entertain the plethora of other factors here cited, perhaps especially the notion that capitalism, *at least* in the form in which it has been handed down to Africa and also, we may want to say, in the forms in which it has been imposed in Russia and Eastern Europe, is 'doomed', an already-given failure that nonetheless will never be admitted to because to do so would be to threaten the validity of the current apparatus of world domination, namely the International Monetary Fund (IMF) and the World Bank.[4]

The depredations of the IMF and the World Bank, their insistence on a single model of development and ruthless erosion of gestures towards independent statehood, have been too well documented for me to attempt to repeat them here. Here, however, is a further brief excerpt from Anne McClintock's excellent essay 'The Angel of Progress', which also substantiates many of the doubts about the 'postcolonial' which I have myself been suggesting in earlier chapters:

> The US's 'development' myth has had a grievous impact on global ecologies. By 1989, the World Bank had $225 billion in commitments to poorer countries, on condition that they, in turn, endure the purgatory of 'structural adjustment', export their way to 'progress', cut government spending on education and social services (with the axe falling most cruelly on women), devalue their currencies, remove trade barriers, and raze their forests to pay their debts.

Under the banner of the world's dominant nations, the World Bank has

> engineered one ecological disaster after another: the Indonesian Transmigrasi programme, the Amazonian Grande Carajas iron-ore and strip-mining project, and Tucurui Dam deforestation project, and so on. The Polonoreste scheme in Brazil carved a paved highway through Amazonia, luring timber, mining and cattle ranching interests into the region with such calamitous impact that in May 1987 even the President of the World Bank, Mr Barber Conable, confessed he found the devastation 'sobering'. (McClintock, 1992, 95)

What we have here is the disappearance of a 'real' economy, in the sense of an economy that can retain some responsiveness to local needs and conditions, behind the screen of a 'virtual' economy in which local activities are mere shadow-play compared with the 'distant action' that in fact controls production, markets and profits. This 'global grid of currency speculation and capital transfer' (Appadurai, 1990, 8) – which is where I started in the first chapter – has also of course now gone through a further 'virtual' transformation for it is this system, a system for globalisation and for the erosion of local 'difference', that forms the basis of the 'world-wide web', whose ability to speed and develop communication only thinly conceals its potentially deathly relation to regional difference and self-determination, its ready assimilation to reactionary forces the world over.

The concerns of such writers as McClintock and Appadurai, however, are economic and systemic in their direction; it has been and continues to be my concern to 'turn' these concerns towards the literary and the 'postcolonial' in their problematic interrelations. For our purposes, then, a more reliable witness than Barber Conable, even when 'sober', is Edward Brathwaite. In a section of *The Arrivants* called 'The Cabin' he writes a thinly veiled discourse about the 'tidal' incursions of global capitalism into Caribbean life:

> But the tide creeps in: today's
> insistence laps the loneliness of this
> resisting cabin: the village grows and bulges:
> shops, super-
> market, Postal Agency
> whose steel spectacled mistress
> rules the town. But no one knows
> where Tom's cracked limestone oblong lies.
> The house, the Postal Agent says,
> is soon to be demolished:
> a Housing Estate's being spawned
> to feed the greedy town.
>
> (Brathwaite, 1973, 71)

The quasi-anonymous 'Tom' cannot be uncovered, the secret is too deeply buried; the supposed coming of improved communications in the significantly named form of the 'Postal Agency' serves only to sever communication and community, just as for those falsely enmeshed in the 'web'. There are reminiscences here of Coetzee's speculations in *Life & Times of Michael K* on the relation between host and parasite, between the urban and the rural, with the 'housing estate' suitably taking the place of the 'rehabilitation camp'; echoes also, against the odds, of Meera Syal and the fairy-tale ending of *Anita and Me*, whereby what the family escape through the miraculous good offices of Harinder Singh is precisely the perilous devaluation of their property through finding themselves too close to ... a housing estate.

Brathwaite's indictment continues:

> It is not enough
> to tinkle to work on a bicycle bell
> when hell
> crackles and burns in the fourteen-inch screen of the Jap
> of the Jap of the Japanese-constructed
> United-Fruit-Company-imported
> hard sell, tell-tale tele-
> vision set, rhinocerously knobbed, cancerously tubed
> (Brathwaite, 1973, 223)

This is a brilliant compendium and condensation of postcolonial themes and anxieties. First, the 'bicycle bell' reminds irresistibly of the 'unheroic heroes' of writers like Naipaul and Kiran Desai, whose small-scale theatrics are continually reduced to rubble by the escalation of the world of exploitation that surrounds them. This is the world of the 'tele' – in other words, literally the world of distance, the world of the 'far away' – of television, certainly, but also of telephony, telepathy, telekinesis, the quasi-magical moving of perspectives, voices, goods and bodies from place to place in a parody of communication that prices individual and communal agency 'out of the market'.[5] And what is induced by this massive imposition of incomprehensible power is here, as we might expect, the stutter: the stutter as a sign of abuse, as the living vocal record of damage but also, as in this case, as evidence of the transference of a painful stereotyping onto a still more distant ethnic other in an endless search for blame for the conditions and effects of expropriation (see Freud, 1953–74, II, 48–105).

The outward and visible signs of what Brathwaite is describing are many. They call themselves by the names of Benetton, Monsanto, McDonald's – let us take just one as an exemplar, one which is especially symbolic because of its long years under the ban in one of the world's largest markets, India (a ban which was, naturally, ultimately doomed): Coca-Cola. Emblematically, the ascension to guru-hood of the hero of Desai's *Hullabaloo in the Guava Orchard* takes its place in a sequence of events of which Coca-Cola is part –

and so, interestingly, is the 'postal service', and also the 'tele'-medium of the newspaper, whose relevant article reads thus:

> 'Fleeing duties at the Shahkot post office, a clerk has been reported to have settled in a large guava tree. According to popular speculation, he is one of an unusual spiritual nature, his child-like ways being coupled with unfathomable wisdom.'
>
> There it was – a modest column introducing Sampath to the world, along with news of a scarcity of groundnuts, an epidemic of tree frogs and the rumour that Coca-Cola might soon be arriving in India. (Desai, 1998, 67)

Which, we might ask, is the most apocalyptic of these events; which the most 'developmental'? 'Coca-Cola: the Real Thing', the protagonist of Foden's *Last King of Scotland* notices on a sign as he overhears comment on the problems of Uganda's chronically unstable regimes (Foden, 1998, 35); what, we might ask, is the '*real* thing' here – Amin's mother after all was known, so we understand, as Pepsi Cola, although I think we would be wrong to think of this as evidence of commercial rivalry …

Coca-Cola, Arundhati Roy observes in *The God of Small Things*, is not always good for you, although for Naipaul's Tulsi widows trying to eke out a living while saving family face Coca-Cola is only a stage on the road to a recognition of the horror, but also the at least temporary possibilities, afforded by Western addictions:

> Then the Americans came to the village. They had decided to build a post somewhere in the mountains, and day and night army lorries rolled through the village on skid chains. The lane next to the cemetery was widened and on the dark green mountains in the distance a thin dirt-red line zigzagged upwards. The Tulsi widows got together, built a shack at the corner of the lane and stocked it with Coca Cola, cakes, oranges and avocado pears. The American lorries didn't stop. The widows spent some money on a liquor licence and, with great trepidation, spent more money on cases of rum. (Naipaul, 1961, 407)

What, after all, is in a name? What is in a name even when it is coupled with an addiction? What is in a name when it threatens the very roots of the culture into which it is supposedly 'acculturated'? What is in a name, even a religious name, when it is violently transplanted – as is the case in one of Chandra's stories in *Love and Longing in Bombay*, when Sanjeev's mother sees that he is wearing a

T-shirt with a picture of 'a blond, scruffy-looking man and the single word "Nirvana"' (Chandra, 1997, 67)?

Perhaps, seen from one perspective, not a great deal; perhaps we can even treat such matters with the humour that Desai and Chandra bring to them. But there are further perspectives, and again despite the overriding comedy we might find a certain disorientation present in Foden's recounting of a very real incident in which Idi Amin made his famous offer, in the face of the near-starvation of most of Uganda's people, to help out the World Bank:

> the World Bank is very happy with Uganda. In fact, I have decided to help the World Bank. I have decided to offer food relief to countries with food problems: millet, maize and beans shall be sent in sacks to all thin countries. And cassava also. (Foden, 1998, 11)

Let us immediately place this account of a peculiar distortion, a distortion which in the shape of Amin was simultaneously economic and military, alongside the more ubiquitous distortions documented by Gray:

> In a world in which market forces are subject to no overall constraint or regulation, peace is continually at risk. Slash-and-burn capitalism degrades the environment and kindles conflict over natural resources. The practical consequences of policies promoting minimal government intervention in the economy is that, in expanding regions of the world, sovereign states are locked in competition not only for markets but for survival. The global market as it is presently organised does not allow the world's peoples to coexist harmoniously. It impels them to become rivals for resources while instituting no methods for conserving. (Gray, 1998, 196)

Slash-and-burn capitalism (or 'insuranburn', as Naipaul has it in a related context); 'ludicrous' and 'doomed', in Achebe's words. Interestingly, Foucault hardly mentions across a wide swathe of works the dimension of the international labour market, preferring to remain anchored in a fantasy of the nation-state; Spivak, although she talks of 'super-exploitation' (Spivak, 1995, 197–205), treats it as though she is herself succumbing to Enlightenment meta-narratives of progress. The literary question would be of how to recognise the intolerable pressures under which postcolonial narratives emerge, especially when they take on themselves, as narratives from the dominant powers no longer often do, the responsibility of speaking for and on behalf of 'the folk'.

The 'free market', says Gray, in a term that he treats with an unremitting and well-deserved irony, 'nullifies precedent'; it 'snaps the threads of memory and scatters local knowledge' (Gray, 1998, 37). If it does this on a cultural level, than we can rapidly see that it is also the agency that prolongs trauma at the personal level and thus ensures the trope of the conversion of 'freedom' into total control which marks so many postcolonial texts.

In Kureishi's *The Black Album* both Chili, the sharp but hopeless addict, and his wife Zulma, who is concerned with relationships only for the money they might bring her, are arch-supporters of British Thatcherism. In Welsh's *Marabou Stork Nightmares* one of the insistent questions is about the identity of the Marabou stork itself, constantly referred to as a vicious scavenger/predator. At one level it is Roy Strang himself who is revealed in the role – or rather, who finally finds it impossible to complete the hugely strenuous work of disavowing his own predatory tendencies. But at another, the label attaches itself to characters who appear in Roy's African/imperial fantasies, the character, for example, of Dawson, whose whole rule in life is acquisition and 'development': 'I want the land they have. It's over two hundred square miles. With my smaller park joined to these resources, we could be in business. Big business' (Welsh, 1995, 54).

'I want the land they have ... Big business'; in the joining of those two crucial phrases the absolute continuity between imperial expansionism and capitalist resource exploitation is perfectly summarised; the neocolonial web is seamless and complete. The question thus raised is one that strikes at the very heart of the postcolonial, namely, whether it is politically accurate or helpful to use the term 'postcolonial' at all in a world where the ending of formal colonial status has in most cases succeeded only in prolonging economic subjugation and indeed in many cases in intensifying economic differences between the industrialised nations and those other parts of the world for which there is, indeed, not even an agreed name.[6] Loomba and Kaul describe the situation from an Indian point of view:

> not only is the agricultural, industrial and financial infrastructure in India being altered under pressure from the International Monetary Fund and the World Bank, but some of the 'cultural' formations that have been the definitive indices of Indian rural and semi-urban life are being simultaneously destroyed. The capitalisation of agricultural practices and markets

> must lead to greater agricultural prosperity, but it does little to support those landless peasants who are dispossessed when older traditional (semi-feudal) arrangements give way. The construction of big dams and hydroelectric projects is vital to the industrial and urban sectors, and totally destructive of rural and tribal communities, who are dislocated from their geographical and cultural coordinates. If our central governmental-IMF practices are profoundly altering economic and social relations in India it will be hardly possible to study the 'post-colonial' without seeing it as constantly in response to, and structured by, the neo-colonial. (Loomba and Kaul, 1994, 25)

Yet what is truly extraordinary about this analysis is the way in which, despite seeing clearly the depth of the social fractures being caused by IMF policies, the authors can still assert – without the slightest supporting evidence – that such capitalisation 'must lead to greater agricultural prosperity'. Even *if* there were any such evidence – and such evidence as exists all points in the other direction – a further question would remain: *whose* prosperity?

The point, though, is that so monolithic have economic ideas become, so subservient to a single US-sponsored notion of 'development', that it is becoming, or has become, impossible to conceive of alternatives; and when we are thinking about conceiving of alternatives, we are back on the terrain of the literary. Postcolonial writing, we might say, is continually involved in a battle – not directly with colonising forces, not even with the 'native neo-colonialists' now in charge of so much of the ex-colonial world, but with the 'closure of the alternative', the imposed perception of the impossibility of ways of life that do not promise 'convergence' with global norms.

Globalisation is everywhere; in Coetzee the death camps are ubiquitous, the ironically inescapable 'rule of life'. A crucial question confronting the study of the postcolonial remains, as it has now been for many years, whether the very ways in which the writing is studied, in which it is 'written about' in both senses, are complicit with this globalisation. As we have earlier seen Gareth Griffiths put it,

> the problem has arisen that with the realisation of the danger that post-colonial theory may act as a globalising international force to wipe out local differences and concerns, an opposite and equally different reaction has developed in the form of a resurgence of atavistic, essentially nativist theories. (Griffiths, 1996, 168)

Griffiths does not explain what he might mean by an 'atavistic theory', but what does appear to me crystal clear is that the problem inheres in the term – by which I inevitably mean the *use* of the term – 'theory' itself. Consider, for example, this passage by the editors of *The Post-Colonial Studies Reader*, one of whom is Griffiths himself: 'Most recently a flurry of theoretical activity has made the nation and nationalism one of the most debated topics of contemporary theory. We have sought to illustrate the importance of this attempt at retheorising nationalism ...' (Ashcroft, Griffiths and Tiffin, 1995, 152) and so forth. Or consider this comment, by the same editors, which appears to express incredulity that thinking can occur outside the industrialised world: 'although "theory" has emerged more often in the post-colonial *creative* text, theoretical texts such as Wilson Harris's *Tradition, the Writer and Society*, which offers many conclusions of an apparently poststructuralist nature, actually *precede* the writings of Derrida and Foucault' (Ashcroft, Griffiths and Tiffin, 1995, 117).

There can surely be no doubt that what lies behind such rhetoric is an assimilation of the notion of theory to an unthought acceptance of the necessity of a convergent 'development', that theory is taken – mistakenly – to refer to a 'next stage' in the progress of thought, an Enlightenment model if ever there was one. Consider, finally, the ludicrous lengths to which this discourse of 'theory' drives otherwise excellent black critics, in this passage from Barbara Christian:

> people of colour have always theorised – but in forms quite different from the Western form of abstract logic. And I am inclined to say that our theorising (and I intentionally use the verb rather than the noun) is often in narrative forms ... My folk, in other words, have always been a race for theory ... (Christian, 1987, 52)

Apart from the massive generalisation and 'essentialism', if we want to use the term, that lies behind the passage, it is clear that what is being talked about is not *theory* in any recognisable form but *thinking in general*. But then, what can one say in the face of such remarkably smug generalisations as those offered, albeit in a 'protected' discourse, by W.J.T. Mitchell:

> The commonplace is simply this: the most important new literature is now emerging from the former colonies of the Western empires – from (for instance) Africa, South America, Australia, New Zealand; the most provocative new criticism is emanating

> from research universities in the advanced industrial democracies, that is, from the former centres of the 'Western empires' – Europe and the United States. (Mitchell, 1992, 56)

There are so many evasions and fallacies here that I have space only to mention one, the idea that domination by the imperial 'centres' is somehow a thing of the past, something that formerly happened; a fatuity which would of course, if accepted, prevent us from thinking at all about the phenomena Mitchell claims to be observing.

Let us try to put international relations and questions about writing and thought into a different and more probable context by looking at a fascinating passage from Walcott, in which he is speaking of New World writers from a Caribbean perspective, and thus to an extent of the 'new world order' in general:

> to most writers of the archipelago who contemplate only the shipwreck, the New World offers not elation but cynicism, a despair at the vices of the Old which they feel must be repeated. Their malaise is an oceanic nostalgia for the older culture and a melancholy at the new, and this can go as deep as a rejection of the untamed landscape, a yearning for ruins. To such writers the death of civilisation is architectural, not spiritual, seeded in their memories is an imagery of vines ascending broken columns, of dead terraces, of Europe as a nourishing museum. They believe in the responsibility of tradition, but what they are in awe of is not tradition, which is alert, alive, simultaneous, but of history, and the same is true of the new magnifiers of Africa. For their deepest loss is of the old gods, the fear that it is worship that has enslaved progress. (Walcott, 1974, 63)

What I want to pick up on here is a rhetoric that can embrace 'melancholy', 'ruin', 'loss', for it is such a rhetoric alone that can provide an alternative viewpoint to the mad progressivism, the riotous but essentially reactionary lust for 'enlightenment', that is signalled in the higher and higher stages to which theory appears, in a bizarrely inappropriate travesty of evolution, to believe that it can ascend. What need to be recognised here are the loops, twists and defiles of the *literary*, which involves recognising the necessity of incarnating the divergent, the alternative – looking at texts not through 'the framework of theory' but looking instead for that of which 'theory' might be merely a temporary and limited instance. To conduct such a search it would be necessary to abandon the triumphalist stance of the theorist, to break with the disavowal of pain and exclusion that lies behind this stance, and to re-encounter again the melancholy, the ruin and the loss, the ineradicable fact of genocidal violence in the past and the equally ineradicable fact of its continuation in the present day.

It would be necessary, as Walcott here hints, to look again and with growing seriousness at the myth of 'development' and at all it leaves behind, at all it excludes from a fantasised body politic. It would be necessary to continue to examine strenuously, at whatever cost, the role and impact of 'modernisation' wherever it is to be found and its negative impact on the possibilities for radical change. It would be necessary, for example, to think further about the implications of Chandra's story of the two elderly accountants who are replaced by a computer (Chandra, 1997, 204–6). It would be necessary to learn lessons, some salutary and others not, from the most conspicuous of the world's battles with the force of modernisation, which is still being fought on the ex-imperial and ex-colonised site of China. It would be necessary to hear the words Gurnah in *Paradise* puts into the mouth of the native Sultan Chatu when he rejects the Arab merchant's gifts, his mind having been 'poisoned' by European traders:

> We did not ask you to come, and we have no welcome for you. Your intentions are not generous, and by coming among us you only bring us evil and calamity. You have come here to do us harm. We have suffered from others like you who have preceded you, and have no intention of suffering again. They came among our neighbours and captured them and took them away. After their first visit to our land only calamities have befallen us. And you have come to add to them. Our crops do not grow, children are born lame and diseased, our animals die from unheard-of diseases. Unspeakable events have taken place since your presence among us. You have come and brought evil into our world. (Gurnah, 1994, 160)

It would be necessary to place this stunning indictment of trade, with its thinly disguised subtexts of slavery and the spread of disease, alongside the recurring myths of the 'new world order' in all its many forms and to enquire, as Harris does, into what the relation might be between this new world order and the state of the imagination. It would probably be necessary, at the end of the day, to recognise that the term 'postcolonial' itself contains the seeds of its own destruction and that what is going on, the exigencies, desperations and emergencies to which 'postcolonial writing' is responding, is a condition that is more adequately described by a term like 'delocalisation', a term that refers directly to capitalism's current central imperative, which is to strip away local difference in the name of the unhindered flow of commodities. And it would, of course, be necessary to insist, time and time again, that the trajectory of this unhindered flow can only be towards steepening the world's economic gradient, towards restricting manufacturing to areas where the labour market is cheapest, restricting agriculture to those areas where peasant labour can best be bent to the service of agri-business conglomerates, in order to cream off profit from these enterprises and to channel them into the already affluent parts of the world; as, for the self-proclaimed 'theorists', the cream of the writing is scooped off and served up for the benefit of the 'Western framework'.

The notion of the postcolonial, I am thus saying, can in the end be considered only under the heading of the alibi; of that which stands in for something else, that which is perennially 'elsewhere', that which is everywhere marked as what I have referred to as the 'text instead'. This is the opposite, it is important to reiterate, of the silencing of the subaltern; it is a matter of a complex reading, a complex listening, whereby the plethora, the multitude of voices can be heard even as they speak the melancholy inevitability of their loss. Neither should my remarks about the development of capitalism be read as though they could be made to fit with the Marxist and neo-Marxist frameworks of Ahmad or San Juan; as I said in my Introduction, I feel more in sympathy with the drift of these critics than with the fellow-travellers of a misnamed 'high theory' but the fact remains that Marxism, for all its early insights into the internationalisation of labour, remains like other Enlightenment and neo-Enlightenment systems a narrative of progress, and thus stands in disavowal of its own melancholy, its own defeat and loss.

Soyinka speaks of the dangers that arise when black intellectuals generate 'fantasies of redemptive transformation in the image of alien masters' (Soyinka, 1976, xii); San Juan suggests that 'postcolonial literature' will attain to a new stage of significance when it takes on 'universalist' ambitions, when it speaks of plights that are held for the species in general (San Juan, 1998, 267–9, 273). If we put together the more important aspects of these two insights, what we would get would be a literature, and an attention to literature, that would be able to look squarely at its own paradoxes, that would be able to own to prior damage while at the same time insisting that such damage is, in a sense, 'common property'. This is not to argue for a moment against the specificity of particular national or communal situations; but it is to remind that the peculiar condition of the literary will always be to effect a link between the actuality, the presence of such conditions, however painful and terrifying, and the imaginary, universality held in its proper position, in absence; and thus we would be able to focus properly on all that stands 'between' the two realms.

What stands between them in respect of the 'postcolonial' is, as I have tried to demonstrate, massive cultural trauma, such trauma as condemns to repetition and remains enthralled by, as Soyinka puts it, 'the image of alien masters'; it is the trauma produced by the imposition of what, after Deleuze and Guattari, I have been referring to as a 'desiring machine'. As Young puts it,

> This desiring machine, with its unlimited appetite for territorial expansion, for 'endless growth and self-reproduction', for making connections and disjunctions, continuously forced disparate territories, histories and people to be thrust together like foreign bodies in the night. (Young, 1995, 98)

Young's concern is to show how this mechanism produced exactly the effect it apparently sought to prohibit, in the form of 'the unlimited and ungovernable fertility of "unnatural unions"' (98); my concern is with a different sort of 'unnatural union', the unnatural union of presence and absence that characterises writing, and in particular with how we may see the shaping of this unnatural union as it emerges under the specific pressures of the 'new world order'; whether, indeed, writing or criticism can sustain the force of resistance that would enable them to maintain the spirit of differentiation in the face of globalisation; whether the writing itself can generate a critical response that will not smother and neutralise, cover it in the foam of the ever-ready Western fire extinguisher; whether the condition of the postcolonial can point the way towards a truer decolonisation of the world, while all the while remembering, as the literary constantly does, that the only way is via the detour, it is by not forgetting the trauma, by not losing sight of the melancholy, by not succumbing to the utopian lure and by thus continually remembering to investigate the fictionality of the – or, indeed, any – 'new world order'.

# Notes

## Chapter 1

1. There are, unsurprisingly, many other ways of classifying types of colonial rule: see, e.g., Walvin, 1992, 1–23; Hargreaves and Heffernan, 1993, 21–38, 77–94; Engels and Marks, 1994, 19–84, 267–76.
2. There have historically been many different versions of the 'new world order', all related in one way or another to different versions of modernity: for examples see Polish Ministry of Information, 1942; Fletcher, 1982; Ekins, 1992; Grugel, 1995.
3. Some of the most interesting speculation in this area occurs in Mishra and Hodge, 1991, who attempt to distinguish between complicit and non-complicit formations:

   > The echoes of guilty partnership in an illicit affair are set off by the word 'complicit', and these overtones hold back the difficult task of defining the 'new' postcolonialism which would take us beyond the oppositional postcolonialism of non-settler colonies that pivots around the moment of independence. (413)

4. For cognate, though different, views of the literary, see the work of Maurice Blanchot, perhaps especially on literature and death (see, e.g., Blanchot, 1982, 85ff.) and on 'the absence of the book' (Blanchot, 1993, 285–434); cf. also Bennett and Royle, 1995, perhaps especially 170–7.
5. Cf. Jonathan White in the surprisingly immodestly titled *Recasting the World: Writing after Colonialism*:

   > Throughout the world departments of English (so named) are increasingly teaching postcolonial or 'new' literatures ... But they are *wrongly named* for doing so. Even for those many literatures written in the English language, *English* as the umbrella term for the study in question seems (however unintentionally) like a continuation of imperial sway. (White, 1993, 17)

   But this, of course, does not get to the heart of the larger linguistic problem.

6. There has been plenty of recent discussion of the postcolonial in both its Scottish and its Irish dimensions; on Scotland see, as one recent example, Andrew Lincoln on Scott and the 'infant colony' (Lincoln, 1999); on Ireland, see particularly David Lloyd on Irish writing and the 'postcolonial moment' (Lloyd, 1993).
7. I would also hope the book to have other pedagogic values. For example, I hope that the second and third parts of the Bibliography might provide students and interested readers with working lists of primary and secondary texts for consultation; I have also intended my chapter structure to provide, or at least suggest, a ground-plan for the appropriate topics for such a course.
8. This is by no means the most bizarre of the contortions into which Spivak is driven by the peculiar exigencies of 'high theory'. For example, there is her description of herself as a 'practical deconstructivist feminist Marxist', on which she expands in her 'Interview with *Radical Philosophy*' (Spivak, 1990, 133–7) and which appears to demonstrate a deep and complex allegiance to those very 'master-narratives' which elsewhere she claims to reject.
9. In particular, on the psychoanalytic side I am interested in ideas of the uncanny and the phantom; in Deleuze and Guattari in ideas about deterritorialisation and reterritorialisation. References, particularly to Freud and to Deleuze and Guattari's *A Thousand Plateaus*, are given where appropriate. As a key to the postcolonial dimensions of such texts, perhaps the following passage from Deleuze and Guattari on Freud and psychoanalysis might be suggestive:

> Problems of peopling in the unconscious: all that passes through the pores of the schizo, the veins of the drug addict, swarming, teeming, ferment, intensities, races and tribes. This tale of white skin prickling with bumps and pustules, and of dwarfish black heads emerging from pores grimacing and abominable ... Freud tried to approach crowd phenomena from the point of view of the unconscious, but he did not see clearly, he did not see that the unconscious itself was fundamentally a crowd. (Deleuze and Guattari, 1988, 29)

## Chapter 2

1. Other commentators on this flawed and damaging notion of 'development' include Arjun Appadurai and Arturo Escobar as well, of course, as Marx: see Appadurai, 1990; Escobar, 1995; Marx, 1969.
2. Recent critics are now also invoking a notion of a 'fourth world'. Quoting David Callaghan's claim that the 'culture of Australia's indigenous people is more akin to those of the American Indian, the

tribespeople of the Kolahai, the Ainu of Japan, the eskimo ...' (Callaghan, 1988, 13), Adam Shoemaker describes this as a 'Fourth World connection' which provides Aboriginal Australians with 'important terms of reference' (Shoemaker, 1989, 277).

3. My objection to Bhabha's notion of 'hybridity' can perhaps best be grasped if we look at a brief passage from Bhabha:

> I am attempting to write of the western nation as an obscure and ubiquitous form of living the *locality* of culture. This locality is ... more hybrid in the articulation of cultural differences and identifications – gender, race or class – than can be represented in any hierarchical or binary structuring of social antagonism. (Bhabha, 1990, 292)

Thus hybridity appears as a prop to the reactionary attempt to salvage a concept of the local in the face of the uncanny ubiquity of delocalisation.

4. We can find this criticism at its most politically bitter in Aijaz Ahmad's *In Theory* and in E. San Juan's *Beyond Postcolonial Theory*. For example:

> Despite its prima facie radicalism, I contend that in general postcolonial discourse mystifies the political/ideological effects of Western postmodern hegemony and prevents change. It does so by espousing a metaphysics of textualism, as in Gayatri Spivak's fetishism of 'the archives of imperial governance', or in Bhabha's analogous cult of linguistic/psychological ambivalence. Such idealist frameworks of cognition void the history of people's resistance to imperialism, liquidate popular memory, and renounce responsibility for any ethical consequence of thought. (San Juan, 1998, 22)

5. On the binary voice see, e.g., Bhabha, 1994, 67ff.; Tiffin, 1996, 153–5; also, more obliquely, Neil Lazarus on the necessity for 'hating tradition properly' (Lazarus, 1999, 1–15).
6. My identification of the 'text instead' follows on from previous work of mine: see, e.g., Punter, 1998, 2, on the 'text always more perfect, more preserved from arbitrary incursion than the text we have, in any reasonable or "daylight" scenario, succeeded in writing or reading ourselves'.
7. For these controversies, see Moore-Gilbert, 1997, *passim*; as a particular instance, Simon During's essay 'Rousseau's Patrimony: Primitivism, Romance and Being Other' provides an interestingly challenging deployment of a range of psychoanalytic concepts in essential relation to the anthropological (see Barker et al., 1994, 47–71).
8. I have expressed my anxiety at this 'pseudo-magical' trick before: see the remarks on the 'unlocking of the crypt through the (post-funerary) use of the magic word' in Punter, 1999, 49.

9. Gray puts it thus:

> It is fashionable to see multinational corporations as constituting a kind of invisible government supplanting many of the functions of nation-states. In reality they are often weak and amorphous organisations. They display the loss of authority and the erosion of common values that afflicts [sic] practically all late modern social institutions. The global market is not spawning corporations which assume the past functions of sovereign states. Rather, it has weakened and hollowed out both institutions. (Gray, 1998, 63)

Cf. Hirst and Thompson, 1996, 76–98.

10. The crucial texts here would be Freud, 'Inhibitions, Symptoms and Anxiety' (1926) (Freud, 1953–74, XX, 87–172); Klein, 'The Importance of Symbol-Formation in the Development of the Ego' (1930) (Klein, 1988, 219–32); and Bowlby, 1969–80.

11. 
> This sense of loss, then, we may interpret as a kind of textual deficit; as the impossibility of sealing up the fragments of the 'lost' manuscript (which is clearly, in its very textual incarnation, no longer lost, yet which remains haunted by its own provisionality). Or we may interpret it as loneliness, as the primal ground of the law of the orphan ... (Punter, 1998, 203)

12. The whole complex issue of psychoanalysis and South America is best illuminated in the pages of the *Journal of Psychoanalysis of the SPPA*, published from October 1993 onwards.

13. John Earl Joseph provides an interesting linguistic perspective on what some of the consequences of this situation might be:

> If complete stability is demanded of the standard language, then the gap between it and its underlying dialect base can only widen as the dialects continue their normal rate of change. ... When the absolute standard becomes this powerful, the language ceases to be standard and becomes classical. ... By ceasing to be tied to a living community of speakers, by ceasing to change, classical languages give up much of what it means to be a language. (Joseph, 1987, 172–3)

The question here, though, might be about what a 'normal rate of change' could mean under conditions of induced 'development'.

## Chapter 3

1. 
> Individual or group, we are traversed by lines, meridians, geodesics, tropics, and zones marching to different beats and differing in nature. ... There are different animal lines of flight:

> each species, each individual, has its line. ... it should be borne in mind that these lines mean nothing. It is an affair of cartography. They compose us, they compose our map. (Deleuze and Guattari, 1988, 202–3)

2. Young's references are to Deleuze and Guattari, 1988, 260, 202 (see also n. 1 above).
3. On the cultural situation of the First Nations in North America and in Australasia, see, e.g., the relevant American documents and commentaries in Milner, 1989; Shoemaker, 1989, especially 265–82; and Narogin, 1990, *passim*.
4. Clearly the last few years have seen a crucial reorientation in the intellectual and practical domains of geography; see, e.g., Virilio, 1977; Benterrak, Muecke and Roe, 1984; Agamben, 1993; Chatterjee, 1993; Harvey, 1996; Gupta and Ferguson, 1997.
5. There is, it seems to me, some care to be taken in considering Deleuze and Guattari's characterisation of the nomad; in particular, to what extent it falls under the sign of a kind of instant exoticisation that obscures the plight of displacement. Would this comment, for example, be free from the idealistic trace?

   > If there is no history from the viewpoint of nomads, although everything passes through them, to the point that they are like the *noumena* or the unknowable of history, it is because they cannot be separated from [the] task of abolition which makes the nomadic empires vanish as if of their own accord ... (Deleuze and Parnet, 1987, 142)

6. It may also be the case that this 'act of multiplicity' has further connotations. See, for example, James Hillman on the 'underworld' as 'an innumerable community of figures' (Hillman, 1979, 41).
7. The postcolonial motif of Paradise is ubiquitous; what needs to be brought into focus is its intrinsic connection with what Annie E. Coombes, in 'The Recalcitrant Object: Culture Contact and the Question of Hybridity', refers to as the '"disappearing world" phenomenon' – referring back to Chris Pinney's comment, 'The structural need which Disappearing World [a TV series] has for a fragile exoticism (a world as yet unrepresented) demands ... difference and ... disappearance is the only way of maintaining that distance' (Barker et al., 1994, 106; Pinney, 1989, 27).
8. This image of the ambiguously destined letter refers us back, of course, to many 'subsidiary sources'; to Lacan, 1972, for example, and also to Derrida's 'Le Facteur de la vérité' and its emphasis on the way in which the letter 'may have no fixed location, not even that of a definable hole or assignable lack' (see Derrida, 1987).
9. Critical theorists twenty years ago were fond of talking about

successive 'Copernican revolutions'. This is how Lacan spoke of Freud in 'The Freudian Thing, or the Meaning of the Return to Freud in Psychoanalysis' and 'The Agency of the Letter in the Unconscious or Reason since Freud' (see Lacan, 1977, 114, 165), and it was the image Catherine Belsey attempted to extend in utopian vein in her *Critical Practice* (see Belsey, 1980, 130–7).

10. On anthropology and its political functions, see Perry Anderson's famous essay 'Components of the National Culture', where he speaks of the ways in which 'British anthropology developed unabashedly in the wake of British imperialism' (Anderson, 1969, 264–5).

11. I have in mind such passages as the following:

> He had become so much a creature of twilight and night that daylight hurt his eyes. He no longer needed to keep to paths in his movements around the dam. A sense less of sight than of touch, the pressure of presences upon his eyeballs and the skin of his face, warned him of any obstacle. His eyes remained unfocussed for hours on end like those of a blind person. (Coetzee, 1983, 158)

12. The image of the spider resonates with, among others, Brathwaite on Kwaku Ananse, who 'gleams/in the darkness/and captures our underground fears' (Brathwaite, 1973, 149).

> Creation has burned to a spider.
> It peeps over the hills with the sunrise
> But prefers to spin webs in the trees.
>
> (Brathwaite, 1973, 164)

13. See Appadurai, 1990:

> the disposition of global capital is now a more mysterious, rapid and difficult landscape to follow than ever before, as currency markets, national stock exchanges, and commodity speculations move mega-monies through national turnstiles at blinding speed, with vast absolute implications for small differences in percentage points and time units. (8)

14. The imperial rhetoric here is reminiscent of Paul Scott's *Raj Quartet*, as indeed of *The Jewel in the Crown* in particular, which offers us near the end an image not so much of wealth and comfort as of destitution and disturbance. I will not, says Lady Chatterjee, become 'the repository of a tradition', for

> A repository sounds like a place for storing furniture when you bash off to some other station. I suppose an Englishman could say that the whole of India is that sort of place. You all went, but left so much behind that you couldn't carry with you wherever you were going, and these days those of you who come back can more often

> than not hardly bother to think about it, let alone ask for the key to go in and root about among all the old dust sheets to see that everything worth-while that you left is still there and isn't falling to pieces with dry rot. (Scott, 1976, 450–1)

## Chapter 4

1. On the question of the implication of English language and literature in the imperial project, see, among many other examples, Laura Chrisman on 'representations of imperial discourse' (Chrisman, 1990) but also, more directly, the sections on 'Universality and Difference' and 'Language' in Ashcroft, Griffiths and Tiffin, 1995, 57–82 and 285–318.
2. As is made evident in Thomas Mun's treatise of 1664 when he points out that 'the true form and worth of forraign Trade' is to do not only with 'The great Revenue of the King, The honour of the Kingdom' but also with 'The Sinnews of our wars, The terror of our Enemies' (Mun, 1928, 88).
3. The connections between imperialism and the adventure story are made in classic form in Martin Green's *Dreams of Adventure, Deeds of Empire*. In this context, see particularly his comments on popular literature and children's literature (Green, 1980, 203–34).
4. Fanon's works are, of course, emblematic in any study of the postcolonial:

   > Let us waste no time in sterile litanies and nauseating mimicry. Leave this Europe where they are never done talking of Man, yet murder men everywhere they find them, at the corner of every one of their own streets, in all the corners of the globe. For centuries they have stifled almost the whole of humanity in the name of a so-called spiritual experience. Look at them today swaying between atomic and spiritual disintegration. (Fanon, 1965, 251)

5. On the rhetoric of ruin, it is perhaps also worth thinking about the intellectual and institutional ruins discussed in the essays by Bill Readings and Diane Elam in volume 17 of the *Oxford Literary Review* (see Readings, 1995; Elam, 1995).
6. > the law, while it serves in itself to arrest development, cannot abide the thought of another agency which may do so, however fantastic its ... aspirations; and therefore this evil must be punished, says the law, without contemplating the possibility that the evil that is to be punished is, in many respects, akin to the 'evil' associated with the law itself. (Punter, 1998, 208)

7. For commentary and background on the devastating series of allegations and admissions appearing in the Australian context, see, e.g., Narogin, 1990, 9–15; Hodge and Mishra, 1991, xvi, 23–49, 136–42; Davidson, 1991, 82–7.
8. On the 'relic', see Derrida, for example on the 'dead body resting there in the interminable decomposition of relics' or on 'a remain(s) that would no longer be – neither relic nor remainder [*reliquat*] – of any operation' (Derrida, 1986, 91, 257).
9. Perhaps H. G. Wells expresses it most brutally in *The Island of Doctor Moreau*, with its endless and madly accretive repetitions of 'the Law':

   > And so from the prohibition of these acts of folly, on to the prohibition of what I thought then were the maddest, most impossible, and most indecent things one could well imagine. A kind of rhythmic fervour fell on all of us; we gabbled and swayed faster and faster, repeating this amazing law. (Wells, 1993, 57)

10. This might remind us of the crucial arguments that have taken place around the text of *Heart of Darkness* in recent years; see Achebe, 1977; Frederick Crews' chapter, 'Conrad's Uneasiness – and Ours', in Crews, 1975; Parry, 1983; and, in general, Hamner, 1990.
11. For part of the history of this series of disastrous cross-contaminations, see the thorough account in Vaughan, 1991; for what one might think of as its 'psychic equivalent' see Fanon, 1965, 200–50.
12. I am thinking, for example, of poems like 'The Spoiler's Return', the magnificent 'The Schooner *Flight*', 'Names', and large parts of *Another Life* (see Walcott, 1992, 432–8, 345–61, 305–8, 291ff.).
13.
   > They do not ask us, master,
   > do you accept this?
   > A nature reduced to the service
   > of praising or humbling men,
   > there is a yes without a question,
   > there is assent founded on ignorance,
   > in the mangroves plunged to the wrist, repeating
   > the mangroves plunging to the wrist,
   > there are spaces
   > wider than conscience.
   >
   > (Walcott, 1992, 280)

14.
   > The real aim of colonialism was to control the people's wealth: what they produced, how they produced it, and how it was distributed; to control, in other words, the entire realm of the language of real life. ... The domination of a people's language by the languages of the colonising nations was crucial to the domination of the mental universe of the colonised. (Ngugi, 1986, 16)

## Chapter 5

1. In Fred Botting's 'Whither Theory', this haunting is usefully figured in terms of theoretical excess: 'The excess of positions, the more and more theoretical talk, is singularly perceived to be doing the same thing [sic], repeating the same desire by trying to win the battle for theoretical authority' (Botting, 1993, 215).
2. There are, however, some suggestive paragraphs that permit a potential shifting of this framework. For example, in his editor's note to the section of *The Shell and the Kernel* called 'Secrets and Posterity: The Theory of the Transgenerational Phantom', Nicholas Rand claims that the phantom has 'the potential to illuminate the genesis of social institutions and may provide a new perspective for inquiry into the psychological roots of cultural patterns and political ideology' (Abraham and Torok, 1994, 169).
3. As Derrida says in his Foreword to *The Wolf Man's Magic Word*,

   > The cryptic enclosed within the self, but as a foreign place, prohibited, excluded. The self is not the proprietor of what he is guarding. He makes the rounds like a proprietor, but only the rounds. (Abraham and Torok, 1986, xxxv)

4. An interesting, if slightly oblique, contribution to the discourse can be found in Derrida's meditations on circumcision, the body and 'foreignness', and Geoffrey Bennington's 'commentary' thereon (see Bennington and Derrida, 1993, 242–53). See also Royle, 1995, 143–58.
5. The imagery betrays the unthinkability and the violence:

   > Void makes loss a reality. Do not think about righting the balance, but live close to the painful reality and try to relate it to what is good. What is needed here, and is so difficult to achieve, is a new orientation of our desires, a re-education of our instinctive feelings. We may think here of Plato's image of the soul as a charioteer with a good horse and a bad horse, struggling with the bad horse and pulling him up violently, 'covering his jaws with blood' (*Phaedrus* 254E). (Murdoch, 1992, 503)

6. For example:

   > Let us keep in mind the speech of the depressed – repetitive and monotonous. Faced with the impossibility of concatenating, they utter sentences that are interrupted, exhausted, come to a standstill. Even phrases they cannot formulate. A repetitive rhythm, a monotonous melody emerge and dominate the broken logical sequences, changing them into recurring, obsessive litanies. (Kristeva, 1989, 33)

7. See in particular Deleuze and Guattari, 1983, *passim*.
8. See Freud's 'Mourning and Melancholia' (Freud, 1953–74, XIV, 239–57); Abraham and Torok's 'Mourning *or* Melancholia: Introjection *versus* Incorporation' (Abraham and Torok, 1994, 125–38); Kristeva, 1989, especially 97–100; and Butler, 1997, 132–50.
9. Karel Gijsbers' paper, 'Phantom Limbs and the Haunted Brain', was delivered at the *Phantom fx* conference, University of Stirling, 24 May 1997.
10. D'Aguiar's work includes, however, two other novels, *The Longest Memory* and *Dear Future*, as well as poetry, the most recent volume of which is *Bill of Rights*.
11. The topic of trauma is one of great complexity. See in particular Caruth, 1991; Healy, 1993; Leys, 1994.
12. On the complexities of the 'limbo gateway', see Harris, 1981, where he also describes what he terms the '*limbo-anancy* syndrome'.
13. Although she is talking in terms of gender relations, it would be worth thinking through remarks such as these by Judith Butler in *The Psychic Life of Power* in a postcolonial context:

> in melancholia not only does the ego substitute for the object, but this act of substitution *institutes* the ego as a necessary response to or 'defence' against loss. To the extent that the ego is 'the precipitate of its abandoned object-cathexes', it is the congealment of a history of loss, the sedimentation of relations of substitution over time, the resolution of a tropological function into the ontological effect of the self. (Butler, 1997, 169)

14. As Freud engagingly puts it in a related context, 'Children have no scruples over allowing animals to rank as their full equals. Uninhibited as they are in the avowal of their bodily needs, they no doubt feel themselves more akin to animals than to their elders, who may well be a puzzle to them' (Freud, 1953–74, XIII, 127).
15. See Bhabha, 'Of Mimicry and Man: The Ambivalence of Colonial Discourse', but also 'Signs Taken for Wonders: Questions of Ambivalence and Authority ...' and 'DissemiNation: Time, Narrative and the Margins of the Modern Nation' (Bhabha, 1994, 85–92, 102–22, 139–70, or original versions as cited in the Bibliography).
16. 'I dropped the tribute to Victorian England', Achebe adds, 'when I went to the university although you might find some early acquaintances still calling me by it. The earliest of them all – my mother – certainly stuck to it to the bitter end' (Achebe, in Ashcroft, Griffiths and Tiffin, 1995, 190).
17. We might consider, for example, how 'emergent anti- and post-colonial cultural and theoretical discourse was formed as much through transnational dialogue with other Third World discourses and movements as it was through dialogue with the West' (Williams

and Chrisman, 1993, 16). The specific examples they cite are the influences of Afro-Americans (Booker T. Washington, W. E. B. du Bois), Caribbeans (Marcus Garvey) and West Africans (Joseph Casely-Hayford) in black South Africa.

## Chapter 6

1. Captain Cutteridge's remarkable contribution to West Indian education, and various later comments by those subjected to his pedagogy, are alluded to in Tiffin, 1996, 147–9.
2. See Freud, *The Psychopathology of Everyday Life*, on automatic actions and their psychic functioning (Freud, 1953–74, VI, 132, 177, 214).
3. On repetition, see Freud, *Beyond the Pleasure Principle* (Freud, 1953–74, XVIII, 21–2); also John Forrester's discussion of this passage in the context of his developing treatment of Lacan (Forrester, 1990, 210ff.).
4. Hanuman, monkey deity of the Ramayana, is also known as the 'highest of the lesser gods'.
5. The whole topic of modernity is clearly crucial in relation to postcolonialism and the myth of development; the Chinese model may be the most instructive. Emblematic in the cultural field would be a paper given by Rey Chow at the 1988 conference on Modernism and Contemporary Chinese Literature at the Chinese University of Hong Kong; the paper was called 'In Feminine Detail: Modernity and Narration in Four Chinese Writers', but began memorably with an assertion of *continuity* between modernity and 'the details of old Chinese clothes', which were 'astonishingly pointless ...'.
6. > You should have hidden, Michaels. You were too careless of yourself. You should have crept away in the darkest reach of the deepest hole and possessed yourself in patience till the troubles were over. ... Well, the laws of nations have you in their grip now: they have pinned you down ... (Coetzee, 1983, 206)
7. On the exotic in general, see Dorothy M. Figueira's *The Exotic*, in which exoticism is seen as

   > an experience the structure of which is predicated upon the impossibility of fulfilment. Nevertheless, the nihilistic gesture which foregrounds the exotic quest is not abandoned. The subject continues to seek reification in an endeavour whose ephemerality stands revealed and, in a capitulation of reason, is embraced. (Figueira, 1994, 168)
8. See Freud on the etymological and epistemological complexities of these terms in 'The "Uncanny"' (Freud, 1953–74, XVII, 220–6).

9. Kristeva's remarks in *Strangers to Ourselves* on this constellation of alienation, foreignness, exile are curiously misguided (Kristeva, 1991, 1–19), although not as bizarre as some of the things she said some years earlier in the entirely reprehensible *About Chinese Women*. There she speaks of a society that has 'nothing exotic about it' (Kristeva, 1977, 12) and then proceeds to extraordinary generalisations such as this: 'the *faces* of Chinese women: smooth, placid, closed without hostility, clearly unaware of us in the shadows ... A fragile, flexible reserve, an unbridgeable distance ... And myself, an eternal stranger ...' (157).
10. This raises the whole question of the law in a postcolonial context, and here we would come upon one way of interpreting some of Derrida's remarks in *The Other Heading*:

    > Just as it is necessary earnestly to analyse and earnestly address – and this is the whole problem of ethico-political responsibility – the disparities between law, ethics, and politics, or between the unconditional idea of law (be it of men or of states) and the concrete conditions of its implementation, between the structurally universalist pretention of these regulative ideas and the essence or European origin of this idea of law (etc.), is it not also necessary to resist with vigilance the neo-capitalist dogmatism in those states that had incorporated it? (Derrida, 1992, 57)

    This, of course, goes far (but brilliantly) beyond the current issue.
11. Some of the connections between the ghostly and the machinic are outlined in Deleuze and Guattari, 1988, 303–8.
12. And incest itself, we might think, bears a curious relation to narrative. In *The Romantic Unconscious*, I have examined *Emma* and *Wuthering Heights* as 'recourses against incest ... Incest figures here as the short-circuiting of narcissism' (Punter, 1989, 137).
13. There are also some curious connections here with the pornographic gaze, which is perhaps after all not so far from the fascination with the 'savage' that we find in early anthropology or on the covers of *National Geographical Magazine* (see Assiter, 1988, 101–2). On race and pornography in general, see Forna, 1992; Kappeler, 1986, 150–4.
14. In thinking of some of the most inept attempts to make use of this inadequate concept, I am reminded of Annie E. Coombes' warning 'to avoid the uncritical celebration in museum culture of a hybridity which threatens to collapse the heterogeneous experience of racism into a scopic feast ...' (Barker *et al.*, 1994, 92).
15. One of the recent texts on addiction and textuality is Avital Ronell's *Crack Wars: Literature, Addiction, Mania*, but it is deeply flawed by a kind of ludic idealism. Far more helpful in considering the wide-ranging issues raised by addiction in such contexts would be to attend properly to the materials contained in Ben Whitaker's *The Global Fix* and Alfred W. McCoy's *The Politics of Heroin*. Even thirteen years

ago, a reading of Whitaker reminds us, illegal drug sales in the United States exceeded the combined budgets of the USA's five hundred largest industrial corporations (see Whitaker, 1987, xv; McCoy, 1991, *passim*).

16. In Chinese culture these 'paper replicas' are themselves haunted and haunting, as we see in the scenario of a poem by Li Ho:

> The shamaness pours a libation; clouds come crowding thick;
> Fragrant smoke rolls from the charcoal fire in the jade incense
> burner.
> Sea god and mountain spirit descend among the worshippers.
> Paper money rustles noisily in the gusty wind.
>
> (Soong, 1985, 139)

17. On Gothic locations that can be visited only under conditions of the greatest secrecy, see Punter, 1999, 46.
18. With Keats I am thinking particularly, of course, of 'On First Looking into Chapman's *Homer*' (Cook, 1990, 32), though also of a more general trope of 'conquest'.
19. And could be compared interestingly with the sometimes personified form of 'Evil Forest' in Achebe's *Things Fall Apart*, which has an interesting fate:

> Every clan and village had its 'evil forest'. In it were buried all those who died of the really evil diseases, like leprosy and smallpox. It was also the dumping ground for the potent fetishes of great medicine-men when they died. An 'evil forest' was, therefore, alive with sinister forces and powers of darkness. It was such a forest that the rulers of Mbanta gave to the missionaries. They did not really want them in their clan, so they made them that offer which nobody in his right senses would accept. (Achebe, 1996, 105)

## Chapter 7

1. With Gray's formulations we might also compare, for instance, James Der Derian on the inevitable conflict between a 'universalist "new world order" [which] inevitably fails to live up to its lofty ideals' and 'the rebirth of an authoritarian "new order"' (Der Derian, 1992, 163).
2. But one might prefer to speak of it as a 'hypnotic' text, using Borch-Jacobsen's remarks in *The Freudian Subject* to connect hypnosis, death and a certain kind of addiction to leadership:

> The object-put-in-the-place-of-the-ego-ideal, then, is not loved – it hypnotises. Medusa-like, it paralyses, freezes, the ego. And this object is the leader, the *Führer*. For the political bond that binds the

> members of the group to their shared ideal object ... is the hypnotic, hypnotico-suggestive bind. (Borch-Jacobsen, 1989, 226)

3. Or:

> The plague is met by order; its function is to sort out every possible confusion: that of the disease, which is transmitted when bodies are mixed together; that of the evil, which is increased when fear and death overcome prohibitions. (Foucault, 1977, 197)

4. We can look back here to Kincaid's *A Small Place*; but also to Ngugi's thinking about imagistic incommensurability in, for example, 'Literature and Double Consciousness'; cf. also Ngugi's own deployment of the term 'new world order' in essays like 'Culture in a Crisis: Problems of Creativity and the New World Order' and 'The Allegory of the Cave: Language, Democracy, and a New World Order' (see Ngugi, 1997, 37–52, 126–31; Ngugi, 1998, 71–101).
5. See San Juan, 1998; but also what Deleuze and Guattari have to say about the transformation of the war machine after the Second World War, and their challenging assertion that '*it is peace that technologically frees the unlimited material process of total war*' (Deleuze and Guattari, 1988, 467).
6. As opposed to, for example, Homi Bhabha's attempt to establish a 'hybrid location of cultural value', which he sees as the base from which 'the postcolonial intellectual attempts to elaborate a historical and literary project' (Bhabha, 1994, 173); it is the sheer absence here of a sense of both multiplicity and limitation which is so alarming.
7. On obsessive/compulsive disorder, see Van Ornum, 1997. It would surely be right to see it as connected in to an opposition which Deleuze and Guattari describe:

> If there exists a primitive 'geometry' (a protogeometry), it is an operative geometry in which figures are never separable from the affectations befalling them, the lines of their becoming, the segments of their segmentation ... On the contrary, State geometry, or rather the bond between the State and geometry, manifests itself in the primacy of the theorem-element, which substitutes fixed or ideal essences for supple morphological formations, properties for affects, predetermined segments for segmentations-in-progress. (Deleuze and Guattari, 1988, 212)

The Blake reference is to 'There is No Natural Religion' (First Series) (Blake, 1966, 97).

8. For a basic history of one aspect of colonial indenture, see Gillion's *Fiji's Indian Migrants* (Gillion, 1962).
9. Perhaps here too, as in a case that Freud discusses in '"A Child is being Beaten": A Contribution to the Study of the Origin of Sexual Perver-

sions', 'an elaborate superstructure of day-dreams ... [has] grown up over the masochistic beating-phantasy' (Freud, 1953–74, XVII, 190).

10. There has been a long debate about Tutuola's English; for some of the key moments in it, see the essays collected in Bernth Lindfors' *Critical Perspectives on Amos Tutuola*: e.g., Eric Larrabee, 'Palm-Wine Drinkard Searches for a Tapster'; anon., 'Portrait: A Life in the Bush of Ghosts'; Harold R. Collins, 'Founding a New National Literature: The Ghost Novels of Amos Tutuola'; Taban Lo Liyong, 'Tutuola, Son of Zinjanthropus'; A. Afolayan, 'Language and the Sources of Amos Tutuola' (Lindfors, 1975, 6–9, 25–8, 43–54, 77–83, 148–62).
11. For example, we might enquire as to the explicatory tone of passages like this:

    > Before reaching my town, there was a great famine (FAMINE), and it killed millions of the old people and uncountable adults and children, even many parents who were killing their children for food so as to save themselves after they had eaten both domestic animals and lizards etc. Every plant and tree and river dried away for lack of the rain, and nothing for the people to eat remained. (Tutuola, 1952, 118)

12. See, e.g., Bhabha, 1983; also Stephen Slemon on 'conceptual influence in the discipline' and 'confusion over the role of social and political theory in the field' (King, 1996, 184).
13. Behind this line of thinking could also lie a recapitulation of the work of the neo-Jungian James Hillman, although I am aware of the controversy surrounding the presumed Eurocentrism of his mythical constructs. See, e.g., Hillman, 1975, 66ff.
14. I could put it in the kind of terms most frequently found in post-colonial criticism: 'the problematic spatio-temporality implicit in the term "post-colonial" has repercussions for the conceptualisation of the past in post(anti)colonial theory' (Shohat, 1996, 330).
15. San Juan speaks, in the context of a specific piece of textual criticism, of the 'fissure between the patronising endorsement of the "model minority" archetype and the factual errors compounded with a self-righteous paternalism', regarding both as 'symptomatic of the doctrine that Asian immigrants, like all aliens, should be measured against a white supremacist standard' (San Juan, 1998, 171).
16. The most significant voice on these issues remains that of Ngugi wa Thiong'o, a voice all the more powerful for its refusal to renounce the possibility of a culturally prejudiced silencing; see especially the essay (and previously Clarendon lecture) 'The Allegory of the Cave: Language, Democracy, and a New World Order' (in Ngugi, 1998, 71–101); on how 'the post-colonial state and intellectual ... steal ... to enrich the languages of Europe', his next essay, 'Oral Power and Europhone Glory: Orature, Literature, and Stolen Legacies' (103–28), is even more powerful.

17. Summarised in the egg that, as we have seen, feeds the world, but can also produce a world of vengeance and torture:

> When he commanded it to produce anything it could, the egg produced only millions of whips and started to flog them all at once ... All the king's attendants were severely beaten by these whips and also all the kings. Many of them ran into the bush and many of them died there ... (Tutuola, 1952, 123–4)

18. On the international labour market, see particularly San Juan, 1998, 220–6. In an unintentionally hilarious account of the 'optimistic' and 'pessimistic' possibilities for the future division of labour, Hirst and Thompson, having pointed out that manufacturing labour costs in Indonesia are less than 2% of those in Germany, nevertheless stoutly claim that 'the threat of collapsing employment and output in the First World as jobs fly to the Third World is at present quite unreal ...' (Hirst and Thompson, 1996, 117, 119–20). I write this as Marks & Spencer, a company that has previously prided itself on domestic sourcing, announces that it has given up and will be shifting its purchasing away from the UK.

## Chapter 8

1. Among recent work in this area, most notable has been Chris Baldick's *In Frankenstein's Shadow*. See in particular Baldick, 1987, 10–29.
2. Jacqueline Howard, for example, writes of such issues in her chapter 'Pseudo-Scientific Gothic: Mary Shelley's *Frankenstein: or The Modern Prometheus*' (Howard, 1994, 238–84).
3. I am thinking here, among other things, of Blanchot's argument that 'humanism is not to be repudiated' provided we recognise it 'where it adopts its least deceptive mode, never in the zones of authority, power, or the law, not in those of order, or culture or heroic magnificence, any more than in the lyricism of good company, but rather such as it was borne even to the point of the spasm of a cry. Among others by he who, refusing to speak of himself as a man, evoked only *the mental animal* ...' (Blanchot, 1993, 262).
4. See, for example, Timothy Brennan's emphasis on the notion of the 'cosmopolitan intellectual' in his *Salman Rushdie and the Third World* (Brennan, 1989, 59–70), as well as Rushdie's own remarks in '"Commonwealth Literature" does not Exist' (in Rushdie, 1991, 61–70).
5. See, e.g., Bruce King on 'new centres of consciousness' in King, 1996, 3–26. But it is becoming clearer, at last, that such a set of 'geographical' conventions is increasingly beside the point; although the

excesses of 'teletheory' may in the end contribute to a reactionary anxiety about the perception of material conditions, the fact remains that the 'old geographies' have been replaced at the cultural level by virtual trajectories; location becomes a question of tax regime.

6. See Rushdie, 1983, 219; also Freud, 1953–74, XVII, 227ff., although it is true that in his search for the topography of the uncanny Freud is here in fact *distancing* himself from Jentsch's emphasis on the automaton as the principal source of epistemic doubt.
7. In connection with the implications, violences and residues of partition, it is interesting to read and think about the remarkably neutral account by Hermann Kulke and Dietmar Rothermund (Kulke and Rothermund, 1998, 281–93); cf. the more challengingly insidious argument about domination and discourse in Inden, 1990.
8. As Rushdie himself says: 'Throughout human history, the apostles of purity, those who have claimed to possess a total explanation, have wrought havoc among mere mixed-up human beings' (Rushdie, 1991, 394).
9. On the significance of disability as a key term in the histories of textuality, see, e.g., Punter, 2000b.
10. I have already cited some references in previous notes; to these we may add the whole debate about literature and orature, as outlined by Ngugi, who speaks of the coining of the term 'orature' by Pio Zirimu 'to connote a system of aesthetics, an oral narrative system, for instance, which could be differentiated from the system of visual narratives' (Ngugi, 1998, 111).
11. See, e.g., C. I. Macafee's 'Ongoing Change in Modern Scots: The Social Dimension', which concludes that 'Scots is already a long way along a trajectory which is taking it towards integration with English as the continuum between the two shrinks, apparently inexorably, towards the English pole' (in Jones, 1997, 546).
12. See Foucault's arguments around 'the body of the condemned': 'systems of punishment are to be situated in a certain "political economy" of the body ... it is always the body that is at issue – the body and its forces, their utility and their docility, their distribution and their submission' (Foucault, 1977, 25). Cf. Butler on 'bodily subjection' (Butler, 1997, 31–62).
13. Cf. the arguments about dehumanisation and the banishing of the physical in Baudrillard's *The Evil Demon of Images* ('a logic of the extermination of its own referent, a logic of the implosion of meaning in which the message disappears on the horizon of the medium' (Baudrillard, 1987, 23)).
14. Two resonant instances of variously imagistic dealings with this 'new geography' are to be found in Appadurai, 1990, and its discourse of -scapes ('ethnoscapes', 'mediascapes', 'technoscapes', 'finanscapes', 'ideoscapes') and in much of the fiction of J. G. Ballard; see, for

example, 'The Cloud-Sculptors of Coral D' and 'Studio 5, The Stars' (Ballard, 1973, 11–30, 145–84) for examples of a specific architecture of indifference.

15. The alibi, I take it, is the crucial term here. See also, for example, my comments on Poe's 'Ligeia' and the problems of graves, evidence and the alibi in Punter, 1998, 111ff.

## Chapter 9

1. Sometimes referred to, with a subtle change of emphasis, as 'selective' mute (see Kratochwill, 1981). Another instance would be Faith in Farida Karodia's *A Shattering of Silence*, who also enters into an impossible world between trauma and the sign: 'Was this what prison was like? I wondered. Angie had once told me that not being able to speak was like being imprisoned in your own body. She had assured me that sign language would ultimately free me' (Karodia, 1993, 59).
2. In the helpful wording of Anne Whitehead's unpublished dissertation, 'Trauma, Gender and Performance: Theorising the Body of the Survivor', Cathy Caruth argues

   > that the traumatic event profoundly disrupts the chronological process which is integral to history – and to narrative – because it is only experienced belatedly. The traumatic experience thus no longer coincides in temporal or spatial terms with the precipitating event: it is experienced in its possession of the individual after an interval of time has elapsed and (usually) in a different place. It is thus not only meaning which is problematised, but history itself, which enters the 'pathology' of trauma and becomes 'symptomatic'. (7)

3. Cf. Judith Butler in particular on the subject status of 'women' (Butler, 1990, 1–6).
4. On the dangers of the 'multicultural fallacy', see for example the Introduction on 'Black Britain and the Cultural Politics of Diaspora' in *Welcome to the Jungle*, by Kobena Mercer, and the various further references given there. See also, in the same volume, his chapter on 'Recoding Narratives of Race and Nation' (Mercer, 1994, 1–31, 69–96).
5. The comparison, of course, is with Coleridge's 'Rime of the Ancient Mariner'. One might also be put in mind of another somnambulistic part of the poem:

   > The helmsman steered, the ship moved on;
   > Yet never a breeze up-blew;
   > The mariners all 'gan work the ropes,
   > Where they were wont to do;

> They raised their limbs like lifeless tools –
> We were a ghastly crew.
>
> (Coleridge, 1935, 200)

6. This, of course, is fundamentally different from the neo-romantic assumptions Kristeva makes in *Strangers to Ourselves*, where in the case of the foreigner, for example, 'the insistent presence of a lining – good or evil, pleasing or death-bearing – disrupts the never regular image of his face and imprints upon it the ambiguous mark of a scar – his very own well-being' (Kristeva, 1991, 4).
7. Rob Nixon puts together the catalogue of derision (while not, of course, subscribing to it): '"a despicable lackey of neo-colonialism", "a cold and sneering prophet", "a smart restorer of the comforting myths of the white race", or, for that matter, a "Gunga Din" who performs "while the cold smiles of the Pukka Sahibs applaud his antic agility"' (Nixon, 1992, 4). Mostly what is thus revealed is the agility of racism's contortions.
8. The origin of 'khaki' is Urdu and refers to the colour of dust; its 'translation' into the sign of the military was effected via imperial troops in India, Afghanistan, the Sudan and South Africa.
9. Hodge and Mishra, among many others, chart some of the (in this case Australian) contexts for such abuse; they speak, for example, of 'the attraction of the innocence/nakedness' of the Aboriginal woman and also of 'the condemnation of it as justification for a punitive response' (Hodge and Mishra, 1990, 34).
10. And thus to the schizo:

    > Scotland as 'country' is, then, a landscape of the mind, a place of the imagination. As such, notions of the essential Scotland are what people want it to be. In this respect, many argue that Scotland is peculiarly prone to myths and legends about itself, because it lacks the formal political institutions of state autonomy. ... the image of Scotland as a divided, schizophrenic society is a very powerful one, corresponding in part to the separation of state (British) from society (Scottish). (McCrone, 1992, 17)

11. The 'respectability' of the four violent youths is firmly established by, of course, the law (see Welsh, 1995, 207ff.).

## Chapter 10

1. It is now generally accepted that slavery still occurs in, to take just one example, the war-torn areas of the southern Sudan. See also Willemina Kloosterboer's now rather old but still devastating study, *Involuntary Labour since the Abolition of Slavery*, where she describes

various circumstances in which 'nothing but terror ... keeps the people at work' (Kloosterboer, 1960, 199).

2. See, for example, the depiction of the 'savages' in Cooper's *The Pathfinder*, or, on more of a cusp between the wild and the domesticated, the emblematic figure of the Tuscarora who stands 'slightly raised on tip-toe, with distended nostrils, like the buck that scents a taint in the air, and a gaze as riveted as that of the trained pointer, while he waits his master's aim' (Cooper, 1989, 11).
3. One example would be the peculiar position in anthropological debate occupied by 'degenerationist' arguments. Annie E. Coombes, in 'The Recalcitrant Object', describes some of the difficulties of 'producing a unified colonial subject which fitted neatly into the evolutionary mould' (Barker et al., 1994, 98ff.).
4. Interestingly, even early Marxist attacks on the eugenics movement 'did not want to stamp out eugenics altogether' but rather to separate it from 'its racism and its bourgeois class-bias' (Mazumdar, 1992, 148).
5. On these issues of ethnic stereotyping, the title of Kobena Mercer's *Welcome to the Jungle* is obviously unforgettable, as is his formulation, 'white ethnicity constitutes an "unknown" in contemporary cultural theory – a dark continent that has not yet been explored' (Mercer, 1994, 217). See also Solomos and Back, 1996.
6. Or it may be better to speak, with Christopher Bollas in *The Shadow of the Object*, of projective identifications, 'acts of expulsion which may reflect defensive manœuvres against primitive anxieties over annihilation' (Bollas, 1987, 167).
7. The point I am making here about Rastafarianism would follow from Kobena Mercer's general argument about 'black counterdiscourse' in 'Black Hair/Style Politics':

    The counterhegemonic tactic of inversion appropriated a particularly romanticist version of nature as a means of empowering the black subject; but by remaining within a dualistic logic of binary oppositionality (to Europe and artifice) the moment of rupture was delimited by the fact that it was only ever an imaginary 'Africa' that was put into play. (Mercer, 1994, 109–10)

8. See, for example, Donna Haraway's *Simians, Cyborgs, and Women*, and especially the first two chapters, 'Animal Sociology and a Natural Economy of the Body Politic' and 'The Past is the Contested Zone' (Haraway, 1991, 7–42).
9. One of the most compelling texts on this logic of extermination is Barry Lopez's *Of Wolves and Men*, which asks the salient question, 'when a man cocked a rifle and aimed it at a wolf's head, what was he trying to kill?' and adds that 'in the wolf we have not so much an animal that we have always known as one that we have consistently *imagined*' (Lopez, 1995, 138, 204).

10. A particularly unfortunate and damaging example of this remains Spivak's treatment of the subaltern who, as Neil Lazarus puts it, becomes in her work 'not a colonised person but a discursive figure in a battery of more or less integrated dominant cultural texts. ... [Spivak's] work ... characteristically defers any detailed presentation of the mass politics of the colonised' (Barker et al., 1994, 205–6).
11. This would be the question which would increasingly serve to undermine whatever is meant by 'deep ecology', which is capable of coming up with economic naivetés of this kind: 'Cultural diversity today requires advanced technology, that is, techniques that advance the basic goals of each culture' (Devall and Sessions, 1985, 73). See also Pepper, 1993, on deep ecology and the political.
12. See Deleuze and Guattari, 1988, 291:

> Why are there so many becomings of man, but no becoming-man? First because man is majoritarian par excellence, whereas becomings are minoritarian; all becoming is a becoming-minoritarian. ... In this sense women, children, but also animals, plants, and molecules, are minoritarian. ... [but] becomings, being minoritarian, always pass through a becoming-woman.

13. The example to which I am referring can be found in Haraway, 1991, 109–24; see also Moore-Gilbert, 1997, 201.
14. This, of course, brings to the fore in particularly contentious fashion a long-running argument about Freud and women. See, for example, *The Memory Wars*, a compendium of argument by Frederick Crews and his opponents in the area of 'recovered memory', which inevitably, via the contested site of hysteria, raises crucial issues about Freud's dealings with women; see also Appignanesi and Forrester, 1992, *passim*.
15. The phrase is in fact from Sartre's Preface to *The Wretched of the Earth*, and the wording and context are important: 'Our enemy betrays his brothers and becomes our accomplice', Sartre says; 'his brothers do the same thing. The status of "native" is a nervous condition introduced and maintained by the settler among colonised people *with their consent*' (Fanon, 1965, 17).
16. The issue of patriarchal silencing is hardly a new one, but Elaine Showalter sheds an extraordinary light on a different aspect of it when, in *The Female Malady*, she offers us the example of the silenced soldier and his astonishingly agonistic 'cure' (though without apparently noticing the all-important detail that the man's mutism had lasted for *nine months* (Showalter, 1985, 176–7)).
17. This would invalidate such utopian fantasies as those of Diana Brydon when she speaks of writings which,

> like the post-colonial criticsm that seeks to understand them, are searching for a new globalism that is neither the old universalism

> nor the Disney simulacrum. This new globalism simultaneously asserts local independence and global interdependencies. It seeks a way to cooperate without cooption, a way to define differences that do not depend on myths of cultural purity or authenticity ... (Ashcroft, Griffith and Tiffin, 1995, 141).

18. There is, for example, Achebe's trenchantly delicate characterisation of the man who

> spoke of the great African novel yet to be written. He said the trouble with what we have written so far is that it has concentrated too much on society and not sufficiently on individual characters and as a result it has lacked 'true' aesthetic proportions. I wondered when this *truth* became so self-evident and who decided that ... this one should apply to black as well as white. (Achebe, 1975, 47)

19. Examples I have in mind (but perhaps I am merely projecting my own tastes) would include the covers to the Heinemann book of South African short stories; the companion volume of contemporary African short stories; Farida Karodia's *Coming Home*; and any of Buchi Emecheta's works.
20. In, of course, America above all. Ihab Hassan quotes from an unpublished manuscript:

> The fall of the People, the rape of the Land, the liquidation of the Indian – these were the formative sins of God's Country, the consciousness of which contributed to the birth of culture. Concretely, the fall contributed to secularism, the rape to materialism, and genocide to imperialism. (Hassan, 1961, 36)

21. Cf. some of the implications of B. W. Higman, 'Slavery and the Development of Demographic Theory in the Age of the Industrial Revolution', in Walvin, 1982, 167–94.
22. Soyinka's description of European habits of interpretation is to be found at its most succinct in his *Myth, Literature and the African World*: see Soyinka, 1976, 37ff.

## Chapter 11

1. My source for this is very probably underestimating the figure; see Overy, 1996, 183.
2. This is recognised also in, for example, Rey Chow's attempt in *Writing Diaspora* to characterise the situation of migrants in general (see Chow, 1993, 179–80) and in various essays in Peter van der Veer's collection of essays on the South Asian diaspora (Van der Veer, 1995).

3. On Marquez and the postcolonial, see Roberto Gonzalez Echevarria's powerful essay on *Cien anos de soledad*, which connects colonialism to issues of myth, genealogy and the archive in Marquez (Bloom, 1989, 107–23).
4. Part of the history of the 'mother-of-separation' may be glimpsed in Marshall Edelson's essay 'Two Questions about Psychoanalysis and Poetry' (in Smith, 1980, 113–19). See also Punter, 2000a.
5. And yet perhaps, as Achebe suggests, the name itself is merely an alibi. 'Admittedly', he says, invoking names associated with imperial adventuring, 'if a John Hawkins were to fit out a slave ship from Plymouth today, he would be universally condemned. The world would not stand for it' (Achebe, 1975, 79). Yet the world 'stands for' Chinese snakeheads and their human cargoes; and, more remarkably, it 'stands for' the conditions of near-slavery in which many contemporary ships' crews operate.
6. The references here include Ishiguro, 1986, and Golden, 1997, both of which have to do with problems of marginal inscription in a specifically hierarchical (in this case Japanese) context.
7. The example is from Jamaica Kincaid, 1988, 43.
8. The crucial moment in the history of mahogany comes when the name of a tree indigenous to Central America and the islands of the Caribbean (a name attributed to the Caribs but apparently of unknown origin) is transformed into the name of a wood desired in Europe and thus, further, into a synonym for the expensive tables made from it.
9. I am here speaking of 'narco-democracy' in two senses: first, as the particular illusion that an 'addicted state', or a state dependent on addiction, can nevertheless accede to Western notions of 'democratic development'; and secondly, as the increasing succumbing of the global body to ideas and images based on 'narco-culture'. That the two are interlinked in a somnambulistic economy designed to evade questioning of the complicities of capitalism seems to me self-evident.

## Chapter 12

1. All this, of course, was evident to Fanon forty years ago, speaking of the

> under-developed world, a world inhuman in its poverty ... a world without doctors, without engineers and without administrators. Confronting this world the European nations sprawl, ostentatiously opulent. This European opulence is literally scandalous, for it has been founded on slavery, it has been nourished with the blood of slaves and it comes directly from the soil and from the subsoil of that under-developed world. (Fanon, 1965, 76)

2. Brecht, perhaps, on 'painful discrepancies in our environment, circumstances that were barely tolerable, and this not merely on account of moral considerations. It is not only moral considerations that make hunger, cold and oppression hard to bear' (Brecht, 1974, 75). Cf. Deleuze and Guattari on extermination, generalised terror and the struggle (Deleuze and Guattari, 1988, 471–3).
3. The literature here is enormous. See, for example, the wide-ranging global implications outlined in the various papers, mostly derived from UN-sponsored projects, in *Deforestation*, edited by J. Ives and D.C. Pitt, and the arguments, especially in the Amazonian context, in Susanna Hecht and Alexander Cockburn's *The Fate of the Forest* (Ives and Pitt, 1988; Hecht and Cockburn, 1989).
4. Even a liberal economist like William Keegan grants that 'there is hardly an example of a capitalist or market economy which does not depend, directly or indirectly, on some degree of cheap labour – at home and (especially) abroad. Traditionally it has been highly convenient for market economies that so many countries offering them cheap commodities are "left behind" and stay behind' (Keegan, 1992, 101). Robert Miles puts it a different way: 'an adequate explanation for unfree relations of production (which includes racism) is best sought in the context of a general theory of capitalist development' (Miles, 1987, 225).
5. Perhaps this notion of parody should better be regarded in terms of scorn or contempt. Certainly this would seem to be the mood behind the ludicrous optimism of Gregory Ulmer's concept of 'teletheory':

   > Teletheory is concerned with discovering and inventing the kind of thinking and representation available for academic discourse in an electronic age. My working assumption is that the mode I seek is modelled in the simple form of the joke. (Ulmer, 1989, 61)

   Ulmer opposes this to the 'melancholy seriousness' otherwise associated with academic work, and hysterically quotes Michel Serres: 'At its birth, knowledge is happy' (Serres, 1974, 75).
6. One among many books that puzzles about this is Immanuel Wallerstein's *Geopolitics and Geoculture*. Wallerstein speaks of the Third World; of the 'extra-European' world; of 'Americanism'; of 'North Atlanticism' (in decline); of the North/South divide. Perhaps in the end his main point is the simple if evasive one that

   > The collapse of Leninism is very bad news indeed for the dominant forces of the capitalist world-economy. It has removed the last major politically *stabilising* force on the planet. It will not be easy to put Humpty-Dumpty together again. (Wallerstein, 1991, 14)

# Bibliography

This bibliography is divided into three parts. The first part lists the primary texts I have had mainly in mind in writing the book, and have referred to most. The second part contains both a range of other postcolonial writing and also other literature referred to on occasion; it would be interesting to know whether any of these latter texts could be referred to as definitively *not* postcolonial. The third part lists relevant critical writing – literary, political, philosophical, economic. Not all the titles listed sit comfortably within one of these categories.

## Main Texts


Achebe, Chinua (1987). *Anthills of the Savannah*. London: Heinemann.

——(1996). *Things Fall Apart* (1958). London: Heinemann.

Armah, Ayi Kwei (1978). *The Healers: An Historical Novel*. London: Heinemann.

Atwood, Margaret (1973). *Surfacing* (1972). London: André Deutsch.

Banks, Iain (1984). *The Wasp Factory*. London: Macmillan.

Barker, Elspeth (1991). *O Caledonia*. London: Hamish Hamilton.

Behl, Aditya, and David Nicholls, eds (1995). *The Penguin New Writing in India*. Harmondsworth: Penguin.

Brathwaite, Edward (1973). *The Arrivants: A New World Trilogy*. London: Oxford University Press.

Chandra, Vikram (1997). *Love and Longing in Bombay*. London: Faber and Faber.

Coetzee, J. M. (1983). *Life & Times of Michael K*. London: Secker and Warburg.

——(1990). *Age of Iron*. London: Secker and Warburg.

D'Aguiar, Fred (1997). *Feeding the Ghosts*. London: Chatto and Windus.

Dangarembga, Tsitsi (1988). *Nervous Conditions*. London: The Women's Press.

Deane, Seamus (1996). *Reading in the Dark*. London: Jonathan Cape.

Desai, Kiran (1998). *Hullabaloo in the Guava Orchard*. London: Faber and Faber.

Foden, Giles (1998). *The Last King of Scotland*. London: Faber and Faber.
Gibson, William (1984). *Neuromancer*. London: Victor Gollancz.
Gupta, Sunetra (1993). *The Glassblower's Breath*. London: Orion.
Gurnah, Abdulrazak (1994). *Paradise*. London: Hamish Hamilton.
Harris, Wilson (1988). *The Palace of the Peacock* (1960). London: Faber and Faber.
Hulme, Keri (1985). *The Bone People*. Auckland: Spiral; London: Hodder and Stoughton.
Kelman, James (1994). *How Late It Was, How Late*. London: Secker and Warburg.
Keneally, Thomas (1987). *The Playmaker*. London: Hodder and Stoughton.
Kureishi, Hanif (1995). *The Black Album*. London: Faber and Faber.
Morrison, Toni (1979). *The Bluest Eye*. London: Chatto and Windus.
——(1987). *Beloved: A Novel*. London: Chatto and Windus.
Naipaul, V. S. (1961). *A House for Mr Biswas*. London: André Deutsch.
Narayan, R. K. (1955). *Waiting for the Mahatma*. London: Methuen.
Ondaatje, Michael (1982). *Running in the Family*. New York: W. W. Norton.
Power, Susan (1994). *The Grass Dancer*. New York: G. P. Putnam's Sons.
Riley, Joan (1985). *The Unbelonging*. London: The Women's Press.
Roy, Arundhati (1997). *The God of Small Things*. London: Flamingo.
Rushdie, Salman (1983). *Shame*. London: Jonathan Cape.
Soyinka, Wole (1970). *The Interpreters*, introd. Eldred Jones. London: Heinemann.
Syal, Meera (1996). *Anita and Me*. London: Flamingo.
Tutuola, Amos (1952). *The Palm-Wine Drinkard*. London: Faber and Faber.
——(1962). *Feather Woman of the Jungle*. London: Faber and Faber.
Walcott, Derek (1992). *Collected Poems 1948–1984*. London: Faber and Faber.
Welsh, Irvine (1995). *Marabou Stork Nightmares*. London: Jonathan Cape.

## Other Primary Texts

Achebe, Chinua (1964). *Arrow of God*. London: Heinemann.
——(1966). *A Man of the People*. London: Heinemann.
——, and C. L. Innes, eds (1992). *Contemporary African Short Stories*. London: Heinemann.
Aidoo, Ama Ata (1965). *The Dilemma of a Ghost*. London: Longman.
—— (1977). *Our Sister Killjoy*. London: Longman.
Anand, Mulk Raj (1977). *Selected Short Stories*, ed. M. K. Naik. New Delhi: Arnold–Heinemann.
Anthony, Michael (1993). *The Chieftain's Carnival, and Other Stories*. London: Longman.
——(1996). *In the Heat of the Day*. London: Heinemann.
Armah, Ayi Kwei (1979). *Two Thousand Seasons*. London: Heinemann.
Atwood, Margaret (1983). *Murder in the Dark: Short Fictions and Prose Poems*. Toronto: Coach House Press.

Ballard, J. G. (1973). *Vermilion Sands*. London: Jonathan Cape.

Banville, John (1986). *Mefisto*. London: Secker and Warburg.

——(1989). *The Book of Evidence*. London: Secker and Warburg.

Berry, James, ed. (1984). *News from Babylon: The Chatto Book of Westindian-British Poetry*. London: Chatto and Windus.

Blake, William (1966). *Complete Writings*, ed. Geoffrey Keynes. London: Oxford University Press.

Brathwaite, (Edward) Kamau (1994). *DreamStories*, introd. Gordon Rohlehr. London: Longman.

Brecht, Bertolt (1962). *Mother Courage and her Children*, trans. Eric Bentley. London: Methuen.

Butlin, Ron (1997). *Night Visits*. Edinburgh: Scottish Cultural Press.

Chang, Jung (1993). *Wild Swans: Three Daughters of China*. London: Flamingo.

Coleridge, Samuel Taylor (1935). *Poems*, ed. Ernest Hartley Coleridge. London: Oxford University Press.

Conrad, Joseph (1973). *Heart of Darkness* (1899). Harmondsworth: Penguin.

Cook, Elizabeth, ed. (1990). *John Keats*. Oxford and New York: Oxford University Press.

Cooper, James Fenimore (1989). *The Pathfinder* (1840), introd. Kay Seymour House. Harmondsworth: Penguin.

D'Aguiar, Fred (1994). *The Longest Memory*. London: Chatto and Windus.

——(1996). *Dear Future*. London: Chatto and Windus.

——(1998). *Bill of Rights*. London: Chatto and Windus.

Emecheta, Buchi (1994). *The Joys of Motherhood* (1979). London: Heinemann.

——(1995). *The Bride Price* (1976). London: Heinemann.

Farmer, Beverley (1992). *The Seal Woman*. St Lucia: University of Queensland Press.

Findley, Timothy (1990). *The Butterfly Plague* (1969). Markham, Ontario and London: Penguin.

Frame, Janet (1980). *Faces in the Water*. London: The Women's Press.

Garcia Marquez, Gabriel (1978). *One Hundred Years of Solitude* (1967), trans. Gregory Rabassa. London: Pan.

Ghose, Zulfikar (1967). *Jets from Orange: Poems*. London: Macmillan.

Ghosh, Amitav (1988). *The Shadow Lines*. London: Black Swan.

Gibson, William (1986a). *Burning Chrome, and Other Stories*. London: Victor Gollancz.

——(1986b). *Count Zero*. London: Victor Gollancz.

——(1988). *Mona Lisa Overdrive*. London: Victor Gollancz.

——(1993). *Virtual Light*. London: Viking.

Golden, Arthur (1997). *Memoirs of a Geisha*. London: Chatto and Windus.

Gordimer, Nadine (1991). *Crimes of Conscience*. London: Heinemann.

Harris, Wilson (1973). *The Whole Armour, and, The Secret Ladder*. London: Faber and Faber.

Heaney, Seamus (1990). *New Selected Poems 1966–1987*. London: Faber and Faber.

Hirson, Denis, with Martin Trump, eds (1994). *South African Short Stories, from 1945 to the Present*. London: Heinemann.

Ishiguro, Kazuo (1986). *An Artist of the Floating World*. London: Faber and Faber.

Kafka, Franz (1930). *The Castle* (1926), trans. Willa and Edwin Muir. London: Secker and Warburg.

Karodia, Farida (1988). *Coming Home, and Other Stories*. London: Heinemann.

——(1993). *A Shattering of Silence*. Oxford: Heinemann.

Kelman, James (1987). *Greyhound for Breakfast*. London: Secker and Warburg.

——(1991). *Not not while the Giro, and Other Stories*. London: Minerva.

——(1992). *The Busconductor Hines*. London: Phoenix.

Keneally, Thomas (1972). *The Chant of Jimmie Blacksmith*. Sydney and London: Angus and Robertson.

Kincaid, Jamaica (1988). *A Small Place*. London: Virago.

Kureishi, Hanif (1997). *Love in a Blue Time*. London: Faber and Faber.

Lamming, George (1970). *In the Castle of my Skin*. Port of Spain and Harlow: Longman.

Larkin, Philip (1990). *Collected Poems*, ed. Anthony Thwaite. London: The Marvell Press.

Laurence, Margaret (1964). *The Stone Angel*. London: Macmillan.

Lee, Dennis (1972). *Civil Elegies, and Other Poems*. Toronto: Anansi.

Lorde, Audre (1995). *The Black Unicorn: Poems*. New York: Norton.

McCarthy, Cormac (1994). *The Crossing*. New York: Alfred A. Knopf.

Mansfield, Katherine (1974). *The Complete Stories*. Auckland: Golden Press.

Mapanje, Jack (1981). *Of Chameleons and Gods*. London: Heinemann.

Melville, Herman (1993). *Billy Budd, Sailor, and Other Stories*, ed. A. Robert Lee. London: Dent.

Milton, John (1980). *The Complete Poems*, introd. Gordon Campbell. London and Melbourne: Dent.

Morrison, Toni (1988). *Song of Solomon*. London: Chatto and Windus.

——(1990). *Sula*. London: Chatto and Windus.

Naipaul, V. S. (1967a). *The Mimic Men*. London: André Deutsch.

——(1967b). *A Flag on the Island*. London: André Deutsch.

——(1971). *In a Free State*. London: André Deutsch.

——(1994). *A Way in the World: A Sequence*. London: André Deutsch.

Narayan, R. K. (1961). *The Man-Eater of Malgudi*. New York: Viking.

——(1967). *The Sweet-Vendor*. Oxford: The Bodley Head.

——(1976). *The Painter of Signs*. London: Heinemann.

Ngugi wa Thiong'o (1968). *A Grain of Wheat*. London: Heinemann.

——(1977). *Petals of Blood*. London: Heinemann.

——(1987). *Devil on the Cross* (1982), trans. the author. London: Heinemann.

Nichols, Grace (1983). *I is a Long Memoried Woman*. London: Caribbean Cultural International.

Nkosi, Lewis (1965). *Home and Exile*. London: Longman.

Nwapa, Flora (1966). *Efuru*. London: Heinemann.

——(1970). *Idu*. London: Heinemann.

Okara, Gabriel (1970). *The Voice*, introd. Arthur Ravenscroft. London: Heinemann.

Okri, Ben (1991). *Flowers and Shadows*. London: Longman.

Ouloguem, Yambo (1971). *Bound to Violence*, trans. Ralph Manheim. London: Heinemann.

Phillips, Caryl (1994). *Crossing the River*. London: Pan.

Plaatje, Solomon (1978). *Mhudi* (1930), ed. Stephen Gray. London: Heinemann.

Poe, Edgar Allan (1960). *Tales of Mystery and Imagination*. London: Pan.

——(1967–78). *Collected Works*, ed. Thomas Ollive Mabbott. 3 vols. Cambridge and London: Harvard University Press.

Rhys, Jean (1997). *Wide Sargasso Sea* (1966), ed. Angela Smith. Harmondsworth: Penguin.

Rice, Anne (1976). *Interview with the Vampire*. London: Raven Books.

Riley, Joan (1987). *Waiting in the Twilight*. London: The Women's Press.

——(1988). *Romance*. London: The Women's Press.

——(1992). *A Kindness to the Children*. London: The Women's Press.

Rushdie, Salman (1981). *Midnight's Children*. London: Jonathan Cape.

——(1992). *The Satanic Verses*. Delaware: The Consortium.

——(1995). *The Moor's Last Sigh*. London: Jonathan Cape.

Sahgal, Nayantara (1975). *A Time to be Happy*. New Delhi: Sterling.

Scott, Paul (1976). *The Raj Quartet*. London: Heinemann.

Selvon, Samuel (1972). *The Lonely Londoners*. London: Longman.

Senior, Olive (1989). *Arrival of the Snakewoman, and Other Stories*. London: Longman.

Serote, Mongane Wally (1981). *To Every Birth its Blood*. London: Heinemann.

Shelley, Mary (1994). *Frankenstein* (1818), introd. Paddy Lyons. London: Dent.

Soyinka, Wole (1973–4). *Collected Plays*. 2 vols. London: Oxford University Press.

Stevenson, Robert Louis (1985). *Treasure Island* (1883), ed. Emma Letley. Oxford: Oxford University Press.

Tam, Amy (1989). *The Joy Luck Club*. New York: G. P. Putnam's Sons.

Thomas, D. M. (1981). *The White Hotel*. Harmondsworth: Penguin.

Tutuola, Amos (1953). *My Life in the Bush of Ghosts*. London: Faber and Faber.

——(1955). *Simbi and the Satyr of the Dark Jungle*. London: Faber and Faber.

——(1967). *Ajaiyi and his Inherited Poverty*. London: Faber and Faber.

Walcott, Derek (1972). *Dream on Monkey Mountain, and Other Plays*. London: Jonathan Cape.

——(1990). *Omeros*. London: Faber.

Wells, H. G. (1993). *The Island of Doctor Moreau* (1896), ed. Brian Aldiss. London: J. M. Dent.

Wiebe, Rudy (1976). *The Temptations of Big Bear*. Toronto: McClelland and Stewart.

Xi Xi (1986). *A Girl Like Me*. Hong Kong: Chinese University Press.

## Critical Writing

Abbas, Ackbar (1997). *Hong Kong: Culture and the Politics of Disappearance*. Minneapolis: University of Minnesota Press.

Abraham, Nicolas, and Maria Torok (1986). *The Wolf-Man's Magic Word: A Cryptonymy*, trans. Nicholas Rand. Minneapolis: University of Minnesota Press.

—— and ——(1994). *The Shell and the Kernel: Renewals of Psychoanalysis*, trans. Nicholas Rand. Chicago and London: Chicago University Press.

Achebe, Chinua (1975). *Morning Yet on Creation Day: Essays*. London: Heinemann; Garden City, NY: Anchor/Doubleday.

——(1977). 'An Image of Africa'. *Massachusetts Review*, 18, pp. 782–94.

Adam, Ian, and Helen Tiffin, eds (1991). *Past the Last Post: Theorising Post-Colonialism and Post-Modernism*. New York and London: Harvester Wheatsheaf.

Agamben, Giorgio (1993). *The Coming Community*. Minneapolis: University of Minnesota Press.

Ahmad, Aijaz (1992). *In Theory: Classes, Nations, Literatures*. London: Verso.

Alazi, Hamza (1973). 'The State in Post-Colonial Societies: Pakistan and Bangladesh'. In *Imperialism and Revolution in South Asia*, ed. Kathleen Gough and Hari P. Sharma. New York: Monthly Review Press.

Amadiume, Ifi (1987). *Male Daughters, Female Husbands: Gender and Sex in an African Society*. London: Zed Books.

Anderson, Benedict (1983). *Imagined Communities: Reflections on the Origin and Spread of Nationalism*. London: Verso.

Anderson, Perry (1969). 'Components of the National Culture'. In *Student Power: Problems, Diagnosis, Action*, ed. Alexander Cockburn and Robin Blackburn. Harmondsworth: Penguin/New Left Review.

Appadurai, Arjun (1990). 'Disjuncture and Difference in the Global Cultural Economy'. *Public Culture*, 2.2, pp. 1–24.

Appiah, Kwame Anthony (1992). *In my Father's House: Africa in the Philosophy of Culture*. London: Methuen.

Appignanesi, Lisa, and John Forrester (1992). *Freud's Women*. London: Weidenfeld and Nicolson.

Arvidson, Ken (1991). 'Aspects of Contemporary Maori Writing in English'. In *Dirty Silence: Aspects of Language and Literature in New Zealand*, ed. Graham McGregor and Mark Williams. Auckland: Oxford University Press.

Ashcroft, Bill, Gareth Griffiths and Helen Tiffin, eds (1989). *The Empire Writes Back: Theory and Practice in Post-Colonial Literatures*. London: Routledge.

——, —— and ——(1995). *The Post-Colonial Studies Reader*. London: Routledge.

Assiter, Alison (1988). 'Romance Fiction: Porn for Women?' In *Perspectives on Pornography: Sexuality in Film and Literature*, ed. Gary Day and Clive Bloom. London: Macmillan.

Baldick, Chris (1987). *In Frankenstein's Shadow: Myth, Monstrosity, and Nineteenth-Century Writing*. Oxford: Clarendon Press.

Barker, Francis, Peter Hulme and Margaret Iversen, eds (1994). *Colonial Discourse/Postcolonial Theory*. Manchester: Manchester University Press.

Baudrillard, Jean (1987). *The Evil Demon of Images*. Sydney: Power Institute of Fine Arts.

Belsey, Catherine (1980). *Critical Practice*. London: Methuen.

Benjamin, Walter (1992). *Illuminations*, ed. Hannah Arendt. London: HarperCollins.

Bennett, Andrew, and Nicholas Royle (1995). *An Introduction to Literature, Criticism and Theory: Key Critical Concepts*. London: Harvester Wheatsheaf.

Bennington, Geoffrey, and Jacques Derrida (1993). *Jacques Derrida*, trans. Geoffrey Bennington. Chicago and London: Chicago University Press.

Bennis, Phyllis, and Michael Moushabeck, eds (1993). *Altered States: A Reader in the New World Order*. New York: Olive Branch Press.

Benterrak, Krim, Stephen Muecke and Paddy Roe (1984). *Reading the Country: Introduction to Nomadology*. Fremantle: Fremantle Arts Centre Press.

Bersani, Leo (1990). *The Culture of Redemption*. Cambridge and London: Harvard University Press.

Bhabha, Homi (1982). 'Signs Taken for Wonders: Questions of Ambivalence and Authority under a Tree Outside Delhi, May 1817'. *Critical Inquiry*, 12.1, pp. 144–65.

——(1983). 'The Other Question'. *Screen*, 24.6, pp. 18–36.

——(1984). 'Of Mimicry and Man: The Ambivalence of Colonial Discourse'. *October*, no. 28, pp. 125–33.

——, ed. (1990). *Nation and Narration*. London: Routledge.

——(1994). *The Location of Culture*. London: Routledge.

Blanchot, Maurice (1982). *The Space of Literature*, trans. Ann Smock. Lincoln (NB) and London: University of Nebraska Press.

——(1993). *The Infinite Conversation*, trans. Susan Hanson. Minneapolis and London: University of Minnesota Press.

Bloom, Harold, ed. (1989). *Gabriel Garcia Marquez*. New York and Philadelphia: Chelsea House.

Boehmer, Elleke (1995). *Colonial and Postcolonial Literature: Migrant Metaphors*. Oxford: Oxford University Press.

Bollas, Christopher (1987). *The Shadow of the Object: Psychoanalysis of the Unthought Known*. London: Free Association Books.

Borch-Jacobsen, Mikkel (1989). *The Freudian Subject*, trans. Catherine Porter. London: Macmillan.

Botting, Fred (1993). 'Whither Theory'. *Oxford Literary Review*, 15, pp. 201–24.

Bowlby, John (1969–80). *Attachment and Loss*. 3 vols. London: Hogarth Press.

Brathwaite, Edward Kamau (1975). 'Caribbean Man in Time and Space'. *Savacou*, 11–12, pp. 1–11.

——(1984). *History of the Voice: The Development of Nation Language in Anglophone Caribbean Poetry*. London: New Beacon.

Brecher, Jeremy, John Brown Childs and Jill Cutler, eds (1993). *Global Visions: Beyond the New World Order*. Boston: South End Press.

Brecht, Bertolt (1974). *Brecht on Theatre: The Development of an Aesthetic*, trans. John Willett. 2nd edn, London: Methuen.

Breckenridge, Carol A., and Peter van der Veer (1993). *Orientalism and the Postcolonial Predicament: Perspectives on South Asia*. Philadelphia: University of Pennsylvania Press.

Brennan, Timothy (1989). *Salman Rushdie and the Third World: Myths of the Nation*. New York: St Martin's Press.

Butler, Judith (1990). *Gender Trouble: Feminism and the Subversion of Identity*. New York and London: Routledge.

——(1993). *Bodies that Matter: On the Discursive Limits of 'Sex'*. New York and London: Routledge.

——(1997). *The Psychic Life of Power: Theories in Subjection*. Stanford: Stanford University Press.

Callaghan, David (1988). 'What Future the Aborigine?' *TIME Australia*, 3.32, pp. 12–15.

Caruth, Cathy (1991). 'Unclaimed Experience: Trauma and the Possibility of History'. *Yale French Studies*, 79, pp. 181–92.

Césaire, Aimé (1972). *Discourse on Colonialism*. New York: Monthly Review Press.

Chakrabarty, Dipesh (1992). 'Postcoloniality and the Artifice of History: Who Speaks for "Indian" Pasts?' *Representations*, no. 37, pp. 1–26.

Chatterjee, Partha (1993). *The Nation and its Fragments*. Princeton: Princeton University Press.

Chow, Rey (1993). *Writing Diaspora: Tactics of Intervention in Contemporary Cultural Studies*. Bloomington and Indianapolis: Indiana University Press.

Chrisman, Laura (1990). 'The Imperial Unconscious? Representations of Imperial Discourse'. *Critical Quarterly*, 32.3, pp. 38–58.

Christian, Barbara (1987). 'The Race for Theory'. *Cultural Critique*, 6, pp. 51–63.

Crews, Frederick (1975). *Out of My System: Psychoanalysis, Ideology, and Critical Methodology*. Oxford: Oxford University Press.

——, et al. (1995). *The Memory Wars: Freud's Legacy in Dispute*. New York: New York Review.

Darwin, John (1988). *Britain and Decolonisation: The Retreat from Empire in the Post-War World*. London: Macmillan.

Dash, Michael J. (1973). 'Marvellous Realism: The Way out of Negritude'. *Caribbean Studies*, 13.4, pp. 57–70.

Davidson, Alastair (1991). *The Invisible State: The Formation of the Australian State 1788–1901*. Cambridge: Cambridge University Press.

Deleuze, Gilles, and Félix Guattari (1983). *Anti-Oedipus*, trans. Robert Hurley et al. Minneapolis: University of Minnesota Press.

—— and ——(1988). *A Thousand Plateaus*, trans. Brian Massumi. London: Athlone Press.

Deleuze, Gilles, and Claire Parnet (1987). *Dialogues*, trans. Hugh Tomlinson and Barbara Habberjam. London: Athlone Press.

Delgado, Richard, ed. (1995). *Critical Race Theory*. Philadelphia: Temple University Press.

Der Derian, James (1992). *Antidiplomacy: Spies, Terror, Speed, and War*. Cambridge (MA) and Oxford: Blackwell.

Derrida, Jacques (1978). *Writing and Difference*, trans. Alan Bass. London: Routledge and Kegan Paul.

——(1986). *Glas*, trans. John P. Leavey, Jr, and Richard Rand. Lincoln (NB) and London: University of Nebraska Press.

——(1987). *The Post Card: From Socrates to Freud and Beyond*, trans. Alan Bass. Chicago: University of Chicago Press.

——(1992). *The Other Heading: Reflections on Today's Europe*, trans. Pascale-Anne Brault and Michael B. Naas. Bloomington and Indianapolis: Indiana University Press.

——(1994). *Spectres of Marx: The State of the Debt, the Work of Mourning, and the New International*, trans. Peggy Kamuf. New York and London: Routledge.

Devall, Bill, and George Sessions (1985). *Deep Ecology*. Salt Lake City: Gibbs Smith.

Dharwadker, Vinay (1996). 'The Internationalisation of Literatures'. In King 1996, pp. 59–77.

Dirlik, Arif (1994). 'The Postcolonial Aura: Third World Criticism in the Age of Global Capitalism'. *Critical Inquiry*, 20, pp. 328–56.

During, Simon (1985). 'Postmodernism or Post-colonialism Today'. *Landfall*, 39.3, pp. 366–80.

Ekins, Paul (1992). *A New World Order: Grassroots Movements for Global Change*. London and New York: Routledge.

Elam, Diane (1995). 'Literary Remains'. *Oxford Literary Review*, 17, pp. 145–56.

Engels, Dagmar, and Shula Marks, eds (1994). *Contesting Colonial Hegemony: State and Society in Africa and India*. New York and London: British Academic Press.

Escobar, Arturo (1995). *Encountering Development: The Making and Unmaking of the Third World*. Princeton: Princeton University Press.

Fanon, Frantz (1965). *The Wretched of the Earth*, trans. Constance Farrington. London: Macgibbon and Kee.

——(1967). *Black Skin, White Masks*, trans. C. L. Markmann. New York: Grove Press.

Farah, Nuruddin (1994). 'Homing in on the Pigeon'. *Brick*, 48, pp. 4–9.

Featherstone, Mike, Scott Lash and Roland Robertson, eds (1995). *Global Modernities*. London: Sage Publications.

Fieldhouse, D. K. (1973). *Economics and Empire, 1830–1914*. London: Weidenfeld and Nicolson.

Figueira, Dorothy M. (1994). *The Exotic: A Decadent Quest*. Albany: State University of New York Press.

Fletcher, Miles (1982). *The Search for a New Order: Intellectuals and Fascism in Prewar Japan*. Chapel Hill: University of North Carolina Press.

Forna, Aminatta (1992). 'Pornography and Racism: Sexualising Oppression and Inciting Hatred'. In *Pornography: Women, Violence and Civil Liberties*, ed. Catherine Itzin. Oxford: Oxford University Press.

Forrester, John (1990). *The Seductions of Psychoanalysis: Freud, Lacan and Derrida*. Cambridge: Cambridge University Press.

Foucault, Michel (1972). *The Archaeology of Knowledge*, trans. A. M. Sheridan Smith. London: Routledge.

——(1977). *Discipline and Punish: The Birth of the Prison*, trans. Alan Sheridan. London: Allen Lane.

Franco, Jean (1988). 'Beyond Ethnocentrism: Gender, Power and the Third-World Intelligentsia'. In *Marxism and the Interpretation of Culture*, ed. Cary Nelson and Lawrence Grossberg. Basingstoke: Macmillan.

Freud, Sigmund (1953–74). *The Standard Edition of the Complete Psychological Works*, ed. James Strachey et al. 24 vols. London: The Hogarth Press and the Institute of Psycho-Analysis.

Fuery, Patrick (1993). 'Prisoners and Spiders Surrounded by Signs: Postmodernism and the Postcolonial Gaze in Contemporary Australian Culture'. In White 1993, pp. 190–207.

Gabriel, Teshome H. (1989). 'Towards a Critical Theory of Third World Films'. In *Questions of Third Cinema*, ed. Jim Pines and Paul Willemen. London: BFI.

Gates, Jr, Henry Louis (1984). *Black Literature and Literary Theory*. New York: Methuen.

——(1989). *The Signifying Monkey: A Theory of African-American Literary Criticism*. New York and Oxford: Oxford University Press.

Gikandi, Simon (1988). *Reading the African Novel*. London: James Currey.

——(1991). *Reading Chinua Achebe: Language and Ideology in Fiction*. London: James Currey.

Gillion, K. L. (1962). *Fiji's Indian Migrants: A History to the End of Indenture in 1920*. Melbourne: Oxford University Press.

Gordon, Avery, and Christopher Newfield (1996). *Mapping Multiculturalism*. Minneapolis: Minnesota University Press.

Goux, Jean-Joseph (1990). *Symbolic Economies: After Marx and Freud*. Ithaca: Cornell University Press.

Gray, John (1998). *False Dawn: The Delusions of Global Capitalism*. London: Granta.

Green, Martin (1980). *Dreams of Adventure, Deeds of Empire*. London and Henley: Routledge and Kegan Paul.

Griffiths, Gareth (1987). 'Imitation, Abrogation and Appropriation: The Production of the Post-Colonial Text'. *Kunapipi*, 9.1, pp. 13–20.

——(1994). 'The Myth of Authenticity'. In *De-Scribing Empire*, ed. Chris Tiffin and Alan Lawson. London: Routledge.

——(1996). 'The Post-Colonial Project: Critical Approaches and Problems'. In King 1996, pp. 164–77.

Grugel, Jean (1995). *Politics and Development in the Caribbean Basin: Central America and the Caribbean in the New World Order*. Bloomington and Indianapolis: Indiana University Press.

Gugelberger, Georg (1991). 'Decolonising the Canon: Considerations of Third World Literature'. *New Literary History*, 22, pp. 505–24.

Gupta, Akhil, and James Ferguson, eds (1997). *Culture, Power, Place: Explorations in Critical Anthropology*. Durham (NC) and London: Duke University Press.

Hall, Stuart (1980). 'Race, Articulation and Societies Structured in Dominance'. In *Sociological Theories: Race and Colonialism*, ed. UNESCO. Paris: UNESCO.

——(1990). 'Cultural Identity and Diaspora'. In *Identity: Community, Culture, Difference*, ed. Jonathan Rutherford. London: Laurence and Wishart.

——(1996). *Stuart Hall: Critical Dialogues in Cultural Studies*, ed. David Morley and Kuan-Hsing Chen. London and New York: Routledge.

Hamner, Robert D., ed. (1990). *Joseph Conrad: Third World Perspectives*. Washington: Three Continents.

Haraway, Donna (1991). *Simians, Cyborgs, and Women: The Reinvention of Nature*. London: Free Association Books.

Hargreaves, Alec G., and Michael J. Heffernan, eds (1993). *French and Algerian Identities from Colonial Times to the Present: A Century of Interaction*. Lewiston: The Edwin Mellen Press.

Harris, Wilson (1967). *Tradition, the Writer and Society: Critical Essays*. London: New Beacon.

——(1970). *History, Fable and Myth in the Caribbean and Guianas*. Georgetown: Ministry of Information and Culture.

——(1981). 'History, Fable and Myth in the Caribbean and Guianas'. In *Explorations: A Selection of Talks and Articles 1966–81*, ed. Hena Maes-Jelinek. Mundelstrup, Denmark: Dangaroo Press.

——(1983). *The Womb of Space: The Cross-Cultural Imagination*. Westport (CT) and London: Greenwood Press.

——(1985). 'Adversarial Contexts and Creativity'. *New Left Review*, no. 154, pp. 124–8.

——, et al. (1975). *Enigma of Values: An Introduction*. Aarhus, Denmark: Dangaroo Press.

Harvey, David (1985). *The Urbanisation of Capital*. Oxford: Blackwell.

——(1996). *Justice, Nature and the Geography of Difference*. Oxford: Blackwell.

Hassan, Ihab (1961). *Radical Innocence: Studies in the Contemporary American Novel*. Princeton (NJ): Princeton University Press.

Healy, David (1993). *Images of Trauma: From Hysteria to Post-Traumatic Stress Disorder*. London: Faber and Faber.

Heaney, Seamus (1980). *Preoccupations: Selected Prose 1968–1978*. London: Faber and Faber.

Hecht, Susanna, and Alexander Cockburn (1989). *The Fate of the Forest: Developers, Destroyers and Defenders of the Amazon.* London and New York: Verso.

Hillman, James (1975). *Re-Visioning Psychology.* New York: Harper and Row.

——(1979). *The Dream and the Underworld.* New York: Harper and Row.

Hirst, Paul, and Grahame Thompson (1996). *Globalisation in Question: The International Economy and the Politics of Governance.* Cambridge: Polity Press.

Ho, Louise (1998). 'Apartheid Discourse in Contested Space: Aspects of Hong Kong Culture'. *Comparative Literature and Culture,* no. 3, pp. 1–6.

Hodge, Bob, and Vijay Mishra (1990). *Dark Side of the Dream: Australian Literature and the Postcolonial Mind.* North Sydney: Allen and Unwin.

Howard, Jacqueline (1994). *Reading Gothic Fiction: A Bakhtinian Approach.* Oxford: Clarendon Press.

Huggan, Graham (1989). 'Decolonising the Map: Post-Colonialism, Post-Structuralism and the Cartographic Connection'. *Ariel,* 20.4, pp. 115–31.

Hutcheon, Linda (1988). *The Canadian Postmodern: A Study of Contemporary English-Canadian Fiction.* Toronto: Oxford University Press.

Inden, Ronald (1990). *Imagining India.* Oxford: Blackwell.

Innes, C. L. (1990). *Chinua Achebe.* Cambridge: Cambridge University Press.

Isichei, Elizabeth (1976). *A History of the Igbo People.* London: Macmillan.

Ives, J., and D. C. Pitt (1988). *Deforestation: Social Dynamics in Watersheds and Mountain Ecosystems.* London and New York: Routledge.

James, C. L. R. (1985). *Mariners, Renegades and Castaways.* London: Allison and Busby.

——(1992). *The C. L. R. James Reader,* ed. Anna Grimshaw. Oxford: Blackwell.

Jameson, Fredric (1986). 'Third-World Literature in the Era of Multinational Capitalism'. *Social Text,* 15, pp. 65–88.

——(1991). *Postmodernism, or, The Cultural Logic of Late Capitalism.* London: Verso.

JanMohamed, Abdul (1984). 'Humanism and Minority Literature: Toward a Definition of a Counter-Hegemonic Discourse'. *Boundary 2,* 12.3/13.1, pp. 281–99.

——(1985). 'The Economy of Manichean Allegory: The Function of Racial Difference in Colonialist Literature'. *Critical Inquiry,* 12.1, pp. 59–87.

Jones, Charles, ed. (1997). *The Edinburgh History of the Scots Language.* Edinburgh: Edinburgh University Press.

Joseph, John Earl (1987). *Eloquence and Power: The Rise of Language Standards and Standard Languages.* London: Frances Pinter.

Kanaganayakam, Chelva (1996). 'Exiles and Expatriates'. In King 1996, pp. 201–13.

Kappeler, Susanne (1986). *The Pornography of Representation.* Cambridge: Polity Press.

Katrak, Ketu (1989). 'Decolonising Culture: Toward a Theory for Post-colonial Women's Texts'. *Modern Fiction Studies*, 35.1, pp. 157–79.

——(1996). 'Post-colonial Women Writers and Feminisms'. In King 1996, pp. 230–44.

Kaul, Suvir (1994). 'Separation Anxiety: Growing Up Inter/National in Amotav Ghosh's *The Shadow Lines*'. In Loomba and Kaul 1994, pp. 125–45.

Keegan, William (1992). *The Spectre of Capitalism: The Future of the World Economy after the Fall of Communism*. London: Radius.

King, Bruce, ed. (1996). *New National and Post-Colonial Literatures: An Introduction*. Oxford: Clarendon Press.

Klein, Melanie (1988). *Love, Guilt and Reparation, and Other Writings 1921–1945*, introd. Hanna Segal. London: Virago.

Kloosterboer, Willemina (1960). *Involuntary Labour since the Abolition of Slavery: A Survey of Compulsory Labour throughout the World*. Leiden: E. J. Brill.

Kothari, Geeta (1995). 'Where Are You From?' In *Under Western Eyes*, ed. Garrett Hongo. New York: Anchor Books.

Kratochwill, Thomas (1981). *Selective Mutism: Implications for Research and Treatment*. Hillsdale (NJ): Lawrence Erlbaum Associates.

Kristeva, Julia (1977). *About Chinese Women*, trans. Anita Barrows. London: Marion Boyars.

——(1982). *Powers of Horror: An Essay on Abjection*, trans. Leon S. Roudiez. New York: Columbia University Press.

——(1989). *Black Sun: Depression and Melancholia*, trans. Leon S. Roudiez. New York and Oxford: Columbia University Press.

——(1991). *Strangers to Ourselves*, trans. Leon S. Roudiez. New York: Columbia University Press.

Kulke, Hermann, and Dietmar Rothermund (1998). *A History of India*. 3rd edn, London and New York: Routledge.

Lacan, Jacques (1972). 'Seminar on *The Purloined Letter*', trans. Jeffrey Mehlman. *Yale French Studies*, 48, pp. 39–72.

——(1977). *Écrits: A Selection*, trans. Alan Sheridan. London: Tavistock.

Lamming, George (1960). *The Pleasures of Exile*. London: Michael Joseph.

Lazarus, Neil (1999). *Nationalism and Cultural Practice in the Postcolonial World*. Cambridge: Cambridge University Press.

Leavey, John P., Jr (1986). *Glassary*. Lincoln (NB) and London: University of Nebraska Press.

Lee, Dennis (1974). 'Cadence, Country, Silence: Writing in a Colonial Space'. *Boundary 2*, 3.1, pp. 151–68.

Leys, Ruth (1994). 'Traumatic Cures: Shell-Shock, Janet and the Question of Memory'. *Critical Inquiry*, 20, pp. 623–62.

Lincoln, Andrew (1999). 'Scott's *Guy Mannering*: The Limits and Limitations of Anglo-British Identity'. *Scottish Literary Journal*, 26.1, pp. 48–61.

Lindfors, Bernth, ed. (1975). *Critical Perspectives on Amos Tutuola*. London: Heinemann.

Lloyd, David (1993). *Anomalous States: Irish Writing and the Post-Colonial Moment*. Dublin: The Lilliput Press.

Longxi, Zhang (1988). 'The Myth of the Other: China in the Eyes of the West'. *Critical Inquiry*, 15, pp. 108–31.

Loomba, Ania, and Suvir Kaul (1994). *On India: Writing History, Culture, Post-Coloniality*. Stirling: Oxford Literary Review.

Lopez, Barry (1995). *Of Wolves and Men*. New York: Touchstone.

Lukács, Gyorgy (1962). *The Historical Novel*, trans. Hannah and Stanley Mitchell. London: Merlin.

McClintock, Anne (1992). 'The Angel of Progress: Pitfalls of the Term "Post-colonialism"'. *Social Text*, 21, pp. 84–98.

McCoy, Alfred W. (1991). *The Politics of Heroin: CIA Complicity in the Global Drug Trade*. New York: Lawrence Hill.

McCrone, David (1992). *Understanding Scotland: The Sociology of a Stateless Nation*. London and New York: Routledge.

Macherey, Pierre (1978). *A Theory of Literary Production*, trans. Geoffrey Wall. London: Routledge and Kegan Paul.

Marx, Karl (1969). *On Colonialism and Modernisation*, ed. Shlomo Avineri. New York: Anchor Books.

Mazumdar, Pauline M. H. (1992). *Eugenics, Human Genetics and Human Failings*. London and New York: Routledge.

Mellor, Anne K. (1995). 'A Feminist Critique of Science'. In *Mary Shelley's 'Frankenstein'*, ed. Fred Botting. London: Macmillan.

Meltzer, Donald (1967). *The Psycho-Analytical Process*. Perthshire: Clunie Press.

Mercer, Kobena (1994). *Welcome to the Jungle: New Positions in Black Cultural Studies*. New York and London: Routledge.

Miles, Robert (1987). *Capitalism and Unfree Labour: Anomaly or Necessity?* London and New York: Tavistock.

Milner, Clyde A. (1989). *Major Problems in the History of the American West*. Lexington and Toronto: D. C. Heath.

Mishra, Vijay, and Bob Hodge (1991). 'What is Post(-)colonialism?' *Textual Practice*, 5.3, pp. 399–414.

Mitchell, W. J. T. (1992). 'Postcolonial Culture, Postimperial Criticism'. *Transition*, no. 56, pp. 11–19.

Moore-Gilbert, Bart (1997). *Postcolonial Theory: Contexts, Practices, Politics*. London: Verso.

Morris-Jones, W. H., and Georges Fischer, eds (1980). *Decolonisation and After: The British and French Experience*. London: Frank Cass.

Morrison, Toni (1992). *Playing in the Dark: Whiteness and the Literary Imagination*. Cambridge (MA) and London: Harvard University Press.

Mukherjee, Arun (1988). *Towards an Aesthetic of Opposition: Essays on Literature, Criticism and Cultural Imperialism*. Stratford: Williams-Wallace.

Mun, Thomas (1928). *England's Treasure by Forraign Trade* (1664). Oxford: The Economic History Society/Basil Blackwell.

Murdoch, Iris (1992). *Metaphysics as a Guide to Morals*. London: Chatto and Windus.

Naipaul, V. S. (1962). *The Middle Passage: Impressions of Five Societies*. London: André Deutsch.

——(1972). *The Overcrowded Barracoon, and Other Articles*. London: André Deutsch.

Narogin, Mudrooroo (1990). *Writing from the Fringe: A Study of Modern Aboriginal Literature*. Melbourne: Hyland House.

Ngugi wa Thiong'o (1972). *Homecoming: Essays on African and Caribbean Literature, Culture and Politics*. London: Heinemann.

——(1983). *Barrel of a Pen: Resistance to Repression in Neo-Colonial Kenya*. London: New Beacon.

——(1986). *Decolonising the Mind: The Politics of Language in African Literature*. London: James Currey.

——(1993). *Moving the Centre: The Struggle for Cultural Freedoms*. London: James Currey.

——(1997). *Writers in Politics: A Re-Engagement with Issues of Literature and Society*. Oxford: James Currey.

——(1998). *Penpoints, Gunpoints, and Dreams: Towards a Critical Theory of the Arts and the State in Africa*. Oxford: Clarendon Press.

Nixon, Rob (1992). *London Calling: V.S. Naipaul, Postcolonial Mandarin*. New York and Oxford: Oxford University Press.

Ohmae, Kenichi (1995). *The End of the Nation-State, the Rise of Regional Economies*. London: HarperCollins.

Okely, Judith (1996). *Own or Other Culture*. London and New York: Routledge.

Overy, Richard, ed. (1996). *The Times Atlas of the 20th Century*. London: Times Books.

Pagden, A. R. (1995). *Lords of All the Worlds: Ideologies of Empire in Spain, Britain and France, c. 1500–c. 1850*. New Haven and London: Yale University Press.

Parry, Benita (1983). *Conrad and Imperialism*. London: Macmillan.

——(1988). 'Problems in Current Theories of Colonial Discourse'. *Oxford Literary Review*, 9.1–2, pp. 27–58.

Pepper, David (1993). *Eco-Socialism: From Deep Ecology to Social Justice*. London and New York: Routledge.

Petersen, Kirsten Holst, and Anna Rutherford, eds (1986). *A Double Colonisation: Colonial and Post-Colonial Women's Writing*. Mundelstrup, Denmark: Dangaroo Press.

Petras, James (1993). 'Cultural Imperialism in the Late Twentieth Century'. *Journal of Contemporary Asia*, 23.2, pp. 139–48.

Pinney, Chris (1989). 'Appearing Worlds'. *Anthropology Today*, 5, pp. 26–8.

Polish Ministry of Information (1942). *The German New Order in Poland*. London: Hutchinson.

Punter, David (1986). *The Hidden Script: Writing and the Unconscious*. London and New York: Routledge.

——(1989). *The Romantic Unconscious: A Study in Narcissism and Patriarchy*. London: Harvester Wheatsheaf.

——(1996). *The Literature of Terror*. 2 vols. London: Longman.

——(1998). *Gothic Pathologies: The Text, the Body and the Law*. London: Macmillan.

——(1999). 'Ceremonial Gothic'. In *Spectral Readings: Towards a Gothic Geography*, ed. Glennis Byron and David Punter. London: Macmillan.

——(2000a). *Writing the Passions*. London: Longman, forthcoming.

——(2000b). '"A Foot Is What Fits the Shoe": Disability, the Gothic and Prosthesis'. *Gothic Studies*, 3, forthcoming.

Rajan, Gita, and Radhika Mohanram, eds (1995). *Postcolonial Discourse and Changing Cultural Contexts*. Westport (CT): Greenwood Press.

Ramchand, Kenneth (1969). 'Terrified Consciousness'. *Journal of Commonwealth Literature*, no. 7, pp. 8–19.

Readings, Bill (1995). 'Dwelling in the Ruins'. *Oxford Literary Review*, 17, pp. 15–28.

Ronell, Avital (1992). *Crack Wars: Literature, Addiction, Mania*. Lincoln (NB) and London: University of Nebraska Press.

Rooney, Caroline, ed. (1997). *Knowledge, Learning and Migration*. Stirling: Oxford Literary Review.

Royle, Nicholas (1995). *After Derrida*. Manchester and New York: Manchester University Press.

Rushdie, Salman (1991). *Imaginary Homelands: Essays and Criticism 1981–1991*. London: Granta.

Rutherford, Anna, ed. (1992). *From Commonwealth to Post-Colonial*. Sydney and Conventry: Dangaroo Press.

Said, Edward (1978). *Orientalism*. New York: Vintage.

——(1983). *The World, the Text and the Critic*. Cambridge (MA): Harvard University Press.

——(1986). 'Orientalism Reconsidered'. In *Literature, Politics and Theory: Papers from the Essex Conference 1976–84*, ed. Francis Barker et al. London: Methuen.

——(1993). *Culture and Imperialism*. New York: Alfred A. Knopf.

San Juan, E. Jr (1998). *Beyond Postcolonial Theory*. London: Macmillan.

Serres, Michel (1974). *Hermes III: La Traduction*. Paris: Minuit.

Shoemaker, Adam (1989). *Black Words, White Page: Aboriginal Literature 1929–1988*. St Lucia: University of Queensland Press.

Shohat, Ella (1996). 'Notes on the "Post-Colonial"'. In *Contemporary Postcolonial Theory: A Reader*, ed. Padmini Mongia. London and New York: Arnold.

Showalter, Elaine (1985). *The Female Malady: Women, Madness and English Culture, 1830–1980*. New York: Pantheon.

Slemon, Stephen (1988). 'Post-colonial Allegory and the Transformation of History'. *The Journal of Commonwealth Literature*, 23.1, pp. 157–68.

——, and Helen Tiffin, eds (1989). *After Europe: Critical Theory and Post-Colonial Writing*. Sydney: Dangaroo Press.

Smith, J. H., ed. (1980). *The Literary Freud: Mechanisms of Defence and the Poetic Will*. New Haven and London: Yale University Press.

Solomos, John, and Les Back (1996). *Racism and Society*. London: Macmillan.

Soong, Stephen C. (1985). *A Brotherhood in Song: Chinese Poetry and Poetics*. Hong Kong: Chinese University Press.

Soyinka, Wole (1976). *Myth, Literature and the African World*. Cambridge: Cambridge University Press.

Spivak, Gayatri Chakravorty (1985). 'Can the Subaltern Speak? Speculations on Widow Sacrifice'. *Wedge*, nos. 7/8, pp. 120–30.

——(1986). 'Three Women's Texts and a Critique of Imperialism'. *Critical Inquiry*, no. 12, pp. 243–61.

——(1987). *In Other Worlds: Essays in Cultural Politics*. New York and London: Routledge.

——(1990). *The Post-Colonial Critic: Interviews, Strategies, Dialogues*, ed. Sarah Harasym. New York: Routledge.

——(1995). 'Afterword'. In Mahasweta Devi, *Imaginary Maps*. New York and London: Routledge.

Stasiulis, Daiva, and Nira Yuval-Davis, eds (1995). *Unsettling Settler Societies: Articulations of Gender, Race, Ethnicity and Class*. London: Sage Publications.

Suleri, Sara (1992). *The Rhetoric of British India*. Chicago: University of Chicago Press.

Sunder Rajan, Rajeswari (1993). *Real and Imagined Women: Gender, Culture and Postcolonialism*. London and New York: Routledge.

Taussig, Michael (1993). *Shamanism, Colonialism and the Wild Man: A Study in Terror and Healing*. Chicago: University of Chicago Press.

Tiffin, Chris, and Alan Lawson, eds (1994). *De-Scribing Empire: Post-Colonialism and Textuality*. London: Routledge.

Tiffin, Helen (1996). 'Plato's Cave: Educational and Critical Practices'. In King 1996, pp. 143–63.

Todorov, Tzvetan (1997). 'The Coexistence of Cultures'. In Rooney 1997, pp. 3–17.

Trinh, T. Minh-ha (1989). *Woman, Native, Other: Writing, Postcoloniality and Feminism*. Bloomington: Indiana University Press.

Ulmer, Gregory (1989). *Teletheory: Grammatology in the Age of Video*. New York and London: Routledge.

Van der Veer, Peter, ed. (1995). *Nation and Migration: The Politics of Space in the South Asian Diaspora*. Philadelphia: University of Pennsylvania Press.

Van Ornum, William (1997). *A Thousand Frightening Fantasies: Understanding and Healing Scrupulosity and Obsessive Compulsive Disorder*. New York: Crossroad.

Vaughan, Megan (1991). *Curing their Ills: Colonial Power and African Illness*. Cambridge: Polity Press.

Virilio, Paul (1977). *Speed and Politics*, trans. Mark Polizzotti. New York: Semiotext(e).

Walcott, Derek (1974). 'The Muse of History'. In *Is Massa Day Dead?*, ed. Orde Coombs. New York: Anchor.

Walder, Dennis (1993). 'V. S. Naipaul and the Postcolonial Order: Reading *In a Free State*'. In White 1993, pp. 82–119.

——(1998). *Post-Colonial Literatures in English: History, Language, Theory.* Oxford: Blackwell.

Wallerstein, Immanuel (1991). *Geopolitics and Geoculture: Essays on the Changing World-System*. Cambridge: Cambridge University Press.

Walvin, James (1992). *Slaves and Slavery: The British Colonial Experience.* Manchester and New York: Manchester University Press.

——, ed. (1982). *Slavery and British Society 1776–1846*. London: Macmillan.

Weinstock, Donald J., and Cathy Ramadan (1978). 'Symbolic Structure in *Things Fall Apart*'. In *Critical Perspectives on Chinua Achebe*, ed. C. L. Innes and Bernth Lindfors. London: Heinemann.

Whitaker, Ben (1987). *The Global Fix: The Crisis of Drug Addiction.* London: Jonathan Cape.

White, Jonathan, ed. (1993). *Recasting the World: Writing after Colonialism.* Baltimore and London: The Johns Hopkins University Press.

Whitehead, Anne (1997). 'Trauma, Gender and Performance: Theorising the Body of the Survivor'. Unpublished PhD dissertation, University of Newcastle-upon-Tyne.

Williams, Patrick, and Laura Chrisman, eds (1993). *Colonial Discourse and Post-Colonial Theory: A Reader*. New York and London: Harvester Wheatsheaf.

Young, Robert J. C. (1990). *White Mythologies: Writing History and the West*. London: Routledge.

——(1995). *Colonial Desire: Hybridity in Theory, Culture and Race*. London: Routledge.

Zabus, Chantal (1991). *The African Palimpsest: Indigenisation of Language in the West African Europhone Novel*. Amsterdam and Atlanta: Rodopi.

Žižek, Slavoj (1992). *Looking Awry: An Introduction to Jacques Lacan through Popular Culture*. Cambridge (MA) and London: MIT Press.

# Index